David Tomory was born in London in 1949 and brought up in New Zealand. He first went to India in 1971. Since then he has visited the country many times, travelling and writing. These days he divides his time between India and London.

David is also the author of *A Season in Heaven: True tales from the road to Kathmandu*, published by Lonely Planet.

hello goodnight

A Life of Goa

David Tomory

LONELY PLANET PUBLICATIONS
Melbourne • Oakland • London • Paris

Hello Goodnight: A Life of Goa

Published by Lonely Planet Publications
    Head Office: PO Box 617, Hawthorn, Vic 3122, Australia
    Branches: 150 Linden Street, Oakland, CA 94607, USA
                     10a Spring Place, London NW5 3BH, UK
                     1 rue Dahomey, 75011, Paris, France

Published by Lonely Planet Publications, 2000

Printed by The Bookmaker International Pty Ltd
Printed in China

Map by Natasha Velleley
Designed by Maria Vallianos
Author photograph by Olencio Coutinho/Hollywood Studio

National Library of Australia Cataloguing in Publication Data

Tomory, David.
Hello Goodnight: a life of Goa.

ISBN 1 86450 061 1

1. Goa (India: State) – Social life and customs.
2. Goa (India: State) – Description and travel.
3. Goa (India: State) – History. I. Title.
(Series: Lonely Planet journeys.)

915.47990452

Text © David Tomory 2000
Map © Lonely Planet 2000
LONELY PLANET and the Lonely Planet logo are trade marks of Lonely
Planet Publications Pty. Ltd.

Contents

FOR MY PARENTS

Acknowledgements

I am fortunate to have many friends in Goa, some of many years. They provided information and arranged introductions and helped me in innumerable ways, and though I cannot thank all of them individually here, I could not have done without their help.

Special thanks go to Lucio Miranda and Kim Morarji. Both know Goa much better than I ever will, and they did their best to improve my knowledge of it. Paul and Marion invited me on their taxi tour and lent me books; Brendan and Kate and Eve told me stories of Vagator, Anjuna and Arambol. Dry Ice talked me through techno. Carmel, Manuel and Alex offered me kind hospitality. At the Central Library in Panjim I was much assisted by the staff of the Goa and Rare Books Archive. Paddy and Alan told me Jungle Barry stories; Remo Fernandes directed me to Lucio.

No person mentioned above nor anyone else quoted in this book is in any way responsible for any mistakes of fact, for the use I have made of their words, the context in which those words appear, or for any conclusions I may have drawn from what they told me.

Some names have been changed and identities disguised. Rudyard Kipling called this 'muddying the waters of inquiry with the stick of precaution'.

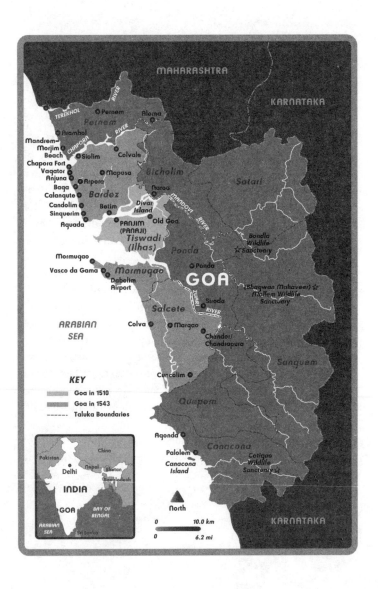

PROLOGUE

Modern Goa begins behind this house. Before it are clumps of cactus, the coconut grove, the dunes, the sea. It is a three-room fishing house made of mud, with old half-round clay roof tiles on top and good cane furniture inside. Only where the roof beams rest on them at the corners do the walls meet the roof; and so the house is open to the air, making the weather inside a refined version of the weather outside. There is no ceiling. When it blows, a fine rain of dust falls from the tiles, from the palm-wood rafters and the bamboo laths between them; and when it rains, you receive a very fine spray.

My diary lists India's seasons: 'The Hot, March to June. The Wet, July to September. The Cool, November to February'. So eager is my diary for the coming of the Cool that it has forgotten transitional October, aftermath to the Wet – and green, bright green. The sand sprouts. The wells are full, which makes the traditional ceremony of jumping into them while drunk much easier. The world is alive with creatures. Years ago, waking one morning to a damp forehead, I found a bright green spatula-fingered tree frog sitting on it.

Goa's one monsoon and long dry winter make it less tropical than Kerala to the south, with its second monsoon and short dry winter; but this October of 1997 is quite tropical enough. By ten in the morning the barometer on the back porch reads 36 Centigrade. The front porch is inviting under its rattan awning, but simmers by midday. An early show of birds – drongos, woodpeckers, bee-eaters, hoopoes – soon disappears. I feel the weight of the sun, not dry and burning, but enveloping like a hot compress, like clingfilm. Sweat springs to the surface of the skin; I wake up with it and shower it off, and back it comes as the water dries.

At dawn in the village the thin smoke of breakfast fires drifts up from mottled red tile roofs into the bamboo thickets and the palms. The morning surf is gently rhythmic from beyond the dunes, and in the distance the bread delivery boys sound their bicycle horns. It is Goa's finest hour.

I had just got in from London. I was sleeping the fitful sleep of arrival when from nowhere a helicopter came in low over the roof, rattling the tiles and filling the room with dust. The howling rotors and the pterodactyl outrage of crows shook me awake and sent me disoriented out of the back door into the half-light. The chopper had gone, but hovering over the house now was a grey and skeletal jungle tenement from a dream. Mist drifted about its concrete feet. I peered at it. It was real enough; the crows evicted from my roof were already settling on it.

I retreated back through the house, made some tea and sat on the front porch for the sound of the surf, the palms, the early birds. Soon it got too hot for someone just in from London, and I went back inside.

The morning wore on. The helicopter did not return. No work began on the tenement. Life does go on in this weather, but out of the sun. Indoors it is dim and atmospheric, like a cave. Spiders straddle webs, stinging hairy caterpillars lurk, and midges flock overhead. Whitewash lies thickly on the walls, which are also thick, but old and dry and hollowed out by the ants, the armies of the day as the flying insects are the armies of the night. One large hole opens into the kitchen, and when they panzer out of the wall in search of sustenance – no food can be left out for more than a minute – there are so many ants that you imagine them leaving behind a subterranean world of empty tunnels held together by whitewash.

The geckoes do not trouble the ants, preferring things that fly by night, that they can stalk like cats. During the day they are merely sentries, patrolling the walls desultorily, clucking hopefully to one another. The cry of the southern house gecko is louder than any gecko in India, but in this house so open to the air it must compete with the surrounding cicadas, frogs, jackals, dogs, squirrels and birds. They call and dispute, and the crows rasp on even through siesta.

For geckoes, the vertical – short of glass or polished steel – is horizontal. They will cling to a wall even in death. They cling on through 'a "dry adhesion" brought about by surface phenomena possibly at the molecular level between the setae and the substratum', the experts think – but contemplative on the wall in the afternoon heat, the geckoes themselves prefer God to science. They mingle with the model saints on the altar shelf, and their eyes flash red in time with the electric Sacred Heart. In the course of a dash along the wall from the shelf to the Madonna calendar, a gecko will suddenly stop. For minutes it will remain inanimate, a piece of pale translucent jewellery.

Sometimes the twentieth century vanishes altogether. Modern life's supports are fragile: when the pipes dry up, water has to be drawn from the well with a rope and bucket. When the power falls below a certain voltage, the fan stops and life is reduced in an instant to somnambulism. But short of a complete power cut, the refrigerator holds on. It ices up and groans, and once it threw me across the room when I unwisely seized a bottle from the ice compartment by its metal cap; but every day the breath of coolness when the door opens is like a blessing. They tell me people use their fridge for an air-conditioner by leaving its door open all day.

When the fan is on I sit beneath it, trying to read a book on the Goa Inquisition, and when it isn't on, it is torture. In a juice bar one lunchtime I share a table with an Italian tourist. I ask him what he does, and he says, 'I sleep.'

Life slows to a crawl. Towards dark it cools down a little. That is when the halting old man in enormous shorts appears. He moves across the coconut grove and into the village, dragging a three-metre-long dried palm leaf behind him. As he passes he calls out 'Hello! Goodnight!' When I first saw him moving so slowly I laughed, but a week later I was that slow myself.

Out in the blackness, the lanterns of the night-fishers bob up and down on an invisible sea. Night falls so quickly that for the first few days I was never in time for sunset on the beach; so, to announce it, a solitary bat began to make a single circuit of the front porch every evening, vanishing as the night came down.

The street lights will be coming on in modern Goa, behind the house where the tenement stands; but here there are none, and in the sudden dark coming in from the sea the front porch is a glowing oasis. Now the armies of the night home in. The geckoes await them on every wall, each to its patch, their missing tails the trophies of turf wars. I close the door and draw the curtain on the kitchen window as the first scarabs, the biggest bugs in the air, come droning in towards the light.

It must be Monday. Through the firecracker din of a birthday celebration can be heard songs of devotion from the big tin speakers of the little Hindu shrine by the roadside. By arrangement in this largely Christian district, the shrine broadcasts only on Mondays.

I stop into Guru Communications for the local paper. It lies humbly on the glass counter beside the glossies and the big national dailies. A recent report has only a third of Goa's mostly literate population ever taking a local newspaper, including the three in English – because of television, apparently, and not because the news is old, misspelt and feebly analysed.

I am scanning the obituaries when a Scooty whines to a halt outside and two English tourists walk in. Both are wearing T-shirts with 'It's Better in Goa' printed on them. We gather by the cash register, surrounded by photocopiers, fax machines, international direct dialling, Cokes, Pepsis and vacuum-packed snacks. At home these accessories would be unremarkable. But to anyone older than a teenager here, they – and the two men – are signs of a changed world.

In this trio of occidental tourists, I am the older model, a serial tourist in Goa, and this changed world is new to me, too. So far the only shock for the other two has been the ride from the airport, in 'a little tin and glass van like a motorised fishbowl'. A gilt St Christopher had swung on his chain wildly to and fro across the windshield. Otherwise they think Goa is so far, so good. A beach destination away from the winter, and cheap. They have been to others like it.

The map they have been given represents this part of north Goa, from Candolim to Baga, as a realm of resorts. No villages are shown. Twenty or thirty hotels are named and numbered, interspersed with restaurants, supermarkets, souvenir shops, money-changing joints and fax, phone and e-mail places.

It amazes me to see this map. Fifteen or even a dozen years ago it would have been blank. Not one of the places on it existed. To me it still looks like a plan, a map of the future – even though the district now resembles the map much more closely than it resembles my memory of it, or the pictures I have of it. In the early 1980s I took a lot of photographs around here. Three years later the road was widened, and the building began; and then the old men in big sun-bleached shorts gave up on the road and began cycling to the bar by the back paths.

To look at, coastal Goa in the early 1980s hadn't changed much since Graham Greene's visit in 1964. Greene arrived only two years after the departure of the Portuguese colonial power, and he called his travel piece 'Goa the Unique'. He thought Goa might stay that way for a couple of years at most, before giant India changed it forever; but when I photographed them, the buildings were still old and the traffic was still mostly bicycles and bullock carts. Once I saw two bullock carts going along at their customary one mile an hour side by side, one driver doing all the talking, not noticing that the other was asleep.

My pictures are of a yellow-and-white house, the window grilles in a pattern of flying birds, and a polished wine-red *balcao,* verandah, with its planter's chair and churchy stained-glass lights. Then there is a courtyard dressed for a wedding; a mysterious old shuttered place; a quaint taverna or two; and the chapel of St Anthony in the middle of the road. On Saturdays still, a congregation dressed in its best attends the evening service as the traffic goes honking by.

Just around the corner from the Hindu shrine there stands a man-high milestone, approximately fashioned at the top into a lion's head. 'Thank You' is painted on its southern face. To signify that you are leaving the limits of the Calangute district and entering those of Candolim, 'Candolim Lions Welcome You' is painted on its northern face. The milestone marks the village of Ximer.

It runs seamlessly into the villages on each side, and they in turn run into other villages, making one long super-village that runs right along the coast from the Mandovi River in the south to the Baga River in the north. The dogs would be after you at night, but by day you used to be able to walk the whole eight kilometres of coastline without ever meeting a wall, jumping drainage ditches where pythons dozed under dead leaves.

People up in Anjuna, a beach and a headland away, have long been calling this area 'the suburbs'. The jibe was not true when they began saying it, but it is true now. Candolim is being walled off. It may be that little Ximer is still a village to itself, but in the real estate ads it is a hyphen in the 'Candolim-Calangute-Baga suburban belt'. Soon it will be part of an eight-kilometre-long super-suburb, welded into a belt for the new millennium.

In his fax office on the road the lean and fastidious proprietor listens intently to his machine. He hears the burble of the access tone. 'The music!' He presses 'send' – to Tokyo or Delhi or Singapore or Berlin or wherever. No more Planet Goa. Next year, he tells me, he'll be opening a cyber café in the new block next door, if they ever finish it. Presently, it is one of a number of modern ruins in the area, a creation of the speculative building boom of the mid-nineties that gave so much of this coast its improvised air and then went bust. 'It's terrible,' I was told. 'Builders are suiciding themselves.' Some modern ruins were born of court injunctions or title disputes – Goa is a paradise for lawyers, too – while others, like this ruin, look dead, but are merely sleeping until the boom resumes.

Someone has given the new block's effigy a pair of trousers. An effigy is always installed in an unfinished building to prevent its occupation by demons. This particular effigy would do for a house, but hung from a railing on the third floor of a cadaverous, monsoon-scoured concrete high-rise block, it is insignificant. Supportive all-night devotional music sessions have been taking place in the echoing garage round the back.

Outside his shop, the proprietor sits with his wife through the slack afternoon hour, sipping from a soft drink called Teem. Smart tourists tour his shelves daily, while their Sumos and Gypsies idle outside. The road brings him ever more custom, but he doesn't care for the noise and the smell of diesel. Over the way they're jamming a narrow dwelling in between a mound and a spreading banyan tree. Once the mound was a small mud-walled café, well kept and bright with advertisements; then it was abandoned. Last year the owners took the roof tiles away, and under the monsoon the walls began to melt back into earth. Soon it was a wet heap. Once dried, it looked prehistoric, not something that had so recently been a café.

The narrow dwelling going in next to it has heavy concrete hoods over its window spaces, a flat slab roof, and air-conditioner slots in the walls. It will be no home beautiful, but at least it's a house, built on a human scale. The shop owner would rather have that than a huge modern ruin: once you're loomed over by multi-storey concrete, that's the view forever. 'At least no one will cut the banyan,' he says. The banyan is sacred to Lord Shiva, and there are ancient and awful sanctions against felling them.

The cars go honking by, the speakers sing, the shrine is wreathed in the smoke of incense and surrounded by people waiting to make an offering to the deity. I cross the road to avoid a certain smelly patch of roadside where, a week earlier, a big dog had been killed by a car. The tropics have no time to waste. Soon that plump – you might even say healthy-looking – dead dog was two bones and a stain.

Once there was an hourly bus, and little else. Here it comes, still with us, the venerable *Rocket*, veering round the shrine. Then they brought the road up to speed for modern times. Under the rush hour it becomes greasy, black and cheesy, fuel-hazed. You trudge along the broken edge of this narrow highway thronged with contending vehicles – scooters, old cars, motorbikes, vans, new cars, posh jeeps, trucks, buses – in ascending order of machismo. The bigger you are, the softer you fall. I once asked a veteran driver what the essentials of driving here were, and he said: 'Good brakes, good luck, good horn.' Then you may drive as if nothing will ever go wrong.

The dogs were slow to catch on because the road was part of their territory, something they slept on while judging to a nicety, with ear to the ground, the arrival of the bullock cart. Then the traffic came. Now, even at one in the morning when the road is its old self, empty and shiny under the moon, when they find you invitingly alone and lit up like a hamburger by the unearthly glow of Benetton-Nike-Lacoste, the dogs are shy. They merely yodel once and then limp off.

'He wouldn't sell his land to me,' a neighbour calls out from amongst the goats at the bus stop. The struggle with her landlord has been going on for years, and it's worth stopping off for a moment to hear the denouement. 'I simply couldn't afford such a price. So he sold outside. Then he fell sick. Only one month later – finish. He went Up. So what good was all that money to him?' The square metre that fetched 250 rupees ten years ago now fetches 4500 or more.

Before me lie kilometres of fresh suburbia, but heading north from Ximer I negotiate a boundary wall as yet surrounding nothing. The enclosure may be a litigation victim, stalled in court at birth, in which case it will grow knee-high grass and end up as a snake park. The walls always go up first, to define the territory. Sometimes they so precisely define it that between one boundary wall and another an alley is left that you have to edge through sideways. But once started, the building is done with alacrity: a friend returning in his car found his route home of years forever barred by a boundary wall that had gone up during lunch.

I think this is Gauravaddo. In the suburban belt, the challenge is to remember which *vaddo* you're in. Vaddo means ward, as in the ward of a town or village, and its name is a signpost to the past. It may signify a trade – like Escrivão Vaddo, the ward of scribes, or Cobravaddo in Calangute, properly Copravaddo, where the coconut white was dried into copra. Or it may signify a community, like Untavaddo, which means Camel Vaddo. The Lobo clan are said to have arrived there on camels.

FX the taxi driver lived here, a block away from St Anthony's, and I used to call in sometimes, before he moved to Bangalore. The site of his old house is now occupied by something like an archaeological dig, rusted steel rods for the piers of a stalled building project jutting from the earth like the ribs of a mechanical mammoth. I look around to make sure. Yes, there's the Ponderosa. Its picture windows and garden fence of bright red wagon wheels were once so modern that people used to come from Ximer especially to see them. It was the only new house in the area, and now I see the owner is doing it up before it becomes the only old one.

From nearby, through the fronds, leaves and vines – patches of jungle survive here – come the cries and exhortations of a building crew invisibly at work. The work itself is quiet. All this newness is being created in the old way, by hand, because machinery is much more expensive than labourers on about four dollars a day. Lamani tribeswomen, vivid in blue and red mirrorwork skirts and long black braids and heavy jewellery, do most of the work. They can pour and level a concrete slab roof in a morning and raise a tenement in a week. It isn't their fault. By the roadside stands the stout developer, adjusting his shades in the wing mirror of his gleaming new Esteem.

The malaria boom isn't their fault either. The labourers – forty thousand or so of them – come from Karnataka, just over the mountains, the Western Ghats, and those with malaria infect the Goan mosquitoes that bite them. The water that construction needs so much of is left lying about for more mosquitoes to breed in. Here by the path to the beach is such an incubator, a deep concrete tank full of water. But no larvae will live long in there. The tank, a refuge from snakes, is packed with frogs.

Animals take change for granted. The crows were outraged only momentarily by the helicopter at dawn, and went on to perch on the new tenement. The ugly concrete tank that saves the frogs from snakes will enable them to grow enormous, to proliferate and chorus through the night, squatting three-deep on each other's heads.

And here in the scrub behind the dunes lie the plastic mineral-water bottles flung away last winter. Bottles that have been here long enough to have an archaeology, brands that went bust years ago, all shapes and sizes, distorted and crisp and browned with age. Half-buried, they have become habitats. For lizards they are an exciting housing development, perhaps even an evolutionary aid: a lizard rushes out, seizes a green caterpillar and rushes back to the perfect refuge of its bottle.

At midday in this heat the beach must have been an Arabia of burned soles and heat haze, and now in the late afternoon there is still no one about, and no breeze. Many prefer the cosier coves to the north, Vagator and Anjuna; they say that eight kilometres of beach is too long, too featureless. Nevertheless, Candolim has a good beach; for the less charitable, Candolim *is* a good beach. Between mid-April and mid-November it is still more fishing shore than tourist seaside. There are more fishermen's shelters than beach cafés, and the narrow wooden sharp-prowed boats eye the turbid sea in a long rank, canted over on their outriggers.

Eventually the flank of my dune cools off. Sunset is imminent, and by now the bat should be circling the porch. At five minutes to six precisely the orange sun goes down – or out, it is so sudden, settling itself for a bare moment on the horizon before being sucked under. No green flash. It does happen, but is very rare, the flash that for an instant electrifies the length of the horizon, turning the sky green. At home, the scarabs will soon come bumbling in towards the porch light. Black and shiny, in repose so elegant and symmetrical, the sacred dung beetles of ancient Egypt are quite useless in the air. Always in pairs, perhaps in husband-and-wife teams, they ricochet ecstatically round the light, lose their bearings, and crash-land. Then they right themselves and struggle off into the darkness on foot, like grounded aviators.

Against a magnificent baroque sunset with flourishes in pink the helicopter reappears, whining in from the west like a bug buzzing the Sistine ceiling.

OLD CONQUESTS

1 Into Goa

The traffic lies gridlocked around the stalled Mapusa bus, filling the road outside the barber shop where I sit for my Dussehra haircut. New beginnings are made at the auspicious festival of Dussehra, in my case everything from the neck up – snipping, scraping, depilation, moisturising, massage. The barber smears my face with an unguent like pink blancmange, then vibrates it with an electric hairdryer-like device with a rubber cup on it. The juddering in the ears will loosen the sand, he says; afterwards, he pummels my head loose-fisted, in time with the rock-breakers outside.

The barbershop was once the Calangute crossroads customs post. It is octagonal, each tall window having a different view of this smuggler's coast – exactly as inside it is a barber's dream, with multiple heads mirrored from every angle. I sit facing the north, the junction, where an angry bus conductor situation is developing. A policeman across the road carefully picks his teeth. The rock-breakers crouch outside the window to my left; I hope they are preparing the trash zone between the shanty shops and the covered market for something better.

A boy wheels his bicycle away from the repair shop, putting to flight a rootling pig wearing a purple supermarket bag over its head. It bounds away through the usual scatter of plastic bottles, plastic bags, juice boxes with straws intact, tampons, broken sandals, imported sunscreen bottles, cans and packets and a burned-out kerosene can. Municipal waste disposal is so far theoretical. The sight brings to mind Hutber's Law, which asserts that progress always means deterioration. Hutber's Law is a sort of economic correlative to the doctrine of the Kali Yuga, the time in which we live, the Hindu era of perishing, in which things – over millennia, admittedly – always get worse. The last days will herald the purifying cataclysm, the cosmic cycle will begin again, and the burned-out kerosene can will still be there.

In the barbershop, religion lives on a human scale. Like many of his trade, my barber is a devotee of the saintly Sai Baba of Shirdi – who is pictured with his own hair hidden in a headscarf. The barber himself is balding. He executes the coup de grâce, the head-and-spine twist and click, and I am ready for auspicious Calangute.

It has so recently become a town of ten thousand inhabitants that Calangute is still called 'the village'. But it doesn't look like one, and you don't have to go to Mapusa (pronounced 'Mapsa') any more for things like electric mosquito-repellers. The pharmacy is a cascade of half-open pill packets, and the hefty Englishwoman heading the crowd at the counter is repeating '. . . whatever's strongest. He hasn't stopped going since we came.' The mosquito-repeller works by heating up little containers of pesticide. The instructions read: 'When you switch on the Mozgo the pleasant aroma arising will tell you . . .'

'Tell me,' I ask the assistant, 'is this stuff dangerous for humans?'

'Not very.'

Out on the street, his wife is holding the glass door shut against the midday din while the man in a yellow phone booth shouts down the line at some distant city. 'I saw the apartment. One bedroom. What? Everything: TV, satellite dish of course, phone, hot water, air-conditioner. Servant or storage space. Four lakh. What? FOUR.' In 1997, four lakh, or 400,000 rupees, is about $9500.

This is enterprise country. Boomtown. Calangute is favoured by retirees, by returning migrants and by people escaping the cities. In the winter it is full of tourists – Indian and foreign. It is the epitome of an old place becoming new; for a place in its third age it is very brash and raw-looking. In its first age it was a village, and the Order of Salesian fathers built their Oratory there. In its second age, with intimations of tourism beginning, the Salesians built a Don Bosco vocational school next to the Calangute church and sold the Oratory to the Tourism Department, who made a dormitory of it in the late 1960s, when the hippies first turned up. It's strange to think that this family holiday town was an émigré youth paradise thirty-odd years ago, when Tommy Butterfly in person saluted new arrivals, and the beach went naked.

In its third age the dormitory has been demolished for something newer and bigger, and surely today's tourists prefer this expanding Calangute. A holiday in India is supposed to be like this, all colour and noise, crowds, cinema posters, snake charmers, fortune tellers and cane-juice machines and ice cream, suave souvenir salesmen, wandering cows and roadside stalls hung with tourist tat.

The visitor seeking a light lunch will never mourn the Cold Porkfat Sandwich Shop, usurped by the Hotel Orfil above and the Arson Shoe Mart below. On the beachfront the amiable crowds know that Calangute is famous, but not when its fame began. It has been a promenade and trysting spot for a hundred years. The locals were putting on musical beach parties ('Goody Servai in his inimitable style with Arunala at the mike') long before the hippies ever did – except that the beach season for Goans was, and is, the broiling summer.

On the corner of the cluttered crossroads, where by day the bus conductors cry their destinations and by night policemen wait to ambush returning partygoers, the barber shop has just ended its evening shift. When it was a customs post, it never closed. To evade it, contraband arriving from the beach might go northwards along the coast, though that road eventually ends up at the river, in Chapora, a notable little smuggling port itself in its day. Or it might turn right. A little way along, the road takes a left round the Don Bosco school and the huge bulk of the St Alex church, and sets off inland towards Mapusa, a much better destination in the great days of contraband.

Mapusa is said to mean 'a place where things are weighed and measured'. Though it too is an old place becoming new, the change is much more a matter of appearances. It has always been a frankly commercial town: in the mid-1970s the first billboard to greet the arriving bus from Calangute read 'The Best Things In Life Aren't Free. Save for them with State Bank Recurring Deposit'. Pictured were a motor scooter, a refrigerator, and a wife. The town itself looks newer than Panjim, which has touches of eighteenth-century elegance, but is in fact much older. Style was never its concern. Before Panjim was built, Mapusa was fattening on the inland trade to greater India, as Portugal's old spice business by sea to Europe was gradually appropriated by the Dutch. In the mid-seventeenth century, huge bullock trains set off at year's end for the mountain passes, with cargoes of coconuts, areca nut and dried fish, to return after monsoon with domestic ware and cloth.

Or the contraband arriving from Calangute beach might avoid the Mapusa turnoff, and instead take the coast road south through Candolim. Along there, past the first rank of resorts and well before Aguada, with its jail, fort, helicopter pad and hotel complex, there are two left turns that end up at the Mandovi bridge into Panjim. The traffic honks and jostles. For safety's sake you seek out the driver who has come through, the older man, the one who through the decades has survived his own driving.

The taxi pulls up, a cramped little Fiat. The driver is a boy. The car will belong to his boss, who reclines all day on the back seat of his own old but still elegant Contessa outside Guru Communications, watching his fleet coming and going along the road. A bicycle is all the boy has ever driven. He sees my expression, and laughs. 'First time in Goa, sir?' Then he pulls the rear-vision mirror in, checks his hair in it, lights a Four Square, leans on the horn with one elbow and drives us out into the Candolim road, grinning as if nothing will ever go wrong.

Two friends and I hire a driver and his little Maruti taxi-van, and early the next morning we set off for the Western Ghats, Goa's inland border, the great jungled scarp that climbs up to the Indian central plateau, the Deccan. It will be differently hot up there. This winter, throughout India, the weather has been a month late – this is said to happen once every decade – and it is still clammy and salty and soporific at sea level, with haze on the beach. Up in the Ghats the humidity will be junglier, richer.

Altitude appeals to us; we have been beachside for some time. I'd recently met a woman who had never been to Candolim before. 'Why, it's lovely,' she had exclaimed, when I'd complained about it. She lived somewhere fully developed, in Bali. Apparently, the beaches there, and in Thailand, were built up years ago. Investment came in big and fast. Perhaps I should see the Candolim-Calangute-Baga suburban belt another way, as an acceptable degree of tourist collateral damage. After all, the belt is very short and narrow; there are beaches in the south which haven't been developed at all. Even in the north, over the Chapora River, development has hardly begun, and plans are monitored by alert environmentalists. Along this road the resorts probe into the palms behind, but not so very far. Back there, ancient landscapes slumber on.

The new road inland out of Old Goa has been cut through a hill, leaving the face of it red and raw; above us stands some light jungle, palms and scrub. At this early pre-commuter hour our taxi quickly crosses the new bridge at Banasterim, the inland border of Portuguese Goa for nearly three centuries, where once men patrolled the walls and crocodiles patrolled the moat. Now we are in another Goa entirely. We rub the condensation from the van windows to see white fog, illuminated by a diffuse sun, still lying beyond the first few trees. We see green lowland paddy fields, creeks and ponds, winding streams and their patient inhabitants: white egrets, all manner of storks, cranes, waders.

The state of Goa is the southernmost segment of the Konkan coast of west India. It comprises three longitudinal strips, the beach and its hinterland, the midlands and the Ghats, all of which are quite distinct from each other in geography and history. The coast is low-lying sandy or estuarine fishing and farming land, with rocky promontories protruding here and there from the midland plateau. Excluding the far northern and far southern coasts, this was the original Portuguese Goa: first, the island and its city of Goa taken in 1510, then thirty years later the provinces of Bardez to the north, including Candolim, and Salcete to the south. Together these made up the Old Conquests, and they remain the heartland of Christian Goa.

The modest rivers and marshes to the north, south and inland became religious and political frontiers. For nearly three centuries after the arrival of the Portuguese, the midland plateau remained part of the ancient Goan world, Hindu in its farmable areas, Hindu and tribal in its marginal ones. The plateau lacks the coastal lushness. From the air it is red-brown, savannah-like in parts, and in others pocked with open-cast pits and streaked here and there with green. It is also an old place made new – but by mining. An earlier newness had arrived in the late eighteenth century, when the midlands were included into the New Conquests, but this was more a change of management. By then the Portuguese Christianising passion was over. The three thousand square kilometres of the New Conquests were taken as a buffer against invaders, and for timber.

To the eye, the midlands are not ancient. The temples are mostly of the seventeenth and eighteenth centuries, and the principal town is Ponda, a village until the mid-twentieth century. Beyond it, on the roads up towards the mines, the destination boards of the dusty, crammed little buses are written in the Marathi script, not in the Romanised Konkani of the coast. Churches are few, and built in modernist concrete. At Tisk the roads turn into wide earthen highways for orange mining trucks barrelling along in clouds of red dust.

The laterite here is ten metres deep, a cap of rock with clay beneath it. Porous and water-bearing, laterite is the wondrous stone that Goa stands upon. It is soft when quarried, and looks like a thick block of terracotta cheese. Then the air hardens it and it darkens, becoming light and strong, the ancestral mother of all building blocks and easily the most attractive. Outside, you walk on it; inside, you live in it. The better houses in the old days were built entirely of laterite, and even in modern high-rises, most walls still are. Plastered over, it stays dry and lasts for centuries, but not forever. Eventually it crumbles into a fine dust which goes on to have a life of its own – on the highway to Tisk, and when it rises in clouds at parties. You come in colours to the laterite dance floor, and go home in khaki.

The Goan designer Wendell Rodricks has created a shade called Laterite Red. In village Goa a stack of laterite waits by every roadside, setting off the greenery to perfection. Red and green, with blue for sea and sky, are the colours of Goa – and white, for the churches. In the old days only churches were allowed to be white.

'In its range of deleterious effects, strip or open-cast mining has done more ecosystem damage to Goa than five-star beach resorts or large factories . . .' Aesthetically speaking, it is laterite's misfortune to be rich in iron. Half of India's iron exports come from Goa. It is her principal industry, more profitable than tourism. The state's second Chief Minister was a mine-owner, and the third was his daughter. Of the exported ore, thirteen million tons of it per year, 90 per cent goes to Japan (which financed and equipped the industry for the purpose), while the thirty million tons of discarded rubble stay at home. This voluminous discard rate – the ore being of low quality – is responsible for most of the 'range of deleterious effects'. Iron has long been recovered from the laterite by the cheapest method, and the resulting detritus heaped up on the landscape. The rehabilitation of the environment one reads about and commends is far less evident than the wanton destruction of it. Near Costi, the landscape as far as you can see is the creation of open-cast mining. 'Open-cast' is the word. The earth is opened and cast aside, and the result is an absolutely defoliated, churned-up world of slag heaps, buttes, peaks and rust-red lakes.

'Look, real mineral water.' We try being funny. 'This must be the mining area,' we say to our hitchhiker, an engineer in an orange construction hat. 'All Goa is mining area,' he replies. It's predicted that the iron will run out in twenty or thirty years. It will have provided a lot of money for the mine-owners, and local employment. It will not have provided a successor industry or improved the quality of life for the people of the iron belt's dust-covered villages.

Onwards and upwards we go, and eventually the orange dumper trucks vanish. The dust blows away, revealing quiet, pitted country roads walled in by vast plantations of cashew, coconut and sugarcane. Then comes the savannah, where big-leaved trees stand in clumps. Itinerant sellers of aluminium cookware doze beneath them. Mongooses and langur monkeys cross the road ahead, vanishing into the high grass.

Jungled spurs begin to invade the savannah; the great scarp looms over us, its tropical evergreen forest hung with cloud and filling the air with humidity. In a couple of weeks it will most likely be raining on the other side. In 1510 Afonso de Albuquerque arrived off the coast to see the Ghats 'hanging over Goa and the sea like an awning'. The Portuguese trekking inland were awed: 'like mounting to the sky, and so rough . . .'

Goa's inland strip is a steepening upward curve. Where it hasn't been 'diverted' for mines or plantations, the forest is dense on the spurs. We breathe rich jungle air. We drive the switchback roads that climb the scarp, the trees brushing the windows on one side, and shading down into the blue on the other. Somewhere we come out onto a ridge and descend into a narrow valley, almost a ravine, full of areca palms. Four men are sitting in a row overlooking this little Eden, smoking and watching for jackals. Virgin forest crowds the mango trees and sugarcane.

We stop the van at a warm waterfall that plays down the rock face right by the road. Opposite, the hill is sliced into neat terraces which are dotted with hayricks the shape of giant beehives. As we stand looking about us, a small, very dark, moustachioed old man of the hills stalks past with his machete and stick, not looking at us.

Our driver has been cautious out here in the boondocks. When asking for directions, his method has been to hear the local man out, and to then ask him what lies in all the other directions, just in case. But he is entranced by this lost valley. 'When do I get to see places like this?'

We sit by a clump of giant bamboo on the crest of the ridge as the sun and tourist Goa sink in the west. Extraordinary to think that in two hours or so from Candolim you can reach any extremity of this state: it is petite, the size of Luxembourg or Delaware, only sixty-five kilometres across and 105 long. In a subcontinent of wearying journeys, Goan journeys are short. We gaze down from the tribal forest across the Hindu midlands to the Christian coast. There lies the Candolim-Calangute-Baga suburban belt – a small place, but a state, or statelet, in the making. When it grows up, it will likely be less a part of Goa than of a multinational empire on which the sun never sets. I think of that empire as Touristhan. The resort map of Candolim that so amazes me is really a map of Touristhan, the kingdom of mass tourism, 'the great destroyer of customs and cultures, and the purveyor of uniformity'.

Fortunately, it was a map of the surface only, even if that surface is disconcerting. Apparent uniformity can be a form of camouflage, just as the uniform of baseball caps and shorts on the beach camouflages some very different types. Cultural variation is resilient, very old and deep and stubborn. Should even the entire coast of Goa turn into Touristhan it will be with a difference. Goa is in India; they do things differently there.

2   THE MARGINS

In the Aryan creation myth of Goa, the hero Parashuram stands upon the crest of the Ghats. Bending his bow, he fires a single arrow into the sea below. He orders the sea to retreat to that point, and so creates the Konkan coast. Parashuram raises the land from the waters, he clears it for settlement, his bow fells game and drives off the primitive men of the jungle.

A warrior-caste hero is something to be. But the feat that made him mythical began as something oddly modern; Parashuram's first experience of Goa was the beach. It is unlikely that the Indo-Aryan peoples of the north ever arrived in the Konkan by way of the Ghats. That steep, jungled descent from the Deccan was virtually trackless then, and inhabited by big cats, pythons and king cobras, boars and bears. Only the tribal people knew the passes. They had been taking salt up onto the Deccan since prehistoric times; it was still being carried over the Ghats on the pack animals of the Lamani in the early 1960s.

An enchantress to the seaborne, a stage for the varied and vivid theatre of India and its visiting players, Goa looked to the Persian Gulf, Arabia, Africa, and finally to Europe. Until big tourism caught her out by flying in, anyone coming by sea she bewitched – and everyone came to Goa by sea. 'Oceans unite. Mountains divide.' The Ghats cut off India to the east, and when you ride south from Mumbai (Bombay) on the new Konkan Railway – which has finally erased the succession of rivers and ridges with a succession of bridges and tunnels – you see that the Konkan is corrugated through its whole length.

It is likely that Parashuram's Indo-Aryans first arrived from the north in the sailing craft of the Gujaratis, somewhere between the seventh and fourth centuries BCE. Parashuram stood on, say, Calangute beach, contemplating a paradisal jungle where the coconut was not yet cultivated, a world so far untouched by north India. The Deccan had been Aryanised for centuries by then, but on this side of the impenetrable Ghats, Goa and all the Konkan still lived in the tribal past. Even centuries later, the Buddhists would be calling Goa Aparanta, 'Beyond the End'.

In the Sanskrit texts Parashuram is literally the maker of Goa. Symbolically, he stands on the Ghats to raise the land below. Here his writers are making a metaphor out of geology, for the Ghats are ancient, Pre-Cambrian; they formed the western edge of India when the laterite shelf below was still the seabed.

The Sanskrit texts call the whole Konkan coast Parashuram's Realm, for his subjugating and ordering of it, for his establishing of the Brahmin ascendancy and the order of caste. *Parashu* in Sanskrit means 'axe'. Parashuram, Axeman, is iron personified. Iron made the Aryan power. The iron plough and axe changed agriculture forever and created landownership, which in turn produced a stratified society with a priesthood, warriors armed with iron weapons, a merchant class.

To clear the wilderness, to drain the rich lowlands and farm them, the incomers had to attract local labour, and this gave rise to an 'almost unique form of pioneer enterprise', the profit-sharing village commune. The best lands were taken into private ownership, and the rest were auctioned off to the local community.

Deals had to be made, force had to give way to persuasion, however ungentle. The texts speak a little of the world displaced by the incomers, of the aboriginals, the Stone Age Mhars and Kols and Mundas. It is through the prism of religion that we see the accommodating of settlers into new surroundings and the submission of the locals to the forceful new culture: in the end, the tribal mother goddesses, 'gruesome and beautiful at the same time', give up power to – and marry – the father gods of the Aryan settlers.

The descendants of the old tribes live on in the forests of the Ghats which, however encroached upon, still cover 10 per cent of Goa. Some go on living the ancient life of slash-and-burn, cultivating the clearing, then moving on. Others get by precariously on the edge of the latest civilisation, ours; they have never quite vanished or been absorbed. The most conspicuous along the coast of Goa are the Lamani, immemorially traders out of Karnataka. Tribal origins are not always so obvious as in the vivid Lamani women; their men are drab beside them.

Soon after the Indian general election of the spring of 1998, I read that Goa's two new Members of Parliament in Delhi would be trying to get 'groups like the Dhangars under ST' (Scheduled Tribe). Numbers of the Dhangars still practise transhumance, travelling seasonally with their flocks and herds, and they are often called the only truly tribal people of the state. All the other communities that the papers call 'the backwards' have official designations of one kind or another – Backward Caste, Other Backward Caste, Scheduled Caste. But Goa remains the only state of India without a Scheduled Tribe, an aboriginal community identified by the authorities as disadvantaged, one of the 'weaker sections', and hence deserving of development money and social welfare schemes. The Dhangars have gone unscheduled perhaps because of their transience; it is difficult to bring progress to those who refuse to stay put.

The Dhangars were Hindu before the Christian era began, but preserve some customs of purely tribal origin. They bury all their dead. (Hindus in Goa cremate their dead but bury certain classes of them, the casualties of epidemics, for instance, and children below a certain age.) A Dhangar man receives no dowry from his bride's family, as Hindus conventionally do, but pays the bride-price – though inflation is making the traditional polygamy unaffordable.

The Dhangars have been nomadic since prehistoric times. In the great Goan historian D. D. Kosambi's 1962 account, they are still gelding their sheep with sharpened flints, a Mesolithic habit. In groups of a dozen people, accompanied by their flocks, they leave eastern upland Goa in the summer for the 300-kilometre trip over the Ghats and onto the Deccan to escape the tremendous coastal monsoon that gives the sheep foot rot. (The coast receives around one hundred inches of rain in three or so months, the Ghats twice that – and the Deccan plateau, twelve.) They stay four months, returning to the coast after the great Dussehra festival of October–November, and the last rains. On the way, local farmers pay them for the sheep dung left in their fields. The wool is sold in the spring.

'In fact, they are not only backward, but are also reluctant to enjoy the modern facilities most of which remain unknown to them'. Development programmes tend to presume – as Norman Lewis puts it, in the context of Indonesia – that 'tribal people's unsatisfactory existences can only be improved by government interference'. When development is underfunded, and/or botched by maladministration, self-sufficiency is undermined; while at the same time, the new, developed life is made unreachable for lack of resources. The tribal girl collecting my empty cans and jars is dressed for the imitation lifestyle, in fake Reeboks and a Calvin Kleen T-shirt.

British anthropologists of the 1920s wrote that to the tribal peoples, their 'godlings', their village deities, totems, were *devaks*. The *devaks* might inhabit statues, trees, rocks or animals. They animated everything inanimate, and were worshipped as living ancestors and propitiated as spirits of the dead. Each tribal clan was subdivided by the worship of one *devak* or another, and all the members of the sub-clan took that *devak*'s name. To marry someone of your own *devak*-name was incestuous, forbidden; in this way, the ancestors guarded genes and sanctified the social order. There was marrying out – but no marrying up. Tribal organisation was 'horizontal', lacking the vertical hierarchy and attendant privileges of caste.

I came across a *devak* once, at Bondla, the smallest of Goa's three wildlife sanctuaries. As you approach it, roadside signs can be seen – 'Carnivore Keep Balance of Nature' – and the night I arrived there with my father, there was chicken curry. The forest encloses a little zoo, where the next morning we found all the animals asleep except for a pair of amorous leopards. A notice nearby read 'No Indecent Behaviour in Front of the Animals'.

'That is an Indian lion,' the keeper said, pointing to a reclining carnivore. My father said no, it wasn't. It lacked the ridges of hair along the belly; it was an African lion. 'Ah, yes,' the keeper said, 'but it was *born* in India.' On to the next cage. It was empty, except for a hunk of dripping meat on a hook, and the door was open. The keeper explained that the zoo's policy was to let the female animals out to breed; the regular meals of home brought them back, and quite often their wild mates as well. A sensible policy for a zoo in a jungle. At night the wild animals outside roared, howled and twittered to be let in while the captives inside clamoured to be let out. We carefully checked our room for snakes, as all the venomous ones had recently escaped the serpentarium, and were out here somewhere.

The *devak*, a 'hero stone', a local village ancestor memorialised probably for dying while resisting a cattle raid, was a statuette under a banana tree. On the back of the postcard of him available at reception, however, he was identified as Vetal, a notable deity of the Konkan, a father god who must not be approached by women and who presides over ghosts and spirits. Here, in this stocky figure with the pagoda crown, neat goatee and knee-length phallus, was a fine example of a local *devak* promoted to the lower reaches of the Hindu pantheon in the interests of peace. He is an early example of politics working through religion. 'Many nameless village gods have risen from gruesome origins to identification with some respectable Brahmin deity.' Vetal, he who must be obeyed – though he looked decorative and disempowered in that municipal park.

Several months later, in a guesthouse in the Himalaya, I pinned the postcard to the wall above my table. One day the cook called by, in his galoshes and balaclava. Himself a hillman from a remote mountain village, he'd had to take the job because his wife had shot someone by mistake, and he had the blood-debt to pay.

Of everything in the room, only the photo interested him. A

devak of the south, I said. He knew that – even if the godlings of his own valley were represented by faces only, masks of silver. I thought he'd be taken aback by this exotic and underdressed figure from a palm-tree coastline two thousand kilometres away, but he wasn't. He frowned over the picture for some time, so when he left, I gave it to him. I passed his room an hour later, and there was Vetal on his god shelf with the fresh marigolds and the pictures of his father and Sai Baba of Shirdi, the Dalai Lama, and the mouth of the sacred cave of Amarnath.

From the anthropology of the 1920s comes a neat epigram: 'The unwilled is the spirit-caused'. The world beyond the (then very short) range of human control was unpredictable and mostly ungovernable. It was a spirit world inhabited by the ancestors in their malign aspect, able to take any form, and by apparitions of the unfulfilled, the ungrateful dead, the unspeakable familiars of Vetal. It was his demons that were responsible for the more workaday afflictions. In the village of Naroa, on the Bicholim bank of the Mandovi River, there is a haunted temple hill. On it stands a tree riddled with iron nails. Each nail entraps a demon once exorcised from some afflicted person and driven into the tree. Human agency was able to deflect at least some of the lesser spirit-caused problems; in the more difficult cases, one consulted a specialist.

The *ghadi* is a figure from the prehistory of religion – priest of the *devak*, shaman, exorcist. Low in caste, high in repute, they were made grants of land in return for their services and given a ward of the village, a *vaddo*, to live in. Some *ghadivaddos* still remain, at least in name. And the *ghadis* themselves continue their work at the edge of our reality – though everyone acknowledges that today our reality is taking over. It has pushed the spirit world back, and psychologists, doctors, social workers and priests of the big religions are swarming over the psychic territory. Among the educated, necromancy is no longer considered useful.

Professionals prefer the psychiatrist to the *ghadi*. It is said that if there were more antivenin in the hospitals, the *ghadi* would be as redundant as the druid.

Yet the elderly snakewoman from Aguada is no less the shaman these days because she spends her time doing house calls for snake-bitten goats, or for a foreigner's dog envenomed by a cobra in Candolim. In snake cases she will certainly be called before the doctor is: snakebite has always been seen as an affliction more mystical than medical.

Every heap of rubble, woodpile and hole in the wall will house a snake at some time. Rodents are parasitic on humans; snakes come for them, so they are always with us but rarely seen, like spirits. Inscrutable, they leave signs such as tracks and discarded skins that preserve their ancient and fabulous reputation. If a cobra appears to a pregnant woman in a dream – or so Auntie, my landlady in Arambol, used to tell me – she will have a boy; and if a water snake, a girl. A snake in the house was a guardian spirit and should be left alone; Auntie was always trying to convert hers by feeding it only on saint's days.

The mate of a murdered cobra is said to come looking for revenge, though the renowned snakeman Romulus Whitaker writes that it is attracted by the musk released at death. Naturally, Whitaker's 'Big Four' most venomous snakes – the cobra, the krait, the Russell's viper, the saw-scaled viper – are most feared, though the cobra is sacred to Lord Shiva, and so gets respect as well.

When a king cobra dies it must be buried, not burnt. It can grow to five metres in length, and is the only snake that builds a nest. This most intelligent of snakes – shy, but armed with enough venom to kill an elephant – is the most celebrated in legend. 'My grandfather is certainly reported to have seen the brilliant light cast at night by the jewel that a king cobra had laid aside while feeding, though no such jewel has ever been found in the head of any cobra in spite of the most active search (for it is traditionally the one effective antidote for snakebite).' Until the jewel is found, the old chicken method, still used today, will have to do. The anus of a live chicken having been applied to the bitten part, 'the chicken sucked the venom till it dropped dead. Several chickens were used . . .'

The tribes lived in the borderlands and followed religions whose method was negotiation with the spirit world. Because that world begins at the edge of our own, anything borderline – marginal, ambiguous, transitional, edgy – was potentially dangerous. Even with us, the bride is carried over the threshold. The snake has always been propitiated because it is the most ambiguous creature, living somewhere between the subterranean world of the dead and our own. The humanoid effigy keeps demons out of the unfinished house. The limits of the village and the sea's or river's edge were the limits of the human realm.

Crossroads, neither the one road nor the other, were once tribal cult sites. Throughout the Stone Age, the aborigines 'whose nomad tracks met at the junction' worshipped their mother goddesses at crossroads. With the arrival of the Indo-Aryans and the dispossession of the mother goddesses by the father gods, the cult sites were demoted. Places of holy dread like the Calangute–Nagoa crossroads were said to be haunted, to bring evil repute upon any house built nearby, condemned to the condition of the cemetery and the deserted temple. A new, male, protector-spirit of crossroads was appointed, the Aryan god Rudra. Then Christianity came, and Rudra was overthrown by St Christopher, patron saint of wayfarers. Finally, the traffic came and overthrew everyone at crossroads everywhere.

In the old days no one from Calangute strayed at night beyond the Convent of Boa Viagem, the Safe Journey, on the Mapusa road. The nearby Fondiem spring, sacred like all healing springs, had a resident sprite who in the manner of the Sphinx posed deadly riddles to anyone seeking the healing powers. Mysterious fires suddenly combusting in a grove on the Anjuna border were declared to have been lit by the shades of departed villagers on their way to the Nagoa church – very old spirits, these, from the days before Anjuna had a church of its own. (Though Nagoa was sacred to still older spirits. As its name indicates, before the church was built a Nag shrine stood there, a shrine of the sacred cobra of Shiva.)

When a cross was built and blessed at the flaming grove, the fires ceased. There is nothing random about the placing of all those Goan crosses. They defy the ghosts of the margins, the hilltops – the Baga hill, for instance – and the seashore. The traveller passing the gloomy copse at dusk, the 'hour of the demons', when it is neither day nor night, saw the white cross and was reassured. The 'cross in Moadys was built because of the evil wind'; another, 'to appease those spirits'. A wayside cross was erected to repel 'the collective ghost' of the village ancestors.

And each human life itself had borders, internal boundaries to be crossed with caution and sanctioned by ritual. Birth, obviously; and then puberty, a marginal time of neither child nor adulthood. For women, menstruation, motherhood, and menopause. But of all the rites, the funerary were the most punctiliously performed – lest the dead become undead and rise again to commit nocturnal nuisances and burden the living with time-consuming and expensive exorcism rites. No threshold in life was more difficult to cross than the one over to the other side.

The anthropologists say that twenty of Goa's thirty-four communities – communities in the sense of castes, hereditary classes – cremate their dead, in the Hindu way. Fourteen of those commit the ashes to the sea. The remainder, including Christians and Muslims, practice burial. The Kunbi, a Backward Caste, an ancient tribal community, bury their dead in east–west alignment, facing the rising sun. The Kharvi, fishing people, seat their dead to bury them. Of the three groups of Gauda, two are Hindu, but all bury their dead – and when the relatives leave the graveside they do not, must not, ever look back.

Everything is animate. Nothing dies. Death may not be the end, even for the dead. They envy the living: if you turn around for one last look, they may follow you. This is the anxiety for the living, that the dead may not be properly dead. The past has to be seen to be past before the living can move on.

Christians still keep round-the-clock vigils, surrounding the newly dead with the living for fear of demonic possession. The first Christians in Goa, sixteenth-century men obsessed by signs and marvels and well used to cohabiting in Europe with the old pagan necromancy and witch-lore, encountered a world crowded with yet more religions and beliefs. And with vast cultural and linguistic variety: 'As a matter of fact, Goan culture has always had . . . a marginal character due to its situation beyond a mountain barrier, at the common apex of two distinct linguistic, perhaps ethnic, groups' – those of Maharashtra to the north and Karnataka to the east and south. This weight of influence compressed a tremendous diversity into a very small unity. D. D. Kosambi wrote that as late as 1924 it was possible to place any Goan by accent to within five miles of their place of origin. The Salcete and Bardez accents are still very different.

Layers of belief were taken on over the centuries, even over millennia. The Indo-Aryans had absorbed primordial cults of the lingam, the serpent and the sacred pipal tree in their making of Hinduism. Then other influences came to Goa – Sumerian possibly, Buddhist and Jain certainly. The most Goan of dynasties, the Kadambas, who ruled a millennium ago, were Hindus converted from Jainism. The Bahmani dynasty, a branch of which ruled Goa until driven out by the Portuguese in 1510, were Turks whose troops were mostly Muslims converted from Hinduism.

Some of Goa's aboriginal communities were Hinduised; some were later Christianised. In the time of cultural revolution from hunter-gathering to farming, from nomadism to settlement, Buddhism was enormously influential in encouraging literacy, the use of iron tools and the plough. Buddhist monks penetrated the wilderness to preach nonviolence to the tribals, to discourage the blood sacrifices practised by their religious cults. They founded their cave-monasteries at the junctions of trade routes, at the approaches to the mountain passes where settlements already stood; in Goa there are at least three known cave sites.

When the cave-monasteries had served their purpose and were abandoned, the tribal sacrifices resumed. 'The people whom [the Buddhists] had helped lead out of savagery . . . had never forgotten their primeval cults.' But Buddhism had discredited the most sanguinary of them, and cult practice now focused on those symbols of tribal solidarity, the *devta*-totems. The *ghadis* who watched over the order of things continued to be revered. For reinforcement, Hindu pandits were engaged to negotiate with the other world; and in their turn, so were Christian priests. And when science came, it too was added to the array of useful intermediaries. The Kharvi employ both *ghadis* and doctors to mediate between themselves and the other world. 'They believe evil spirits are the cause of diseases. They also visit hospitals.'

'Jungles,' says the Forestry Department man. 'Kunbi.' He looks just like them, dark and whippet-thin, not too citified himself in his bare feet and *lungi* and string vest, but now we know he has a government job.

Through open forest, savannah, and oceans of dead leaves, we have driven down to Mollem. Mollem is in the Bhagwan Mahaveer wildlife reserve on the road up to one of Goa's ancient Ghat passes, and its deep forest has for centuries preserved the only remaining intact building of the Kadambas, of Goa's golden age, the temple of Tambdi Surla. The forests of the Ghats also shelter an extraordinary variety of plants, birds, reptiles – including a hundred varieties of mushroom and all eleven species of dwarf gecko – and animals too, judging by the extensive preserved faeces exhibition in the Cotigao cottage museum.

One of the group of quiet Kunbi men goes up a coconut palm as a lizard goes up a wall. In the mid-1920s, whole villages of Kunbi were tricked by British indentured-labour agents into transportation to the Assam tea plantations, three thousand kilometres away to the north-east. None of them had ever left their hills before, and the only trains they knew were the little steam engines that struggled up the one railway line to Castle Rock, to the border of British India. In Assam the clouds hung low over their damp huts, and the children began to die. Eventually they contrived a mass escape, and with extreme difficulty – their dialect of Konkani being everywhere incomprehensible – and with no money, they jumped trains and hid from the uniforms. Crossing the Ghats during the rains, they eventually got home. It had taken them three months, and they were so starved that the mother of one young man couldn't recognise him.

Now the Kunbi cut coconuts, farm, do contract labour, perform their dances for tourists. They are counted with the lower castes in most towns and big villages. The sociologist Olivinho Gomes calls the Kunbi of Chandor 'Christian aboriginals', and adds that in Goa there are a few Kunbi priests. In 1952, in the Basilica of Bom Jesus in Old Goa, Evelyn Waugh unchristianly noted a group of 'monkey-like figures newly baptised in the jungle'. He himself had been converted to Catholicism, though not in the jungle, all of twenty-two years previously.

The Kunbi have always lived in this open forest of trees that stand in great drifts of dry leaves, and what they really like to do is hunt. They are persecuted for it, and for their slash-and-burn – though the decimation of wildlife in Mollem was done in colonial times and later by city people, leaving the doyen of Indian ornithologists, Sálim Ali, to protest at the spectacle of a wildlife reserve nearly devoid of wildlife.

With the end of hunting, animals have returned – wary ones, a flash of fur here, a glimpse of hide there. But one day, bumping along the road in our van, we see a quartet of gaur, huge and unafraid, wading through the scrub. They are the biggest cattle on earth, and Goa's official state animal. The driver remarks that the gaur is too big to be the official animal of such a small state, and anyway, the official animal of a coastal state should be a coastal fish, the renowned and toothsome pomfret. The gaur stalks off. After that, we see a pair of herons and a solitary grey jungle fowl. That's all for today, but then the jungle isn't a matter of how many wild creatures you see: it's how it feels to be somewhere that still belongs to them.

It begins outside the resthouse room, and no one quite wants to go out at night. At dawn you are sure to find a curious spoor in your path, a wild scent, an intriguing feather. You feel you might see anything, a slender loris with spatulate extraterrestrial fingers and saucer eyes, or a slobbering sloth bear, though these are very rare. Porcupines are not. The Forestry man says they sleep on the resthouse porches, snoring loudly, and rattling their quills when they turn over.

We want to walk into the reserve, but it isn't legal, and we end up in the van. This is unfortunate, because in a vehicle in a forest you hear only the vehicle, while the forest hears only you. The track is lumps of mud and stone, and as we grind along it, big solemn birds gaze down upon us, then slowly flap away. We panic a hog deer, flush a honey buzzard, and put a crested serpent eagle to flight. At the top of the rise, we stall. A few quiet men come past, not looking at us, thin black legs and bare feet silent on the path.

3 SWORD AND HAZARD

November brings in the winter. It exchanges the wet heat that follows the summer monsoon for a long succession of dry, blue, cloudless days that seem to erase time until the next spring and the return of heat. The light and the dark come on quickly, without the northerly lingerings and gloom. Dawn can be quite chilly, for a short while, until the sun is up. Then, from the sea, the shore is clearly visible, the mouth of the Mandovi River, the old stone walls of Aguada and the hill behind, the beach and its wooden boats, the tough green dune scrub, the crowds of coconut palms.

In the early morning of 25 November 1510, the twenty ships of Afonso de Albuquerque's fleet arrived off the river mouth. The fishermen on Candolim beach may not have been too perturbed by the sight; they knew the stout, upright little ships had come to attack the Adil Shah in his island city just upstream because they had tried it before, in March. In any case, the doings of rulers affected fishermen very little. The Dessais, the taxmen of the Adil Shah, were most exacting, and the farmers of the village communes wanted to be rid of them, but only farmers paid taxes.

On deck that morning, the military eye passed over the fishermen and came to rest on the promontory commanding the river mouth. There were two freshwater springs up there; it should be called Aguada, the water place. What a very good site for a fort. On the opposite bank, on a sandy spit, stood the Adil Shah's lightly fortified seaside residence, moated on its inland side. Otherwise there was nothing more than a coconut grove, ponds and creeks and paddy fields, a few dunes. Such was the mouth of the Mandovi in 1510, and for another hundred years. Then the

Aguada fort would be built on the promontory, and opposite it, two hundred years later, Panjim.

Afonso de Albuquerque had had a wretched summer. In May the Adil Shah had driven him out, so he had retired down the coast to the island of Anjediv to recover and refit, and wait to be reinforced. The summer climate took no prisoners. (Two centuries later the British, summering on Anjediv, would bury two hundred dead there.) In June the monsoon had come raging in, turning the sky black all the way up to heaven, bringing thunder and lightning and clouds of spray. Tearing offshore gales had made patrolling by the fleet impossible. And the rain: Albuquerque had found that nearly all of Goa's rain fell in the three monsoon months, in drops ten times the size of European ones.

On the bleak haven of Anjediv, he found he agreed with his orders: Goa would indeed make a fine naval base. It was defensible, being almost an island, but not too much of one, close to its supplies. Even if the place did turn out to be more lush than fertile, it would be a change from the dry fields of Portugal; and in any case, his men had not come to India to be farmers. They looked to the sea, as Goans did – though not for the fishing. They intended to own it. And as for the land . . . In one letter to the Portuguese king, Albuquerque had suggested that amongst Goa's advantages might be its usefulness as a base for expeditions into the interior. But the king knew what he knew too, that Covilhã's report had not encouraged notions of conquest. Covilhã had been here in 1488, arriving by the overland route, the first Portuguese to see Goa, and had made his report in Lisbon in 1493, well before Vasco da Gama's expedition by sea.

Surrounding Goa were any number of lesser states – lesser only in contrast to the powers in the north, the Rajput confederacy and the doomed but still ruling Lodi Sultanate of Delhi. Gujarat to the north-west was held by Muslims, as was most of the Deccan and the Konkan coast. The remaining territories paid tribute to the Hindu state of Vijayanagar, itself on the Deccan. Each of these kingdoms possessed at least one hundred thousand infantry. They had cavalry, the latest imported artillery, and fear-some assault troops, each combatant standing three metres tall and weighing five tons. These were the armour-plated and noto-riously excitable elephants; Vijayanagar alone had nine hundred of them, nearly as many as Albuquerque had men. Everything considered, India possessed overwhelming might. It was one of the world's two superpowers, the other being China.

Portugal, on the other hand, was a small country without allies. Her armies were a ten-month, dangerous voyage away from Goa and in any case were undermanned. Only at sea could Albuquerque win; his fighting ships were the best in the world. The caravel had been steadily improved over a century of sailing the West African coast. With a shallow draught and some twenty-one metres long, it could be lateen-rigged like the Arabian craft it was modelled on, and thus made more manoeuvrable. It was built to withstand the recoil of heavy naval gunnery, currently the sole area of military technology in which Portugal might prevail. Just one caravel could stand off from a fleet of oared galleys – the only armed craft here – and sink them all. The previous year, Almeida had sunk an entire Egyptian fleet off Diu on the coast of Gujarat.

Albuquerque could take a coastal city like Goa, dispossess the Moors and civilise the place. He, the admiral, would have to begin this task himself, there being nothing more to be hoped from the elusive Christian monarch Prester John. Covilhã had at last met this legendary figure – in the wrong country, in Ethiopia. There were Christians in India too, but lapsed and lost to Rome, Indian by culture and professing allegiance to St Thomas or the Patriarch of Antioch. And the Hindus had been Christian once, or so Vasco had surmised twelve years before in that 'chapel' in Calicut (Kozhikode, in Kerala), kneeling in gratitude for deliver-ance from the sea before a dimly lit goddess and child, doubtfully genuflecting to saints with 'as many as four arms' and 'monstrous teeth'.

Better to turn one's mind to the practicalities. The pepper trade was already being diverted from the Arabia-to-Venice route, down to the Cape and round Africa; already in Lisbon, Indian pepper cost only one-fifth of what it was costing in Venice. Albuquerque had assured the king that the taking of Goa would perfectly position Portugal for the control of the rest of the Indian Ocean's trade. There would have to be patrols in the Arabian Sea all the way up to the Persian Gulf, backed by coastal forts. In time the east Asia trade could be taken also. And the capture of Goa would bring an alliance with Vijayanagar, City of Victory, one-time ruler of Goa and bitter opponent of the Adil Shah, whose taking of the port city had cut off Vijayanagar's access to the horse trade from Arabia. By retaking Goa, the Portuguese – and Thimayya of Vijayanagar – would restore it. An excellent business. Horses were expensive, they could not be bred here, and did not live long.

Over there sat the fishermen, mending their nets for the new season. They were wishing his flotilla away, those men of the sea unable to imagine the wealth that would soon come from it. Now the sun was rising behind Aguada, drying up the mist. Breakfast woodsmoke drifted through the palms. Afloat on his element, Afonso de Albuquerque contemplated a Portuguese ocean.

No power laid claim to the sea. Nobody owned it; the merchants of the coastal towns sailed a free-trade zone ungoverned by landsmen. And when the Mughals rose to power in the mid-sixteenth century, they, men from that most landlubberly of places, Central Asia, would also have little regard for the sea. The Chinese had readily taken to the ocean; but the eclipse of his outward-looking supporters at Court had eventually seen to the withdrawal of the huge fleets of the eunuch admiral Cheng Ho that had once visited Africa. Possessing the world's best maps, the Chinese might well have gone on to discover Europe. But even without them, the Indian Ocean at the time of Vasco da Gama's arrival in 1498 saw a voluminous trade, especially out of Gujarat, which had been growing since Roman times. The spice trade to Europe was only a small part of it.

So Vasco made his big entrance into an unregulated ocean. It was just that: an irruption, a bid for that unheard-of thing, sea power. The Zamorin of Calicut laughed at this upstart admiral from somewhere on the other side of Africa, at his poor presents of cloth and beads, and Vasco in a rage went out and sank a shipful of pilgrims. He had gunnery, if little else.

'In 1498', the old Indian school mnemonic went, 'Vasco knocked on India's gate'. In 1998 the quincentenary of his arrival came around, and you could hear the knocking still. The problem with this occasion, for those that cared about these things, was that it squeezed a wide-ranging and general argument about the Portuguese time in Goa, all 451 years of it, into one person – who happens to be a hero in one country and an imperialist in another. In the ensuing clash of columnists it tended to be forgotten that the empire that followed Vasco, be it beastly or noble, was so small that contemporary Indian records barely mention it. No living historian noted the arrival of Jesuits for their famous audience with the Emperor Akbar; the putting down of Portuguese pirates appears as a footnote. It is the impact of his arrival in India that keeps Vasco memorable. Compare the British advent two centuries later, a modest affair of merchant adventurers on a muddy riverbank in Bengal that was to end with most of the subcontinent becoming a colony.

One evening a Goan musician told me that government funding for his cultural troupe's visit to Portugal for the Vasco celebrations had been withdrawn. But there were other reactions to Vasco, a whole range of them, and these began to appear as the anniversary impended. One commentator described life under Portuguese imperialism as 'slavery', another replying that this made it difficult to know what to call the life of the actual slaves. Professional historians were sage and dispassionate. A young tourist interviewed on the street said Vasco da Gama was a Brazilian football club; and the Portuguese Ambassador to India, interviewed in the magazine *Goa Today*, thought Goa's meandering backroads very old-style Portuguese, and was diplomatic about the rest.

Some took the view that Vasco hadn't achieved anything, not even nautically. Having rounded the Cape – and it had taken the Portuguese, less a seafaring nation than a fishing one, about one hundred years to get that far – he realised he had no idea where India was. Ignominiously, he'd had to hire a Muslim pilot, the point being that to Christians the Muslims were anathema, the more so for being ubiquitous. 'Moors' (from the Portuguese *mouro*) continued to rule North Africa, just across the Straits of Gibraltar. They controlled all the business on West Africa's Slave Coast, and Christian Portuguese had to buy from them – and they did so copiously, correcting Portugal's severe labour shortage and making their country the biggest slave owner in Europe. Moors held Jerusalem and its Christian holy places, and Constantinople, the citadel of the Eastern Church. It vexed Vasco to be guided across the Indian Ocean by a Moorish pilot. And soon he would find that they ran the spice trade as well, from the buying from Keralans to the selling to Venetians.

Portugal herself had been a Moorish colony – long before Vasco's time, but no longer than the memory for humiliation. Now she was an ex-colony, an emergent nation on the edge of a hostile Spain and of a Europe as disunited as ever, but much more modern. By the standards of the late fifteenth century, Portugal was backward, a condition which made its nobility touchy and provoked it into posturing and overreach. The *fidalgo* class, the nobility, overmanned (numbering some twenty thousand) and uninterested in farming and trade, were always restive and in need of distraction. Kings, always fearful that the devil might make work for idle hands, took to sending the aristocracy to the ends of the earth for gold, or at least for glory. This made the Portuguese empire most unlike the great capitalist empires that would succeed it. It was the *fidalgo* style, extravagantly martial, pious, romantic and aristocratic, that formed the taste (and enduring reputation) of the Portuguese empire for religious fanaticism, great architecture and music.

Gama, Covilhã, Almeida, Albuquerque: all were men of a hinge century, the fifteenth, a time suspended between the Middle Ages and the Renaissance. The quintessential figure is João de Castro, modern scientist and navigator – and a man of antique superstitions, a bigot, a flagellant. His information on newly fashionable and promising Asia came from Marco Polo, most of whose book was reliable – and from Sir John Mandeville, who was someone's pseudonym, and whose *Travels* is a farrago of monsters and marvels as chimerical as Sir John himself. The practical Portuguese intention was to hijack the Indian spice business, and to link up with Prester John, a King Arthur figure of eleventh-century legend, in the hope of his arising at the head of a Christian multitude to deliver Asia from the Moors.

A good deal of pure fantasy went into the Enterprise of Asia. The nautical reality was that Lisbon and Calicut were an ocean and a continent apart. Even one hundred years after Vasco, and in much better ships, half the men leaving Portugal for Goa would never arrive. The epic poet Luis de Camoens wrote that he set out 'as one leaving this world for the next'.

The voyage to India took ten months, and for three of those months Vasco was entirely out of sight of land. He had no idea of his longitude (and nor would anyone for another 250 years). His map, the standard seafarer's map of the time, was a revision of a Ptolemaic one thirteen centuries old, which so underestimated the size of the world that six years before Vasco, Columbus had thought he could get to the Indies by sailing west. For Europe at least, Ptolemy's was better than the medieval maps which placed Jerusalem at the top, Hell at the bottom and Here Be Dragons in the middle. Africa, though, was mostly speculation, and beyond the Cape it was more speculative still. Bartolomeu Dias had found the way around to the Indian Ocean, but its size and bounds were still hearsay. From Malindi in what is now Kenya, Vasco and his clueless mariners contemplated the watery wastes. And so Vasco hired the best available pilot, a Moor, an Arab, Ibn Majid, the most celebrated Arab navigator alive.

At dawn on 20 May 1498 the Ghats were sighted, and

twenty-three days out of Malindi, Vasco made landfall. On the Calicut quayside, as he looked about for a convenient chapel, wandered seafarers from everywhere but Europe. But now Vasco had opened the way for Europeans. Oceans unite. 'If cultures and civilisations are the tectonic plates of world history, frontiers are the places where they scrape against each other and cause convulsive change.' Calicut had been a frontier for India, Arabia and Africa, and the first people to discover Vasco turned out to be North Africans. They looked at him and his scurvy crew and battered ships, and said – in fluent Spanish – 'What the hell are *you* doing here?'

Floating off Aguada at the end of the Candolim beach, on St Catherine's Day in 1510, Afonso de Albuquerque waited for dawn, ordered the guns to be run out, plotted a Portuguese ocean. And so it became – and officially remained through the long centuries until December 1961, when after a brief gunfight the Aguada fort fell to the Indian Army and the last Portuguese fighting ship, an obsolete frigate, sailed out to face the Indian Navy. Its name? *Afonso de Albuquerque.*

Goa was duly taken. In four days, Albuquerque's and Thimayya's men killed six thousand Muslims. Arriving late upon the scene, the Adil Shah cried that the invaders were sons of the devil; after which the defences were hurriedly reinforced against his revenge, which was soon in coming. Sixty years later, his son was still trying to retake Goa.

One Father Brodrick was later to call Goa an island only by courtesy of two rivers and an inlet, but the rivers were broad and once the bank of the inlet was fortified the thousand Portuguese were there to stay – though the Moorish threat did oblige them to employ some of the island's original inhabitants. The estuarine or saltwater crocodile, largest of all amphibians and in 1510 not at all an endangered species, might attain five metres in length, four hundred kilos in weight, and fifty kilometres per hour over the short, gaping, sprint. The chronicler Barros, who was there, says that criminals and prisoners of war were flung down the river-banks 'at times of stress' to keep the amphibians congregated at the vulnerable inland fords of Gandaulim and Banasterim.

Soon every caravel that could be spared was upping anchor and sailing the short distance up the river to the open sea. Under a blue winter sky the admiral's privatisation programme for the public ocean was about to go into operation. He was not originating something here, but only professionalising it: the Konkan coast had been famous for piracy since Roman times.

The caravels didn't so much trade as manage trade, issuing permits to all shipping, sinking the objectors, and collecting 'duties'. The permit system, 'precisely a protection racket', duly outraged the Venetians who handled the spice business in the Arabian ports. Traders pure and simple, they paid for no army or navy and built no fortresses. The Portuguese, more militant than merchant, built or captured them everywhere they went. They ranged west as far as Hurmuz on the Gulf and as far east as Japan. The empire's laureate Camoens wrote of this age of fort-fever: 'And if there had been more of the world, they would have reached it'; though one suspects that if there had been more of the world, as in fact there was, they would have built forts on it.

The hijacking of the spice trade made Portugal rich, for a time. Rebuilding in the recognised style of imperial grandiosity, the city of Goa likewise fattened on the proceeds. The island's Indians hoped that after four changes of regime in forty years there might be a lasting peace; already, after the Adil Shah, there had been tax relief. His imposition of a feudal system run by local vassals, the Dessais, had been universally detested, and Albuquerque's extirpation of the feudals and reinstatement of the village communes had been universally popular. He had banned *sati*, widow immolation, at once, but was otherwise tolerant of Hindu religion. Eventually, all would have to cluster under the umbrella of Christendom. There could be no enemies within, not in vulnerable Goa, and religion was allegiance. But as yet little could be done; there were too few priests, and these few were suspected of preferring oriental pleasures to missionary zeal.

Albuquerque tried to 'Portuguese' Goa from quite another angle. *Fidalgos* might have prospects back home, but the soldiery did not. They would be in Goa forever, and it was best to settle them, so they were offered Muslim women saved from the slaughter on condition of conversion. His soldiery are said to have been more partial to black Africans, but Albuquerque insisted: sixteenth-century Portuguese leaders may have had 'no contempt for subject peoples', but they did have colour prejudice.

The new social engineering was a consequence of the lack of Portuguese women. (In fact, there would be none in Goa for another thirty years.) Albuquerque hoped that land might fall into Portuguese hands through marriage, but it never did. The clinching arguments were that married men did less damage, and that concubinage was about to get out of control: within three years of his victory, Albuquerque saw four hundred of his men married off.

In 1514, a year before his death, Albuquerque was given a rhinoceros. It became the most famous rhino in history. A great fish found stranded in the Mandovi was considered so extraordinary that a portrait of it was sent to the king – but the rhino was to become the subject of a woodcut by the incomparable Dürer, thereby becoming the model for rhino studies for nearly three hundred years, until explorers in Africa observed that Dürer hadn't actually drawn his rhinoceros from life.

The creature was captured in the wilds of Champaner, northeast of Baroda, by a hunting party of Muzaffar II of Gujarat, and given to Portuguese emissaries as a present for Albuquerque, who shipped it to his king. From Lisbon it went by cart to Madrid, where a pupil of Dürer's wrote up a description of it for the German artist. From a first sketch, he made the famous woodcut.

It is unmistakably the profile of an Asian rhinoceros, except that the armour appears to have been put on in separate pieces, like a knight's.

The much-travelled beast was to make one last journey. On its way by sea to the Pope's menagerie it was shipwrecked, drowned and washed ashore, and had to appear before the Pontiff stuffed.

4 The Rigour of Mercy

Follow the road from Ximer south towards Aguada, to the cross-roads and the little market, the Candolim Tinto, which stands opposite the football pitch. South of the old lockup, its roadside wall painted up into a giant Manik Soda sign, the apartment blocks, resorts and tourist shops of Sinquerim begin. Diversification is evident here. The cyber café sells crochet items; the boutique, roofing tiles.

From the Holiday Beach Resort all the way through Candolim and north to Calangute the new money flourishes. The sandy ground that yielded no more than coconut rent twenty years ago now has all kinds of tourist accommodation built on it. It is crowded in the winter, but unappealing in the summer, with monsoon storms lashing gardens and cars and paintwork and salting the air. Most of the old money, which is to say landowning, always lived inland on the rich riverine soil, and now a lot of the new money goes inland too. Piped water and fast new roads have made a desirable address of even a high, dry, bare place like Alto Porvorim. It gets the breeze if there is one, and is handy to Panjim.

Because land in the area is sold in long strips with narrow frontages, most of the resorts along the road probe deep into the old farmlands. By night, tourists drinking their duty free on their Portuguese-style balconies hear the high keening wail of the jack-als from the wild Candolim hill behind, and the enraged reply of the village dogs. By day they gaze down into the ruminative courtyards of quiet farms.

But the Tinto has no resorts, and just behind it, amongst big old trees, stand a few mansions of old Candolim money. Tenancy reforms and emigration and modern mobility have broken the traditional pattern of life. The elegant Pinto house is semi-occupied by the Bosio Hospital; another mansion, its oldest part from the early eighteenth century and with its own chapel and citadel, is now a retirement home; behind it, an orphanage stands on the site of the Faria house. History lives around here. At the dead time, three in the afternoon, you may stroll under the old trees where great events occurred.

The traffic has driven off for siesta. A little way back, by the crossroads, the crows pick over the market debris in peace. Down in the beach shacks Bob Marley plays righteously on as he has done for a quarter of a century, and for a couple of hours the suburban belt, modernity's front line, returns to the museum.

The landscape is still visibly of ancient times. So much of this place called paradise was manmade, about two thousand years ago. The Parashuram legend was made here. The sunken fields that stretch away behind the old village were first reclaimed from the streams and marshes of the estuaries by settlers from the north and their locally recruited tribal labour, and it was they who planted the coconut palms – originally from Malaysia – along the levees.

No early Hindu buildings remain. Their absence is most eloquent on the subject of imperial Christianity in the second half of the sixteenth century. Candolim's five temples were felled during the occupation of the 'counties' of Bardez and Salcete in the 1570s. Buildings begin again with the enormous church – most likely built on temple ruins, like St Michael's in Anjuna, which stands on the Bhumika Devi site. Then come the mansions of the landowners built in the eighteenth and nineteenth centuries.

At this hour no careering bus will force you down off the road and into the reclaimed lands, and you can stop to look across them to the Candolim church standing a kilometre away against the hills. 'Candolim' is the Portuguese form: *kandoli* means dykes, the walled levees and ingenious system of sluices that hold back the waters. Flooding was done on demand to inundate the rice seedlings, or to farm fish. If these coastal reclaimed lands are now neglected, it is because they are waiting for buildings, as those inland are being abandoned as their ebb and flow is blocked by the giant embankments of the new Konkan Railway. These were the most useful fields, the most productive in Goa. When the Portuguese arrived, so Lucio Miranda told me, 'they saw that the richest settlements lay along the northern bank of the Mandovi and the western bank of the Zuari'. Lucio is an architect and musician, from an old and distinguished family of what he calls 'the Christian Brahmin administrative class'.

'The missionaries had a very long-term plan for the conversion of the whole of society. Here was the granary, the best agricultural land, with plantations and rich temples, and they laid a systematic plan for taking over the wealth of the temples by converting the people. Eventually they took over the whole of the Old Conquests, an area about forty to fifty kilometres long and fifteen kilometres deep.

'Within this area they saw the potential of about seventy-five villages; and in them they found operating this ancient institution – community landholding – and they adopted it on the advice of the Brahmin landowners, who knew exactly how to administer the system in their own interest. Each village was about three kilometres in diameter. The centre was held by the Brahmins; the hillside land was community land, auctioned off for mango crops and cashew plantations.

'The missionaries planted churches in all these villages or began new settlements, a massive operation which took the best part of a century.'

The takeover of Bardez and Salcete (to the north and south respectively) provided a buffer for the beleaguered little island and increased Goa's size fourfold. Until then, the men and crocodiles in armour guarding the capital – the jewel – of the

Portuguese empire in Asia were defending a population which remained largely Hindu. Just upriver, the waterfront of Divar Island was a little Benares, a place of pilgrimage in August for up to thirty thousand devotees.

But over in the city the building of the great churches would soon begin. Hindu temples 'able to compete in magnificence with the most superb of ancient Rome' had made the missionaries, the 'spiritual conquistadors', emulous. They built huge imperial-grade churches everywhere; the Sé Cathedral in Old Goa is still the biggest church in Asia. Portuguese Christianity had only recently left home. It brought to Asia an experience of religious encounter – most recently, and painfully, with the new Protestant heresy – that was notably adversarial. Jews and Muslims were the old devils; Protestants and Hindus were the new ones, now that the latter, whom Vasco da Gama had thought were lapsed-Christian, were recognised as true unbelievers.

Secular power established, conversion of the people was the next essential – essential to that unity of the political and the spiritual contained in the word Christendom. Only Christians would be loyal, and only they would be saved. The Pope who received the stuffed rhino, Leo X, had written to the Portuguese king that those of the empire's new subjects resisting the true faith should be put to fire and steel. Conversion was to be spearheaded not by blunt and grizzled Portuguese ships' chaplains but by the sharpest instrument of the Counter Reformation, the new Jesuit order. They were led into their extraordinary career in Asia by Francis Xavier, a companion of the founder himself, Ignatius Loyola. Few Jesuits were Portuguese: Xavier himself was a Basque.

Eventually cow parts were flung into the Mandovi at Divar to drive the pilgrims off. Temples had been destroyed before, during earlier and equally iconoclastic Muslim occupations, but now they began to fall everywhere in what was called, ingeniously, the Rigour of Mercy. As all non-Christians were, Hindus were seen as simply deluded, however awesome their temples, however admirable the asceticism and learning of their yogis (qualities reminding the Jesuits so much of their own). The Jesuits would bring the printing press – the first exported from Europe – to Goa; and they would also be the burners of books.

The Hindu temple was simultaneously a place of worship, library, academy of learning and of music, court of law and art gallery. 'Some were burnt down, others were heaped as garbage, and still others were razed to the ground. Nearly two hundred and eight of these were big ones and some of them very sumptuous and of exceedingly fine workmanship.' The Rigour of Mercy was rigorous for the merciful, too: 'We are here on a battlefield,' a Jesuit wrote, 'in constant struggle with Turks, Moors and Gentiles, and we have no peace.'

Conversions began to be made urgently, with a variety of more or less violent inducements, and in the mass. The result was that thousands of these New Christians were Hindus baptised and left to God – and soon it was noticed that many of them, renamed but otherwise innocent of their new faith, had neglected to give up 'sorcery'. This was how Hindu religious practices were understood: as a kind of magic. The numbers of New Christians being what they were, it became impossible for the friars at once to convert, to instruct the converted, and to chastise the backsliders. As countless of the converted continued to maintain an inexplicable affection for 'magic', sorcery was realised to be endemic. Letters began to reach Lisbon. 'Many Christians from these parts are badly instructed . . . and have started again to adore in their temples.'

Fear of paganism had impelled these rushed conversions, which in turn had created a fear of heresy. To check this creation of one fear by another, Francis Xavier sent to Rome for yet another instrument of the Counter Reformation. The Holy Office did not do conversions, but followed them up. Its job was to inquire into the purity of faith of the converted, and so it was known as the Inquisition.

Christendom, a unity of Church and State, depended on strength of faith. Loyalty to the Church was inseparable from loyalty to the power that had brought the Church to Goa – and so the inquisitors found themselves in a role as much political as religious. It is a very strange task to try to overturn the entire culture of another country, and its enforcement role made the Inquisition very strange indeed. Tested in action on this, the pagan frontier, in time the Holy Office would create around itself a kind of early-modern surveillance state, becoming a scrutineer of conformity and applying itself with diligence to minute deviations such as the wearing of the *dhoti*, in public or at home, because it was not Christian enough.

In Goa the inquisitors had much scope. Francis Xavier had called the Portuguese mariners and soldiery 'men without law, king or captain, all savages, renegades, blasphemers'. Off duty, they collapsed immediately into vice, particularly being accused, as were converts from Islam, of an addiction to sodomy. Then there were the thousands of Hindu New Christian 'sorcerers'; and these were not the only recent and therefore doubtful converts.

Another community, one of traders and financiers, was familiar to the Inquisition from Europe, and lately from Lisbon. Upon being driven from Spain into Portugal, they had been given a generous twenty years to convert on condition of financially aiding the Portuguese Crown. Many took the opportunity to move on with the voyages of exploration. While he was alive, Albuquerque's Goa had been a refuge.

Here and there in Goa on New Year's Eve you come across the 'Old Man', an effigy of straw and old clothes exhibited like Guy Fawkes at the roadside – and for the same reason, to attract a little money. Afterwards, like Guy Fawkes, he is burned, though traditionally the burning was done on the eve of the great Feast of St John in June. Then, the effigy's name was 'Judeu', and he was commonly identified with Judas, but the real origin of the custom is much older: in Portuguese, Judeu means Jew.

In November 1584 Ralph Fitch and John Newbery arrived in Goa, in fetters. The two Englishmen had been arrested in Hurmuz on the Persian Gulf. 'At our coming we were cast into the prison . . .

and charged to be spies . . .' A recent visit of Sir Francis Drake to the area had made Englishmen unpopular. In Goa the Jesuit Thomas Stevens, deviser of the first printed Konkani grammar, interceded for his compatriots and they were released. A month of uncertain freedom, and 'we presently determined rather to seek our liberties . . . for it was told us that we should have the *strappado*.' The *strappado* was a sort of torturous bungee-jump, in which the torturee was roped round the ankles, then dropped from a high ceiling. You couldn't be tortured more than twice for the same offence, according to rules laid down in great detail in the manual, and the water torture was for men only. So, as all Goa's escapers did – 'Not without fear . . . for we durst trust no one' – they made a night crossing of the Mandovi out of the Portuguese jurisdiction and hiked up over the Ghats to Belgaum.

The acquiring of Bardez and Salcete had created a security problem. Porous, the new long borders allowed easy passage to fleeing Protestants, Jews, sorcerers, slaves and Portuguese deserters. (The latter ended up manning the guns for both sides at great Vijayanagar in 1565, when it lost the battle of Talikota and became the village of Hampi.) Hindus in their thousands crossed and recrossed the rivers on a regular basis. Their temples smashed, the pandits had smuggled their deities and whatever else had survived across the rivers into the Muslim territories, where Hindus might worship in freedom. The deity Bhumika Devi from Anjuna went north across the Chapora River into Pernem, not to return till 1971. The idol of Shantadurga from Calangute, once borne into the safety of Bicholim, got as far as Nanora and refused to move. In the temple committee of Nanora there are descendants of the Hindus of Calangute still – and the Shantadurga in the new Calangute temple is a replica.

Stratagems of resistance were always feasible in the newly acquired territories. The imperial forces were always stretched. This was true of the empire as a whole: Portuguese underpopulation meant that the Spanish had more office-wallahs in their colonies than the Portuguese had personnel, including all the military in theirs. In Goa the free territories were so near, so easy to reach through familiar fields and jungle and fordable rivers, that interdiction of Hindu devotees travelling between the exiled shrines was effectively impossible. And zealous pursuers would experience difficulties with secular Portuguese officialdom, which preferred a quiet life and good relations with its Hindu financiers, tax collectors and importers of vital supplies. Consequently, viceroy argued politely with inquisitor. Politely, because the inquisitor's job was to inquire into the purity of faith, including the viceroy's.

In Chandor village, near the site of the ancient Goan capital of Chandrapura, they hold the Beggars' Banquet. Before a wedding – Christian, though the custom is similar for Hindus and Muslims except in its dietary aspects – an odd number of poor people, seven or nine of them, their age and sex approximating those of certain deceased persons of the village, are sat down to a feast of pork, beef, fish curry and rice and liquor. The poor represent the dead. With the feast, the dead are appeased, and the wedding is safe.

This propitiation ceremony has survived from very ancient times into the present, and despite all the efforts of successive highly sophisticated religions. 'So far,' writes Theodore Zeldin, 'being a member of a civilisation has never freed humans from more than a few fears, for civilisations have always had a sense of being surrounded by hostile forces.'

The malevolence of the dead made things go wrong for the living. It was fear of the dead that had created the original propitiation industry controlled by the tribal shamans, the *ghadis*. Then the Buddhists and Hindus came, and after them the Christians. The latter, though naturally preferring their own modish notions of Purgatory and Hell, knew perfectly well what the old crossroads demons and protector spirits were for. The crosses built to keep off those evil dead of the older religions preserved the sense of dread necessary to sustain the power of the new one.

In Sinquerim, a couple of hundred metres up the road from the Candolim Tinto towards Aguada, stand the resorts, and across the road, beachside, are some houses of the new rich. Graham Greene described those of the early 1960s as resembling plastic soapdishes; today's are postmodernly various, from restrained tasteful to Bollywood baroque. Nearer the beach are the older Goan houses, most of them nineteenth century. Amongst them stands at least one chapel 100 years older, and on the beach itself we find an example of the first mark on Goa that Christendom made. It is that simple expression of the religious instinct, the demon-repelling cross.

Demons were the undeclared baggage of the spiritual conquistadors. Old superstition 'set up a habit of mind that there must always be someone to blame, some evil force to fear and attack'. As late as 1578, the unfortunately feeble-minded King Sebastian would spend half the Portuguese treasury on a crusade into North Africa against the those old demons, the Moors, and suffer the worst defeat in Portuguese history. Thousands, and Sebastian, would be killed; his country would be bankrupted by ransom demands and taken over by Spain. The Spanish Captivity would last for sixty years. It was a high price to pay for making old superstition, atavistic Moor-fear, the basis of foreign policy.

The churchmen newly at work in sixteenth-century Goa were from a Europe grossly overpopulated by devils – the new name for the trolls, hobgoblins and fairies of pagan times who, however reclassified, refused to abdicate. The pagan and Christian elements warring in every European of the time agreed that the unwilled was the spirit-caused. Mental illness was believed to be spirit-possession. Outbreaks of the plague (one having halved the population of Lisbon) were countered by recourse to witches or priests or both. Sixteenth-century Portugal was notably unscientific. Revered elsewhere in Europe, the great herbalist Garcia da Orta was ignored in his religiose homeland. All over the country there existed an excess of convents for the orthodox, while any number of plausible millenarian messiahs harangued the bedevilled peasantry beyond the walls.

Throughout the Middle Ages, European science had been made subject to religious dogma. European navigators relying for their lives on something more practical preferred the ancient pagan Ptolemy; he had at least attempted a scientific cartography. But for everyone else at the dawn of the age of European discovery, geography – though the word would not be invented for another fifty years – was a tangled web of fact, Here Be Dragons, and wild surmise.

In Asia the usual effects of culture shock were exaggerated for sixteenth-century Portuguese by their own extravagant and peculiar expectations. 'The same faith that had fantasised the landscape and imprisoned Christians in dogmatic geography would lure pilgrims and crusaders from Europe on paths of discovery to the east.' Europe had for a very long time been a very small world. Focused on its inland sea, the Mediterranean, the European eye was inward. The Portuguese in particular were seen as unlucky in facing the wrong way, upon the terrifying Ocean Sea, a boundless waste, and upon wild and unrighteous Africa.

At the end of the fifteenth century this position became an advantage. Their voyages would change Europe's idea of the world – eventually. Through the ensuing hundred years or so of encounters with Africa, the Americas and Asia, even the longest and most uncertain voyage would be far easier achieved than a change of mind.

The inward European encountering other faiths was customarily unable to imagine anything beyond Christendom. Other beliefs did not exist, only unbelief, delusion. Even the normally perceptive Albuquerque believed he might destroy Islam simply by carrying off the Prophet's bones from Mecca. The inevitable disillusionment provoked rage and violence – a violence focused on others, 'altruistic', self-sacrificial, worshipping martyrdom.

And since unbelief was a negative quality, without substance, there was nothing to be learned from it. Until Jesuits like Robert de Nobili began to doubt it, the religious order with the best brains in international Christendom continued to pronounce ignorance a virtue. In Goa, translations made by converts of confiscated Hindu texts were found useful only as illustrations of superstition. The religion at the heart of Indian life was treated as a collection of fables, as 'bagatelles and . . . tales of old'. It was considered unnecessary to be honest with people who believed in fables, in fantasies, in nothing. In India this would give Europeans, the 'Franks', the *feringhi*, a great reputation for treachery.

5 GOA DOURADA

'It is a fine city,' Ralph Fitch decided, 'and for an Indian town very fair.' European cities were smallish, and Fitch's own London a good deal greyer. Goa in 1600 must have seemed wildly exotic and alive with colour and incident, her bazaars full of the produce of Portuguese Asia and exciting novelties like tea and Chinese restaurants. A great Asian capital – and for the European visitor there was the reassurance of homely things like churches and bars.

The colossal Basilica of Bom Jesus was nearly finished, and the visitor might attend High Mass to the sound of the harp, lute, organ, violin, trumpet and drum. In the arts, clearly the Portuguese gift was in architecture and music, an important communicator of both being the Jesuits, whose contribution to the arts in Goa thus far had largely consisted of denuding it of its architecture and music.

'We have lands,' Lucio Miranda told me, 'about thirty-five kilometres inland, along the Zuari River, and one day I took a Swiss friend there, to show him the interior of Goa. We picnicked in a field, and nearby, people were singing a pre-harvest litany. It is sung to the cross that stands in the middle of the field. After listening for a while, the Swiss – a musician – turned to me and said, "Do you know that those people are singing in three-part harmony?"

' "Yes, I know that."

' "Here we are, miles from anywhere, in rural India, listening to people sing European harmony – and very well, too."

'At the time I hadn't really considered how odd it was. Later I understood that the confinement of the Portuguese to such a small area meant that acculturation could reach deep levels. They didn't have to deal with huge areas and populations as the Spanish did in South America. And they had all the time in the world.

'Music being a very important part of church culture, the Portuguese needed choirs. By now they'd built all these churches: today Goa has more than three hundred and sixty churches and chapels. First they had to teach people the music, and this they did in even the remotest villages. Those first choirmasters were extraordinarily dedicated. The earliest church music – still a great force in the sixteenth century – was Gregorian chant, choir music.

'All Goan Christian music grew out of choir singing: that's the deep musical base that has produced so very many musicians in all fields, from classical to popular. In my generation, by the time we were fourteen years old, eight out of ten of us could pick up a guitar and learn to play by ear.'

The city of Goa, with two great cathedrals nearing completion and the city walls demolished to allow expansion, was bigger than ever before, but not as big as it seemed to foreign visitors. Ralph Fitch hadn't seen Agra yet; he had never seen a big Indian city. The biggest place he knew was London, whose population was then about two hundred thousand. Jean-Baptiste Tavernier, who declared Goa's seaport of Mormugao to be one of the great harbours of the world, had seen nothing greater than Toulon.

The imperial cities of Agra, Lahore and Delhi each boasted a population of at least half a million, and before its destruction, so had Vijayanagar. By Indian standards the city of Goa, with a population of about seventy-five thousand, was middling. No doubt it was a fine sight, but Golden Goa, the wonder of the East, is a traveller's tale that grew more golden with the city's poignant decline.

Goa declined because laterite is porous. If the waste water discarded by its users is relatively clean, and there isn't too much of it, laterite will filter it efficiently enough to make well water drinkable even if unboiled. But this natural filter can easily be overwhelmed. In May 1998 a study of the overbuilt-up Calangute area found that septic tanks, soakpits and hotel waste runoffs were too many and too close to the wells, and were contaminating the water supply.

In the seventeenth-century city of Goa, as elsewhere, the connection between dirt and disease had yet to be made. Swamped by raw sewage from the burgeoning city, the laterite bedrock began to contaminate the wells. By 1635 there was cholera, and as pools and cisterns were abandoned to stagnation, anopheles, the malaria mosquito, began to breed. In that year, the population of a single city parish was thirty thousand; a century later it would be just over one hundred. In 1839, when the population of that parish was thirty and the city a romantic relic surrounded by encroaching jungle, the novelist Captain Marryat wrote of the city's long-gone golden age. 'Goa was then at its zenith, a proud, luxurious, superb, wealthy city – the capital of the east – a city of palaces . . .'

So let us imagine Goa in 1600, in its pomp.

In November a young man arrives at the jetty. He is Gujarati, and has come down to Goa to visit his uncle, a trader. The Mandovi River is gratifyingly full of shipping: the half-dozen ships of the yearly fleet are ready to set sail for Lisbon, loaded with spices from Cochin; there are dhows in from Arabia and Africa. Clutching his *dhoti* to his face – he is downwind of a 'coffin ship', a slave transport – the young man disembarks. He ascends a stone ramp leading into the city, passing under a new archway of unfamiliar design. To his left is heaped a melancholy ruin; to his right, a building is under construction. Of the same design as the arch, it is presumably a temple of the Portuguese. The builders are Indian, the engineers, masons, wood and stone carvers. Three generations of them must have worked on Portuguese temples by now. Before him lies the Rua Direita, Straight Street, long and broad, all shops, ships' chandlers and small trades, and between them the heavy stone façades of inscrutable buildings. The old bazaar is still there, with another

61

massive temple rising beside it, clothed in bamboo scaffolding. A bustling town with the big blockish Portuguese constructions rising up: Goa has come some way from the old horse-port days.

This place was once called Gove. The melancholy ruin must be the old palace of the Adil Shah. Little remained of the original city of Gove, on the Zuari River, to the south. It had been destroyed over two centuries ago, by Sultan Tughlaq of Delhi, along with the Kadamba capital, Chandrapura. According to the Arab traveller Ibn Batuta, who attended the siege, the Chandrapura king had been betrayed by a jealous relative. Upon throwing herself into the Zuari, his queen had wished her fate on all the women of Chandrapura forever, and the curse had worked; even now, two hundred years later, the women of the place are said to die young.

So Gove had been rebuilt here on the Mandovi. Now it was called Goa, and the Portuguese were turning it into an all-Asia emporium. In the bazaar, the young man sees Chinese mother-of-pearl, porcelain and silk. There are curiosities from Malacca and Europe. Cases of wine. Outlandish vegetables: potatoes, some sweet, some not. Maize, tomatoes, tapioca. Dried red chilli peppers – very hot, apparently. Outlandish fruits: guava, papaya, pineapple. Rhubarb, from China. Also local produce, areca nut, sesame oil, vinegar, the ubiquitous coconut. The fish market is a reeking riot of crows and cats.

A European jeweller tries to lure the Gujarati into his shop. 'Look at this. Rubies from Burma, emeralds from the Spanish Indies. Take your time. Looking is free.' But the street is more absorbing. Servants and slaves are out shopping for their masters, there are people of a dozen nations: Chinese, Persians, Malaccans, Europeans, Abyssinians, mestiços, visiting and local Indians.

Next door to the jeweller stands a Chinese eatery with a meat counter facing onto the street: how bizarre to see people buying fish *and* pork *and* beef. Every dietary law broken; these people must be Christians, who ate anything. The eatery seems to be full of soldiers. Weapons lie under the tables now. Later they will be joined by their owners, a raucous, wild-haired mob drinking wine at eleven in the morning. They drink water as he does himself – in a stream from the jug, not touching the lip. Their clothes are poor, loud bazaar-made waistcoats, dirty breeches, big boots. They make large gestures, raising long pipes towards food-flecked beards; the exhalations rise in clouds, unfamiliar-smelling, mingling with steam from the kitchen.

The young Gujarati is expected at his uncle's, but the passing show is too engrossing. A retinue of slaves brings up the rear of a column, and he leaves the eatery to see who is coming. A palanquin passes, and two or three men on horseback, also with beards but in better clothes, their swords sheathed in leather. As they disappear round the corner, shoppers and clamouring children fill the street. Two East Asian men in hooded gowns cross the road. He questions a passer-by: they're Jesuits, monastics, from Japan, wherever that is.

Familiar faces now, Gujarati businessmen. One of them is his uncle. It's good to be in a family house in this peculiar town, but he finds his uncle anxious. You weren't going to *eat* in that place, were you? You didn't drink the water, did you? Don't go out at night: the Europeans are all armed and very touchy.

'They're touchy about religion, for a start. They stole a holy relic from Ceylon – a tooth of the Lord Buddha – and brought it here and burned it and ground it to powder and threw it into the sea. Why would anyone do that? And every three years they hold a festival at which people are sacrificed, mostly locals. They're burned at the stake, and that after calling *sati* barbaric. Christians have the happy privilege of being strangled before being burned. Even people who die in jail are burned – without being strangled – but not because they're dead, as you'd imagine. It isn't an ordinary pyre, it's a punishment for something they did while alive. *They execute dead people.* Mad. A mad place, but good for business, if you're careful.'

His aunt has gone to bed, the young man yawns, his uncle takes a long pipe from a shelf and lights it. That unfamiliar smell again. 'Tobacco. Very relaxing. From South America, apparently.

That's where those newfangled foods come from – have you tried potato yet? And apparently the Spanish have discovered a leaf, also in South America, that you can chew. It gives you a real lift. But the tobacco will do me. The Portuguese have just started to bring it in. Cures gout, they say. It may catch on.'

'Just a moment, uncle. Where on earth is South America?'

In Brazil, sugar plantations were opening up. For settlers from Lisbon and slaves from West Africa, South America was near, four times nearer than Goa. By 1600 there were twenty-five thousand Portuguese in Brazil; in Goa there were two thousand. In fifty years there would be only half as many Portuguese in Goa, and most of those would be celibate members of religious orders. Viceregal reports on the state of the military began to worry about the Europeans' complexions, as the official colour scheme was gradually undone by sexual outreach. A richly diverse and inclusive society was in the making; a society that Albuquerque's marriage policy had helped begin, if not necessarily the one he would have preferred.

'Utterly at variance with our notions concerning the proper demeanour of a native towards a European'. Two and a half centuries later, the young Richard Burton, scrutinising Goan race relations, would be appalled at the overturning of the proper order. 'At Goa,' he wrote, 'all men are equal.' It had not always been so, and not for women, either. A popular joke doing the rounds of the slave auction in 1600 went: A Khurasani woman for work, a Hindu for nursing children, a Persian for pleasure and a Transoxianian for thrashing as a warning to the other three. The capital of the Portuguese Asian empire, Goa was a premier slave mart with an auction block right on Straight Street in the city centre. There, teeth and limbs were examined for acceptability in the *fidalgo*'s entourage, in the household or the fields. 'The Portingales and Mestiços in India never worke.' A judge might own eighty slaves; the ordinary householder made do with ten.

An Asian or African woman cost one-sixteenth of the price of a good horse – though the married man dallied at his peril. One Portuguese noble unknowingly had his favourite African slave girl fed to him for dinner, by his wife. After which, perhaps he dozed off, while she went out. 'Many husbands are fed datura,' wrote the alert Jan van Linschoten, 'by their wives, to drug them while they pursue their amours.'

For the well-found *fidalgo*, Goa in 1600 was a theatre of ceremonial. Albuquerque was long dead now, and opinion held that valour had died with him. The most popular saying was the Arab one: After the fire, the ashes. The only jousting was social. The lavish hospitality of the time cost real money, and so noble connections were everything; the new arrival from Lisbon was forever being asked whom he knew. At a typically roistering sort of banquet, we find Malaccan slave-girls serving meat and wine, captains in their cups, *fidalgos* attended by a eunuch and two pages.

Awed by the tropics, the empire man played the oriental potentate. The theatricality was not without its uses: liveried retainers and trumpeters and folderol, the public display of arms and vanity, did the empire's work, awed the crowd and promoted the myth of omnipotence. One slave held the umbrella over him, another held his sword, and with his retinue falling in fore and aft, the haughty *fidalgo* proceeded 'very slowly forwards, with a great pride and vaineglorious majestie'. It was an act, a kind of magic, on Goa's little stage.

The retinue lodged where it could around the noble mansion. The typical defender of Portugal-in-Asia was a poor man obliged to fight for a living, who arrived with the winter fleet and immediately set about finding himself a patron. A nobleman always needed his men around him in the city, for show or affray. There were faction fights, sometimes a lot of action after dark. In return, he led them toward the loot in the winter fighting season, and in the idling season, the summer, he fed and housed them. As the enormous raindrops fell, the common soldier sat with his fellows – Portuguese, mercenaries of all nations, mestiços, slaves – learning how to be an old India hand, to chew betel, drink arrack and eat Indian-style. ('The Indians eat everything with the hand alone,' a visiting Englishman observed, 'and so do the Portugals.')

Fidalgos consulted the highly rated Indian doctors (the only Indians allowed to use a palanquin in the city, though Gujarati financiers were allowed an umbrella). For the rest there was the Royal Hospital, famous for cures from both East and West that ranged from cow-urine therapy to bleeding with leeches. One stood little chance of surviving any of them. Life was insecure. The soldier without a patron lived in a palm-leaf hut on the beach, soon to be summarily posted in his rusty breastplate to some remote and godforsaken fort.

Some years before, a Lisbon grandee had calculated that the king was paying for seventeen thousand colonial troops when only four thousand existed. The fort captains were neglecting to declare their casualties; they were pocketing the pay of dead souls. The captains of big, profitable forts like Hurmuz on the Persian Gulf stole the pay of the living as well. They were becoming so rich from the practice that it was worth sending a fleet round from Goa every year, just to shake them down. But for the benighted soldiery there was only suffering – or India and freedom. Deserters roamed the fringes of the Mughal empire, smugglers, hired guns, runaways, loners and chancers; men who, like Fitch and Newbery, had fled through the palm groves and over the Ghats to Belgaum. Pirate dens infested inlets in Bengal and Arakan.

The famous remark is the Jesuit leader Francis Xavier's, in a letter of 1545. 'I am astonished at seeing how those who come [from Portugal] find so many moods, tenses and participles to conjugate the verb "to rob".' The licence of distance, *fidalgo* expectations and sheer wild-frontier rapaciousness enabled the growth of corruption in the imperial system until by 1600 it *was* the imperial system. Later that century the great chronicler Diogo do Couto wrote his polemic *The Practical Soldier;* even by the tolerant standards of those times he found the robbery and bribery outrageous.

Corruption was managed, most efficiently, by the permanent officials of the Goa bureaucracy, whose colleagues in Lisbon would see to it that Couto's book went unpublished for almost two hundred years. But the officials' principal collaborator was distance and the slowness of the mail. The viceroy, supposedly omnipotent, was appointed for three years only, and a letter to Lisbon took seven months or so to arrive. If a civic-minded viceroy in Goa wrote a letter to the king exposing an official, he would have to wait, say, fifteen months for the dismissal notice to arrive. All the accused had to do was write for leave to appeal, then appeal, then wait; and before the judgment arrived, the civic-minded viceroy would be on his way home.

There was too little time for any but the keenest viceroy to achieve anything much – and the viceroy was after all a nobleman chosen not for his knowledge of colonial administration, or of Goa, but for his bloodline. Upon arrival in Goa he would find that the contents of the viceregal palace had been appropriated by his predecessor. This was the form. His first year would have to be spent homemaking, though fortunately not at his own expense: the cartloads of necessities for his vast establishment were all complementary, courtesy of his helpful permanent officials. The viceroy would be grateful. And he would know how to be grateful. He would learn not to be keen.

6 THIS BABYLON

In Anjuna in 1628 a Christian priest arriving to baptise a Hindu 'orphan' – the child of a widowed mother – was beaten up and seen off by the villagers. Anticipating vengeance, some escaped in the usual way, over the river, while others were caught and sentenced to the galleys (it was that or the gunpowder factory). Their village was razed, the land salted for infertility, and a minatory pillar set up. It is still there, lying broken on waste ground. When I saw it, a small kerosene-can shrine sanctified with candle stumps, flowers and offerings of coins had been placed next to the pillar. Deposed, but recognised still to be a power-object, the dread stone had been converted to the service of the old religion it had been set up to evict.

Having never bothered to investigate Indian religion, Christians in those early days understood it as a ragbag of outdated myths bound to vanish at the first encounter with the true faith. The persistence of Hinduism, and the incomprehension and rage that followed the puncturing of the illusion that the religion would easily be replaced, are further illustrated by the curious affair of the Cuncolim Four. The *taluka* (administrative district) of Bardez was bestowed as a mission field on the Franciscans, and Salcete on the Jesuits. In Cuncolim, in the south of Salcete, the temples were destroyed as others had been; and in revenge, four visiting Jesuits were killed by the villagers. In time, the Jesuits were promoted to popular martyrdom – but resentment in Cuncolim at this elevation of vandals ensured that the story did not end there. As recently as 1983, the fourth centenary of the event, 'the dominant caste families' installed an image of the goddess Mhamai on the church altar. The priest presiding over this 'Independent Church of Cuncolim' had to be evicted by court order.

During the period of its greatest zeal, a concerted missionary effort throughout tiny Goa managed to convert only half the population. And in those converts to Christianity the social order of Hinduism lived on, mass conversion in haste having simplified caste but preserved it.

Hindu priests became Christian priests. Temple committees re-emerged as church confraternities. Eventually, the Pope would permit Brahmin converts to keep the sacred thread that they wore, and it would be suggested that they hang the crucifix from it. The Goan successors to the Jesuit master builders who had planned the great cathedrals began to incorporate elements of Indian style into their church designs. (In time, their successors would rebuild the Hindu temples, employing elements drawn from the European baroque.) New churches began to be named after those saints most resembling in someone's mind the deities of the temples the churches were built upon. Our Lady of Bethlehem for the *Saptamatrika*, the Seven Mothers; St James for Lord Shiva. Not for the first time in Goa, a new religion was trying to make itself acceptable by giving a place to – while attempting to assimilate – the deities of an older one.

Hinduism was ineradicable, and by the end of the first decade of the seventeenth century the attempt to eradicate it was already weakening. At what seemed the height of its energies, the Portuguese empire was exhausted. Improvised out of the materials to hand, it had always been more size than substance, a vast net, easily torn, of coastal enclaves and forts held together by visiting fleets. Its insubstantial self is exemplified in the false dome of the Calangute church: so protuberant in front, so hollow at the rear, the very image of a sea power without a hinterland.

That fragile net had been holed by the Dutch in 1604, a mere two years after the founding of their company of merchant adventurers, when they impudently appeared in the Mandovi River. It was a declaration of intent. In that year there were about fifty Portuguese forts around the Indian Ocean, but by mid-century there were nine. The net was in shreds, and an empire that had once spanned half of Asia was shrunken to a few enclaves, including Macau. That last piece of the last European empire was returned to China in December 1999.

Class relations had been inadvertently preserved by conversion, and so had economic relations. The initial turmoil over, the pattern of landowning reasserted itself. Tradition asserts that during the Hindu emigrations of the mid-sixteenth century that followed punitive legislation, prudent families left a son behind to consent to conversion in order to keep the lands in the family. Many legends attach to this first great Goan emigration. Rich Hindus were believed to have dropped their treasure down a well before flight, and, for additional security, to have sacrificed a person or animal to haunt the spot and keep looters from the trove. As haunted places were legion, it would be difficult for a potential looter to identify any given ghost as a guard of valuables, and arrange for an exorcism. Only the sighting of a white snake several metres long, with flowing hair and grey moustaches, guaranteed the presence of buried treasure, for he would be a Lord of Snakes, the reincarnation of the owner, now deceased, as a guardian serpent.

There was no Portuguese takeover of land. They did take an interest in forestry, but for shipbuilding and trade. They looked to the sea, and only the religious orders, landlubberly non-Portuguese, ever owned land. The villages were left alone, unless the government was strapped for cash: as customs revenues and Portuguese support began to fade, successive administrations grew rapacious.

In terms of business, Portugal became more remote – eventually, only 5 per cent of her trade would be with Goa – and so the produce of the countryside, and the coastal trade, grew in importance. With the slow wasting away of the island city through the seventeenth century, the economy became steadily more Indian; inland trading towns like Mapusa gained significance. Tax-collection was a Hindu monopoly.

The Portuguese withdrawal obliged the monastic orders in Goa to support themselves; social relations had to be improved, at least to the extent of making business relations easier. Out of economic necessity, cooperation and absolutism began to cohabit, even if lovelessly: one hand saluted the Hindu businessmen and authority figures without whom Goa could not be run, while the other kept trying to show their religion the door. While Jesuit and Hindu financiers met in the counting houses to lend each other impressive sums of money, a blatantly prejudicial tax on non-Christians, imposed in the sixteenth century, trailed on. It would survive until the 1840s.

Through the late 1660s, Maratha horsemen from the north rampaged through Bardez; the forts built to resist them had been stripped of defenders for the sea war against the Dutch, who had been blockading the coast on and off for fifteen years. The Arabian Sea was a Portuguese ocean no longer. They were now dodging Dutch patrols in the same smuggling boats that the Goans had once used to dodge theirs.

Meanwhile, in their black stone headquarters on Straight Street, the inquisitors doggedly pursued their inquiries. Several hundred people – including numberless 'sorcerers', and one Dellon, an innocent and devout French doctor – languished in solitary confinement.

Considering how changed was the world it worked in, there was a kind of perverse heroism in the Inquisition's obsessiveness. The old semi-feudal Catholic empire that had first employed it was dead in the water, sunk by the new capitalist Protestant one. 'The conversion of unbelievers to the true faith could no longer compete ideologically with double-entry book-keeping.' Having narrowly survived the Maratha invasions, *fidalgos* distractedly went on playing the oriental potentate in a city ever more pestilential. All around them, cathedrals of an Asian vastness emulated temples. Discreetly, the great converter Robert de Nobili, whose adopting of Indian languages and customs was already arousing the interest of the inquisitors, tried on his Brahmin vestments.

The Church's reach around the world had always been more certain than her grasp, and the awful vision of variant Catholicisms beyond her control made – and has continued to make – that highly centralised institution overreactive. As witness in recent times the loud disapproval of Anthony de Mello, an Indian Jesuit 'whose best-selling books on meditation the Vatican decided were too close to Buddhism'. In the late seventeenth century the empire of the Portuguese might be collapsing but the empire of the Church – in no such commercial or political distress, and occupying the same territory – was not.

The world being turned upside down all around it helped make the priestly intelligence community yet more stern and superfocused. The Holy Office, with its background in bedevilled and religiose Iberia, did not allow itself modern doubts.

In Captain Marryat's *The Phantom Ship*, the heroine, gazing from her lodgings in the city of Goa, wonders what is the 'massy, handsome pile' opposite. The Santa Casa, the headquarters of the Inquisition, her landlady tells her, crossing herself with alacrity. Later, the heroine is burned for sorcery. 'At Goa the accusations of sorcery and magic were much more frequent than at other places,' wrote Marryat, whose nineteenth-century novel sourced most of its story from the 1687 first-hand account of Dr Dellon.

Dellon is our star witness, a devout Catholic when most foreign observers were emphatically not. Consider Captain Alexander Hamilton, who visited Goa soon after him. Pirate by profession and Protestant by conviction, he describes the Portuguese as 'most zealous bigots', and their city as peopled by 'thirty thousand church vermin'. Reporting on the popular cult of Francis Xavier, declared a saint in 1622, the Captain seriously doubts 'that the amputated right arm, when sent to Rome to stand its trial for sainthood, took hold of the pen, dipped it in ink and fairly wrote *Xavier* in full view of the sacred college'.

In its two active centuries the Goa Inquisition tried over sixteen thousand cases. Of these, Norman Lewis suggests there were about eight hundred executions, by fire. 'Its prisoners,' he writes, 'well fed and housed in two hundred hygienic cells, were subjected to constant psychological pressure in accordance with the most modern practice.'

In our own time, with its horrors eclipsed several times over, the Inquisition survives as a late-night movie, all pits and pendulums and red-eyed Torquemadas in Klannish regalia. The archives of the Holy Office in Rome were at last opened to scholars in 1998, and their report will give us a much a better idea of the Inquisition's real place in the history of European intolerance: if indeed the Holy Office was the ancestor of Big Brother in the quality of its tortures, its innovative use of informers, anonymous denunciations and sensory deprivation, its ideological justifications for murder.

For Dr Dellon, a young French physician enduring his eighteenth month of incarceration in the basement of the Santa Casa, the morning of 16 January 1676 was like every other, until the bell began to ring. Every day, he awoke to a silent whitewashed cell three metres square, its thick stone walls unlit save for a grille high up near the vaulted ceiling. But on that morning the guard arrived without the bread and the bucket. Instead, he bore new garb for the prisoner – white, with black stripes. Dellon realised that this was the day of the auto-da-fé, the Act of Faith. In the hall outside, he joined two hundred others, men and women, European and Indian, dressed like himself. Surely they never burned so many. Then a guard gave bread to them all, and to Dellon he said that he should take it, even if he wasn't hungry now, because he would be hungry afterwards. It much improved Dellon's appetite to know that there would be an afterwards.

All Goa was there to see the parade, this high drama of the saved and the damned. A 'godfather', a local worthy, was deputed to accompany each prisoner. Also present were officers of the civil power, churchmen not being expected to do the killing themselves. The two hundred in stripes were trudging along before the great wooden cross when Dellon, glancing back, saw another group, also walking before a cross, but wearing the Samaria, the costume of the damned – the tall pointed white cap and gown painted with flames. Did being before the cross mean nothing after all? But, as someone whispered down the line, the inquisitors would have their little joke: the flames were painted upside down. Those in the jokey costumes were among the saved, just; they would live, or once their punishment was over, at least continue to exist.

It was behind the cross that the dead men walked. They wore the Samaria with the flames right side up, on its front a portrait of their own heads resting on a burning log surrounded by capering demons. Beneath this the crime was written '*Convicto Invotivo*', guilty without confession. The tall pointed cap was likewise painted, and each of the damned carried a tall wax candle. Behind them were carried lifelike effigies of those who had died in prison; and humbly following behind, their unshriven bones went along in coffins to be burnt.

Dellon heard his sentence, and it was everything he wanted. First, excommunication. This would be revoked one day in France. Next, various penances; fasting and prayer. And everything he owned was forfeit, but that had all gone when he was arrested. Not often in the course of justice was it best to be poor. Finally, he was banished from the Indies, for which he thanked God, and sentenced to five years on the galleys in Lisbon. There would be company there. What had nearly killed him, what had driven him to attempt his own life and risk eternal damnation, were the terrible solitudes of the Santa Casa.

Dellon had arrived in Daman (in Gujarat) two years previously, at the age of twenty-four. A somewhat obtuse and argumentative amateur theologian, he was soon in trouble. His wooing of a local lady aroused the jealousy of a rival, a well-connected priest. A neighbour – probably the priest's *agent provocateur* – saw a crucifix above Dellon's bed and wanted to know what he would do if he brought a girl home. Would he hang a cloth over the cross?

Dellon, of ungoverned tongue, fell for it. Was fornication not a sin, then, if the cross was covered? Did God not see all the secrets of men's hearts? Triumphantly he quoted chapter and verse. Beware the inquisitors, the neighbour warned him; it was they who decided what was sin and was not. So, Dellon asked, did they place themselves above Christ? He thanked God that France had no Inquisition.

But he was not in France. He was on Portuguese territory, and they were reputed to be the most thorough of heretic-hunters. Half the Indians they accused were not even Christians. Nor were Frenchmen immune. So to pre-empt his anticipated denunciation, Dellon called on the Inquisitor of Daman. He made a speech, quoting the liberal conclusions of the holy Council of Trent, and at the end of it the Inquisitor had him thrown into a dungeon so loathsome that forty of the fifty prisoners, all Malabar pirates, had within a week of incarceration hanged themselves with their own turbans.

Dellon survived, so some months later he was sent down to Goa and jailed again, in the dungeon of the Santa Casa. The cell was clean, the food edible. The mosquitoes were a problem, and so was the lack of a candle when the night came swiftly down after sunset, but the real torture was the loneliness and silence. The walls were two metres thick, but had ears: you were punished for praying too loudly. Defence lawyers were provided, whose job was to betray their clients to the prosecution. Your only speech should be a confession before the Inquisitor. Now Dellon found that his crimes had multiplied in his absence. He had refused to kiss a holy image, saying he thought the act idolatrous; he had mocked an obscure aspect of baptism; he had insulted the Holy Office.

He denied it all. He was told that confession was his only chance – and it was only a chance – of survival. Then he was returned to solitary. After a few months he thought he'd go mad, so he confessed to everything and more besides, and without comment was returned once again to the cells, where, in the silence and solitude and dark, he tried to kill himself. The third time, he was caught trying to cut his wrists with a sharpened gold coin he had kept hidden, and was chained hand and foot so he couldn't do it again.

Then, on 16 January, he awoke and heard the bell begin to ring for the Act of Faith.

After two winters on the galleys in Lisbon, he found a kindly compatriot to beg his release. Dellon went straight from the galleys to a liberal cleric, who absolved him from excommunication. Then he went to church; then he returned home to Inquisition-free France, and wrote his book. One chapter is called 'Ostensible Causes of My Imprisonment'. After all his awful sufferings the tone of it is somewhat aggrieved, as if someone had made a mistake.

The Americas show us triumphant conquistadors, conquests coast to coast, captive kings and gold-bearing fleets on the Spanish Main. Floating on his ocean off Aguada nearly two centuries before, had Afonso de Albuquerque ever imagined that he too might have that kind of power? One doubts it. Visibly, India was no New World. There could be no godlike naming of virgin lands here. There were no vacancies, only a busy city on a small island. This India was no trackless jungle or endless prairie an imperialist might call his own, but a bustling human universe in which he might make a few Old Conquests.

Twelve years earlier, Vasco da Gama had known he had discovered nothing. India was a known quantity. In the end he had – most effortfully, it must be said – merely found another way of getting there. The first people he met in Calicut were the old neighbouring enemy, North African Muslims, in the same business as himself and speaking a common language. And Covilhã before him had found a recognisable world in India, though on a daunting scale. India had states and cities, nobles and priests, merchants and financiers, armies armed and horsed like Europeans; and worse, men whose diseases – like malaria – killed the foreigner.

There was no immunity here. This was not America, where a few dozen Spaniards were able to defeat multitudes of men who had never seen armour, a gun or a horse, where the encounter with Europe meant dying of its diseases. In giving the western hemisphere to Spain and the eastern to Portugal, the Pope's Treaty of Tordesillas had seen to it that the Spanish, though they were few, would overcome, and the Portuguese, because they were few, would not.

Compared to America, India was home. Alexander the Great had been there, and Marco Polo, Sir John Mandeville, Cosmas the India Traveller – and St Thomas, Doubting Thomas the architect, apostle of Christ. Goa was the Gouba of Ptolemy, of the Greeks. She had traded with the ancient Middle East, with the Romans. Communities of foreigners had traded out of Indian coastal cities right through the middle ages. Vasco had rounded the inscrutable continent of Africa to arrive at another point on the same continent he came from. Like Portugal, India was part of Eurasia, a single continent, much-travelled, anciently wired together by language and culture and technology and trade.

Portugal was a small nation on the edge of Europe, and India was a vast land of empires. One suspects that Albuquerque saw the limits of Portuguese enterprise in Asia well enough. 'Reflected in hopeful eyes at home, this empire of tatters and patches was seamlessly perfect' – but Albuquerque was in place, and had eyes to see. After his victory he didn't try to be Aguirre,

Wrath of God; he abjured conquistadorial hubris and went in for social engineering. His successors would display less rectitude. When reality dawned on them too, the old buccaneering spirit would swiftly give up and cash in.

It didn't take long. 'This Babylon,' disillusioned Camoens called the Goa of the 1560s, 'whence flows matter for every evil the world breeds.' The poet of imperial glory had expected better.

7 RESISTANCE

The empire might be moribund, but membership of it was a great stimulant to its subjects. In the tradition of the Romans, whose subjects everywhere had been entitled to call themselves citizens of Rome, Goans were now citizens of Portugal. They had a stake in that giant multinational concern, the empire, and many were members of a world religion that might make the lands beyond the seas more congenial. As early as the sixteenth century, Father José Vaz founded the Oratorian Order to facilitate Goan aspirations of the missionary kind, himself becoming a hero of the Church in Sri Lanka.

By the mid-eighteenth century, Goa was being run less from Lisbon than from Panjim. It was now worth seeking power at home, and Goan aspirations began to include the idea of reform, of a government of Goans. The way into politics would be through religion. The priesthood might be reproved, especially in reputedly lax Bardez, for its appetites for boozing and whoring and gluttony: a priest of Siolim was denounced on his Easter visit for drawing up a surreptitious list of his parishioners' pigs and chickens. But in or out of their official capacity, the Goan clergy were nevertheless in constant touch with the people, and expected to intercede on their behalf.

The clergy belonged to the most prestigious of institutions, and one where educated upper-caste Goans like themselves might have power – but they did not have power. A Goan Christian in the Portuguese colonial government might rise to a high administrative post; his brother in the Church could rise no higher than assistant priesthood. The Church was ruled from Rome, not from

Portugal, and was wary of converts. Still, reform would have to come through the Church, not through the government. Secular power was seen to govern only in its own interest, but the Church had a role in social justice. It claimed to have a conscience. It was expected to practise the Christian virtues of love, community and charity, and if it did not, it invited revolt from within.

The viceroy and his cabinet were officially the executive, and the bureaucracy the administration, but there were endless ways for an entrenched and virtually irremovable bureaucracy to frustrate executive action. Nor did kings encourage viceregal independence: one of the very first directives to a Goa viceroy had been 'Do Not Innovate'. The court in Lisbon spent more on its own entertainments than on investment in the colonies; in the Portuguese case, masterly inactivity by rulers at home and their subordinates abroad was a cause of imperial decline.

In other cases, it was a symptom. French officials in the early twentieth century clamoured for postings to Indo-China, there to patronise vinous luncheons, opium evenings and Annamese concubines. Englishmen visiting India at the same time commonly saw their compatriots resident there as smug, spoiled and out of touch, nobodies abroad with malarial tans and saloon-bar politics. 'He may be ill-bred, stupid, uneducated' – so Aldous Huxley wrote in the late 1920s of someone he met on a P&O liner docking at Bombay – 'no matter. His skin is white. Superiority in India is a matter of epiderms. No wonder if he loves the east. For the European, eastern conditions of life are a kind of intoxicant.'

The rulers of Goa ruled confidently by daylight, but when the dark came down they were subject to nightmares. They were few, and a long way from home. They and their local clients ruled not by consent of Goans, but on the orders of Lisbon, and so they were threatened by subversion from within and bullying from without. The twofold pressure made them close and reactionary.

In 1755, in the aftermath of the terrible Lisbon earthquake, and after many manoeuvres, the Marquis de Pombal finally took over Portugal. The resounding reforms that followed, though greeted with joy by liberals all over the empire, were hardly motivated by liberalism: Pombal's was a personal dictatorship with a morbid fear of competition. He outlawed slavery and racial discrimination not out of conviction but because the colonial governments who practised them were potential rivals. For the same reason, the religious orders and the Inquisition were expelled from Portugal and the empire.

In Goa the orders had become the victims of their own success. Eventually they would return, but only when their old power over the state was gone. The state, the Panjim regime, rather enjoyed this. There were the rest of Pombal's reforms of colonial government for them to deal with – but India was still a long way from Lisbon. The regime soaked up the reformist pressure and waited for Pombal to go. It took twenty years, but when the liberal dust cleared, the regime was still in place, as reactionary as ever – and superiority in Church and State was still a matter of epiderms. Pombal's gale of reforms had arrived in Goa as a breeze.

But the reformers had been kept waiting too long. Expectations had been raised too high, and disillusionment ended in armed revolt. The first attempt to overthrow the state ended in the Pinto mansion in Candolim village, thus becoming famous as the Revolt of the Pintos.

It was conceived by one Father Couto, who had been passed over for promotion in the usual way. He was encouraged by a visit to Lisbon in pursuit of Goan émigré backing and finance, and on his return in 1787 he was able to assemble a group of forty-seven disaffected clerics and military officers, all from Bardez save Couto himself and an Italian. The Ponda Legion were to evict the Panjim regime, and the clergy were to raise the people in support. The plotters were confident. Four and a half thousand Goan troops, not including irregulars, would be facing half their number, the Portuguese and mestiços certain to defend the regime.

Albuquerque's marriage policy had eventually produced from his soldiery a mestiço military class that soon outnumbered the Portuguese and threatened to upset the social order. 'There had developed three layers at the top of Goan society, a straightforward class division – which the Portuguese respected throughout their rule – of the descendants of the Portuguese nobility, the Christian brahmins, and the mestiços. The viceroy would have a cabinet made up entirely of Portuguese *descendentes*: throughout the colonial period there were at least a dozen noble families resident in Goa. Educated, aristocratic, in culture and in style they were an example for the Christian Brahmins, who were already a privileged educated and landowning class.

'The mestiços led the army, rising to be colonels and generals. They were ambitious. There was rivalry with the Christian Brahmins, they did try to take over, but the Brahmins won in the end with Portuguese support, and because they were better educated, they were the administrators – and above all because traditionally they had a superior standing in society. This was India, and Indian society had always placed the Brahmins first and the military, the warriors, below them.' *Caudillismo*, the personal rule of military men that at one time or another occurred nearly everywhere in the Iberian empires – and in Spain and Portugal themselves – never occurred in Goa. The social order might be Portuguese at its head, but its backbone was Indian: the immemorial Brahmin supremacy was always sufficient to prevent a takeover.

'The Goans, very much against their temperament . . . rose to a stature larger than life.' At the beginning of August 1787, in the midst of the rains, the leaders of the coup assembled in Candolim, within striking distance of Panjim and the Aguada fort. The attack was set for the tenth. On the fifth they were betrayed to the governor – viceroys by now having been discontinued – by the brother of a conspirator. The governor was incredulous, and it took the confessions of a priest and another defector to convince him. In a bitter echo of Couto's motives, the priest's aim seems to have been promotion.

Loyal troops were dispatched to the Pinto mansion, where they arrested the forty-seven, including Couto and thirteen other priests. Couto told all and was deported with his brother clerics to Portugal, where they remained under house arrest for eighteen years. Couto's man in Lisbon, a priest called Faria, was locked up in a convent.

It would go worse with the soldiers. Portugal was an ally of Britain, which was at war with France; it was suspected that the conspirators were in treasonous league with Tipu Sultan, an ally of the French from southern India, and expected to invade Goa at any time. A Hindu private investigator was hired, but found no evidence. In the end, retribution fell exclusively on the enemy within. The three most senior Ponda legionnaires had their hands cut off before joining the others for hanging and quartering, and the heads of all thirty-three military men were given a public exhibition in Panjim.

The second attempt at an uprising was more quixotic, not to say poignant, but had essentially the same cause: metropolitan reforms frustrated by colonial reaction. And this time Lisbon was not able to keep its own man in power.

In 1821, half a century after Pombal and thirty-four years after the Revolt of the Pintos, a liberal coup in Portugal produced another government committed to reform abroad. For the first time, it was decided to appoint a local man to supreme authority, the popular Bernardo Peres da Silva. After two weeks in power he was ousted by the mestiço military whose fathers had undone the Pintos. Liberal supporters of Silva's interned in the Terekhol fort were murdered. Silva himself fled to Bombay, where he set about organising an invasion fleet; and he appealed for a loan to a wealthy and celebrated compatriot.

Rogerio de Faria (no relation to the Pintos' man in Lisbon), protected by his Portuguese nationality, had since the 1790s been despatching Rajasthani opium out of Daman, north of Bombay, and shipping it across south-east Asia to another Portuguese possession, Macau. In 1815 the British, who claimed an opium monopoly in India, banned the export of the drug from Bombay but could not legally interdict Portuguese ships carrying it from one Portuguese possession to another, and soon two-thirds of all the opium exported to China from western India was leaving from Daman. Nor was this Faria's only interest. On commencing the export of Gujarati cloth to Brazil, he was knighted. To Bombay he was now Sir Roger, whose splendid house in Colaba had a view of the sea. But he did not forget Goa.

Mindful that his knighthood had come from the liberal regime in Portugal, Sir Roger agreed to assist Silva's attempt to retake Goa by sea. The Bombay press reported Silva's wish to repeat the success of the coup in Portugal. His opening move had been to collect 'out of the bazaar a body of nearly three hundred as ragged-looking fellows as ever were seen'. Sensing his destiny, Silva shrugged off the news that a storm was raging northwards, and embarked his men on two modified barges, a corvette and a ketch. On 27 May 1835, the fleet sailed off towards the south. By the rocks of Vengurla it met the storm, and five days later Silva was back in Bombay in full disarray, his transports holed and his motley crew injured and mutinous. The press feared for law and order.

Sir Roger was discreet, and it was a partner of his who submitted the bill to Silva. Silva never paid it, and this large debt was one of those that finally sank the good knight when the British began once again to export opium out of Bombay and put his Daman detour out of business. Bankrupt, Sir Roger was kept from the street by Sir Jamsethjee Jeejeebhoy, the famous Parsi financier, who had once been an employee of his. Goa remained in the hands of the old regime. No one remembered Sir Roger's role in the building of Panjim, the financing of which had come largely from Portuguese government taxes on his opium business.

His son died in an accident. It was as well for Sir Roger that in his twilight years, relaxing after dinner with a waterpipe, he was able to turn to the chief consolation of his precarious trade.

As I walked into my local bar one evening in 1997, I saw a friend of mine wearing a watch with an entirely black face – no hands or display, nothing. I thought this must be a joke about timelessness until he told me it wasn't a watch at all. It was a magnet. Several weeks before, both his wrists had seized up, immobilising his hands, until a friend had given him the magnet-watch. Four days later the magnetised wrist was fully mobile again; now he was working on the other one.

Suddenly magnetism was in vogue. Next day in the paper a naturopath was recommending the application of six magnets at once, to promote circulation 'especially to the genetary organs'. The day after that, in a stained and yellowed *New York Times* that had been making the rounds of the café tables for some time, I read that American doctors were beginning to run pilot tests on magnet medicine – after scoffing for decades at this alternative therapy, a treatment much admired by sportspeople as a cure for pain. They were finding that the application of magnets to the painful parts worked, exactly as the magnet-watch had worked for my friend's wrist. But the doctors were unable to discover *how* the magnets worked, and until they do, magnetotherapy will never be scientifically respectable.

Magnetism has been in search of respectability for centuries. As a physical therapy, it first attracted attention, and notoriety, in late eighteenth-century France. A product of the Enlightenment, it will be forever associated with the name of Anton Mesmer, whose original method was to place magnets on his patients, after which they fell into a hypnotic trance. There was improvement in conditions ranging from piles to paralysis to melancholia and epilepsy; Mesmer attributed his success to the redirection of 'fluids' in the body.

Mesmer despised mesmerism, bitterly resenting the dark suspicions of witch-doctoring and occultism that fell on him. His interest was purely in physical healing. He called the mysterious link between his magnetically hypnotised patient and himself 'animal magnetism', and said there was nothing mysterious about it. But because the therapy meant touching people and sometimes stroking them with magnets, because his subjects fell into hypnotic trances, and because the subjects tended to be women and the magnetisers men, his critics' dark suspicions included those of sexual malpractice. Passes in the air over one's patients might, with only a slight change of direction, become passes directly at them.

Animal magnetism soon began to change its meaning. The word 'hypnotism', just invented, was immediately made pejorative. 'This sect, embraced among voluptuous or credulous women', exclaimed an anonymous tract in 1800, 'surely it is an evil'. The 'sect' included a Jesuit, one Father Hell, who devised a cure for stomach cramps, and the Marquis de Puységur. He had entered the profession by chance: one of his estate workers suffered from terrible fits, and Puységur, trying the magnet as a last resort, had cured him.

Naturally, in a therapeutic realm on the fringes of respectable science – which itself included much worse things – charlatans abounded. And they themselves were pursued by the debunkers and deconstructionists of sceptical Paris. An actor, deploying the disguises of his trade to play the trick again and again, would turn up at public exhibitions of magnetology, feign a hypnotic trance and then, as the magnetiser turned to acknowledge the crowd's applause, cry fraud. Jules Verne was moved to write a farce called *Magnetomania*, and the great Chateaubriand himself denounced hypnotism.

But the magnetisers pressed on. Puységur took the theory forward, declaring that the power to hypnotise had nothing to do with Mesmer's invisible and undiscoverable 'fluids'. The magnets could not be given up – they were a catalyst of some sort – but Puységur was certain that the hypnotic state, its extreme suggestibility, was induced by the will of the hypnotist alone.

It was his most talented disciple who took the final step. José Custodio Faria was Indian by birth, Portuguese by nationality and French by choice; he was also a priest, an *abbé*. Like Puységur, he was a man of the Enlightenment. Insistent on the scientific method, he believed that 'lucid sleep' – his term for the surreal wakeful-unconsciousness of his patients – could be rationally explained and the method 'developed with art, guided with wisdom, and cultivated with caution'. Faria took Puységur's intuition to its conclusion. No animal magnetism, no hypnotist's willpower, no external agency at all imposed the hypnotic state. It might be *induced* – but this depended entirely on the suggestibility of the patient.

The role of the magnet remained mysterious. Faria continued to use them, but his book *On the Causes of Lucid Sleep* firmly places the hypnotic power where it remains, in the subject. In time, the great psychologist Tourette would take careful note. The hypnotic method went on being the stuff of variety shows, but Tourette spotted the crucial insight and passed it on to Charcot (the teacher of Freud), who placed Faria's book in the academic curriculum. Faria had identified the phenomenon of autosuggestion, the founding idea of the modern psychology of the unconscious.

In 1819 the Abbé, living in obscurity in a church home for the aged poor, completed the first volume of his book, and died. He had begun his practice in 1802, at the height of the magnetising fashion, and had been besieged, like Mesmer, by mockery. Alexandre Dumas' *The Count of Monte Cristo* features a mad monk called the Abbé Faria.

The visiting card of the real Faria introduced him as 'a Brahmin from India'. He was tall, and dark – with African ancestors, perhaps. He wore his hair long, and went about dramatically cloaked. Reports describe the audiences attending his magnetising demonstrations as being overwhelmingly young and female.

Hardly a mad monk, nor even an unchaste one so far as we know, inevitably his exotic appearance and origins in early nineteenth-century Paris marked him for the debunkers as a showman fraudster; and had it not been for his immaculate revolutionary credentials he would have had an even worse time from the press.

In 1795, with Parisian radical politics consumed by the struggle between the Convention and the Directoire, Faria had led a demonstration against the Convention. This got him on side with the winners and earned him, with the ensuing friendship of Puységur, an initiation into the mysteries of magnetism. Still, this risky engagement with a foreign cause is something of a mystery – unless the cause was not quite so foreign after all.

Faria is generally supposed to have given up on Goa when he left it. He was born there, in Candolim, in the village of the fine houses behind the Tinto, the market. José Custodio spent his difficult childhood in a house behind the mansion which is now an old people's home; the site now houses an orphanage. When he was eight or nine his parents divorced. Both returned to their first love, the Church, his mother rising to be a famously disciplinarian abbess of the nunnery of Santa Monica – where half a century later Richard Burton would abduct a successor abbess by mistake. The father, having 'waded through the bitter experience of matrimony', also took Holy Orders and when José Custodio was fifteen, left with him for Portugal.

There is no direct evidence that either ever returned to Goa, but the elder Faria at least never ever let go of it. We do not know why he left his homeland; but once in Lisbon, he became the leading intriguer in émigré politics, a keen supporter of the hammer of the Jesuits, the statesman Pombal, and consequently an enthusiast for Goan 'nativist' rights. The failure of Pombal's reforms in Goa prompted the famous revolt hatched in the Pinto mansion across the road from the Farias', and when it was betrayed, Faria the elder was promptly interned. As Couto the chief conspirator's man in Lisbon, he was duly accused of long-distance conspiracy, anti-Portuguese activities, and so on. Faria may have been saved from worse by the failure of the private investigator in Goa to prove a treasonous connection between the conspirators and the French ally Tipu Sultan; but by now his health was ruined. His role – and Portuguese suspicions – passed to his son.

José Custodio was ordained the year after his father's death, and after seven years, of which his chroniclers seem to know nothing, he turned up in Paris. The reasons for his move are disputed, and there were to be several more years of invisibility before his appearance at the barricades. By then the French were at war with the British and their Portuguese ally, and the British were already occupying Goa.

It is reasonable to suppose that the younger Faria was his father's son in his enthusiasm for the Goan cause, that he was enraged by the betrayal of that cause, and in his turn took it up. The missing years leave plenty of time for clandestine trips to India. Tipu Sultan had spies in Goa and emissaries in the French capital. Faria's move to Paris suggests a prudent absence from the Portuguese wrath which, having fallen on his father, was likely to fall on him. The authorities in Lisbon certainly suspected the old émigré's son of having some part in French designs on Goa. For Faria the collateral benefit of an invasion by Tipu would be revenge for the betrayed men of Candolim. In the absence of any other explanation for his sudden passion for French domestic politics, one may reasonably suppose Faria's march on the doomed Convention to have been an attempt to urge an Indian adventure on the coming men of the Directoire.

This is speculation. A successful Tipu/French invasion might have produced a Goan Pondicherry, continuing the Latin theme in Goa's foreign relations, but with policemen in *képis* outside the Hôtel de Ville in Panjim and more *littérateurs* and café controversialists, not to mention the pleasures of the French table. But the invasion never happened. In 1799 the British killed Tipu Sultan. They continued to hold Goa – and in 1807 Napoleon occupied Portugal. Cut off from his past, the Abbé Faria spent the rest of his life in Paris. We know he sent a few religious objects home to his childhood playmate, the orphan Catarina, and that afterwards, Goa heard no more of him. Forsaking revolutionary politics in Asia for revolutionary science in Europe, he took up the magnet. Revolutionary science has much to thank him for.

Faria's statue, sculpted by a Goan from Bombay in 1945 and placed outside the Secretariat in Panjim, would be described twenty years later by Graham Greene as '. . . pouncing like a great black eagle on his mesmerised female patient' – though nobody has ever suggested that the Abbé had *that* kind of animal magnetism.

8 GOA BRITANNICA

One winter's morning in 1847, the captain of the Aguada fort and his orderly took the pilot boat out to inspect a pattimar down from Bombay. We have their portraits, captured by a passenger on that little sailing craft, a junior officer in the British Army on convalescent leave. The captain 'is a rhubarb-coloured man, dressed in the shabby remains of a flashy uniform; his square inch of blackish-brown mustachio, and expression of countenance, produce an appearance which we should pronounce decidedly valiant, did we not know that valour here seldom extends below or beyond the countenance'. The orderly keeps his cigarillos behind 'his enormous flap of an ear'. Below his uniform jacket he wears a loincloth.

The quote is from *Goa and the Blue Mountains*, Richard Burton's first book. London had recently offered Lisbon half a million pounds for what remained of the Portuguese Empire of India – Goa, Daman and Diu – and had been indignantly turned down. In retrospect, it wasn't a bad offer; even fifty years later, those territories' revenues would be a quarter of that. To the British, the 'Goanese' were cooks, waiters, stewards and butlers, and Burton predictably patronises their little imperial backwater. One day he will be Sir Richard, the famous ethnographer, translator and swordsman. He will be a diplomat, poet, polyglot (with twenty-five languages, not including dialects), explorer and master of disguise, *the* Victorian unique; but up until almost the end of his adventure in Goa, Burton plays the gentleman traveller.

But not gentlemanly enough. To Burton, everything about the two mestiços, the captain and his orderly, is wrong. They are neither one thing nor the other, 'mongrel men'. It is 'difficult to find in Asia an uglier or more degraded looking race'. Miscegenation is degeneration, and throughout his book Burton's distaste collapses his travelogue into rancour. 'This race is decidedly the lowest in the scale of civilised humanity we have yet seen.'

Anxious to succeed where the Portuguese had failed, British theorists of empire seized upon the notion that imperial success lay in keeping the rulers and the ruled out of each other's beds. East was east and west was west, and if the twain met, they made mongrel men. 'It has lost the Portuguese almost everything in Africa as well as Asia.' By Burton's time this was the conventional line, and he took it. It was the price of his ticket; the empire employed him and gave him time to indulge his insatiable curiosity, to travel. This was Burton's motive for greatly exaggerating the numbers of mestiços he found in Goa. He may also have been misled. The mestiço population 'was concentrated round Panjim and Old Goa. They were very prominent there, all in the military, and Burton, a military man, would have paid most attention to that.' And he may have assumed that Portuguese names were inherited from a Portuguese ancestor, when the vast majority of them had been acquired by taking in baptism the name of the presiding priest.

Empire was overreach. 'Everyone knows that if the people of India could be unanimous for a day they might sweep us from their country as dust before a whirlwind.' Holding on was a question of finding the friend within, of dividing and ruling. All empires did this, but the severely undermanned Portuguese had taken the next step by marrying the friend within. A human response to perceived necessity, it proved the racial theorists wrong. Ten years after Burton's visit to Goa, the great revolt they called the Mutiny broke out in British India, and it was the arrogance born of racial notions that set the fire.

British condescension towards Portugal had begun early, with the Methuen Treaty of 1703 that reduced it to commercial dependency on Britain, to 'what today would be called a neo-colonial situation'. The Portuguese dream of empire was seen as just that, unreal, it having been forgotten that the term 'British Empire' was first coined by Dr John Dee, the celebrated Elizabethan occultist.

By the beginning of the nineteenth century, British India surrounded Goa, and its forces occupied the enclave whenever their interests seemed threatened. In 1808, during a sixteen-year occupation (effected in order to deny the harbours to the French), one Dr Buchanan arrived in the old city to call on the Inquisitor, curious to know how the Holy Office was getting on in these more enlightened times. By then, Golden Goa was in ruins, with only three or four giant churches surviving. For those alert to the lessons of history, the stricken city was a monument to imperial hubris.

Dr Buchanan found the Inquisition closed for lunch. When they finally met, the Inquisitor, elderly and learned, would go so far as to discuss Dr Dellon's famous book, but not the current state of affairs, not matters still, in 1808, sacred and secret. Buchanan might look around, but not downstairs, not in the places that Dellon had known – the House of Penitence, the Perpetual Prison and the House of Torture.

By the time of Burton's visit, in the mid-nineteenth century, British tourists are poking around Old Goa for bits of black stone. The remains of the Santa Casa have gone into the building of New Goa – Panjim – and there Burton sees 'an unmistakable Lakshmi borne in procession amongst Christian images'. The new capital, with its overlapping religions, had been completed only ten years before Burton's arrival. 'There was tremendous vision on the part of one viceroy in particular, Don Miguel de Noronha, a man of rare quality. Panjim was his project, and he oversaw the building of it from the 1780s. He was fond of Venice, and if he'd lived to do it, he might have made Panjim a little Venice: after all, most of Panjim stands on reclaimed land.'

Burton notes that the police on guard outside Panjim's public buildings are Muslims, and that no office unconnected to religion is closed to Hindus. Pigs run around in the streets; the back alleys are fetid. The dullness of women's lives is relieved at intervals by their enthusiastic participation in domestic violence. Goan law has steadily liberalised in the sixty years since the Pinto Revolt until it is more liberal than England's; the only capital crimes are murder and sacrilege.

He goes to a ball, finds the food (French), the wine (Portuguese), the musicianship and dancing much better than anything in British India. 'Even the dark faces, in uniforms and ball dresses, tend to variegate and diversify the scene.' Racial mixing has its points, socially. In Siroda he will meet dancing girls, some of them 'very fair, having manifestly had the advantage of one European progenitor'.

By this stage in the book, Burton's always powerfully sexual curiosity is being aroused. British military men on leave routinely enjoyed the anonymity that Goa afforded for sex tourism (just as gamblers fled there from their debts), but for the sake of his respectable readers Burton is tough on his compatriots' concupiscence. He recommends that the British in Goa be avoided, and then heads off to Siroda with two British army lieutenants, some cigars and a bottle of cognac. But not before relating the adventure of the amorous raid on the convent, the guards drugged with datura, the beautiful orphan waiting by the window, the rotund, furious abbess abducted by mistake. Burton identifies the perpetrator as a British officer, a clever man of many languages – a man very like himself.

Tales of Siroda appeared in English magazines. There is no 'RB was Here' inscribed on any wall in the vicinity of the Kamakshi temple, but you expect to find it, as Burton found the initials of numerous others carved into the shutters of nearby establishments. Siroda, on the eastern bank of the Zuari, was in the New Conquests, the final territorial expansion of Goa, and had been Portuguese for only seventy-five years. For Burton, it is a touch of the earthy and real in a make-believe empire, and he much prefers it to Panjim.

Burton calls the women of the twenty or so houses '*bayadères*', from the Portuguese *bailadeira*, dancer, and he calls them nautch girls, but this was a North Indian term meaning professional dancers. These women of the south put on dance performances for the public, but they were all *devadasis*, servants of the temple. By 1952, when Evelyn Waugh went to Siroda ('formerly a village of half-caste whores') they were gone, apparently to Bombay – though their secondary profession of prostitution never entirely eclipsed the first. At the Shantadurga temple outside Ponda, D. D. Kosambi recalled seeing two Chinese porcelain lions which had been presented by a *devadasi* and placed on the balustrade around the temple pool. Having been given them by a client in Bombay, she in turn had donated them to her temple during a visit home to Goa in the traditional service of the deity.

Holy women in the distant past, priestesses of the tribal mother goddesses, the *devadasis* had survived the coup by the Aryan father gods, but at a critical cost in status. (Though not invariably: one sixteenth-century *devadasi* was killed leading a revolt during the Hindu migration from Portuguese Goa, and became a local patron goddess herself.) Until the practice was banned in the 1930s, unmarried girls in Goa were affianced to a temple and 'married' to the deity. In neighbouring Karnataka, they still are.

It seems that once this pledge was made, the Goan *devadasi* became the concubine of one of the local gentry, a patron of the temple. He would pay her mother a fee, and the mother would then use this money to buy her other children an education in sacred music. This kept them from concubinage. Numerous distinguished Indian musicians have since emerged from this branch of the *devadasis*. And for an early example of fusion music, Olivinho Gomes believes that the uniquely Goan form, the *mando* invented in the nineteenth century, accompanied on the violin and pottery drum, is '. . . a synthesis of the Italian minuet and the temple *devadasi* dance song'.

'Goan composers had begun experimenting with Indian folk music,' Lucio Miranda told me. 'They added Western harmonic accompaniment – traditional Indian music does not have harmony – and so invented Goan popular music, in Konkani, with Western instrumentation. The *mando* has two parts. The first part follows the traditional melodic line of the Gregorian chant, but in the mode and language of a love song and the time of a two-beat waltz. Then, to include the local flavour, composers added a second part using local rhythms and singing styles – and that part is faster, gradually rising to a crescendo. You hear how gradually the *mando* moves from the European form into an Indian one.'

But as Burton prepares to leave Siroda – its billing as the town of the eastern Amazons having failed to live up to reality – his interest suddenly revives. He is shown the cremation-place of an Englishman, one Major G–, who had moved to Siroda to marry a *devadasi* of the town, and had cut off all contact with his countrymen. He had spent his time with pandits and yogis, becoming 'such a proficient in the ritual of their faith as to be considered by them almost a fellow-religionist'.

For the first time, Burton is sympathetic: he has nothing to say about *this* interracial marriage. One day he himself will make the pilgrimage to Mecca, disguised as a Muslim – right down to the circumcision, for fear of intimate examination – but here he pays homage to the journey he never took: the one over to another culture, not as imposture, but for real.

Entranced by other cultures, but also by his own part in the imperial project, Burton is caught halfway. Throughout *Goa and the Blue Mountains* he works hard for his readers at being the affable Englishman abroad, but it is a pose. He isn't quite the real thing, too dark for the drawing-room. The book was not a success.

By the Siroda episode his Victorian travel writer's companionable 'we' has quite deserted him, and he begins using on his readers the distancing 'you'. His readers bore him now, for he has found someone tantalisingly like himself, part military man, part cultural defector – but one who in the end went over to the other side. Burton is fascinated. Major G– shares his love of arcana. His books, when Burton sees them, are worm-eaten, but show the Major to have been an expert on the dream theory of the Arabs, on mantras, on geomancy (as in Indian *vastu* or Chinese *feng shui*), on Hindu astrology, the conjuring of devils and divination from bones or the hand.

'He preferred their society to that of his own countrymen.' But Burton himself still has his imperial part to play, and he has to leave the grave of Major G– the Hindu, for whom there had been no way back.

9 GEOGRAPHY AND DESTINY

Travel is in the blood. The Dhangar herdsmen were always nomads, in and out of Goa every year, like the modern Goan who comes and goes with ease now that air travel has taken the finality out of migration. The culture of Goa, right down to its place names, was made by travellers – by nomad tribesmen and migrant Aryans and itinerant Buddhist monks, by migrant dynasties and sailors and traders and exiles who left traces of themselves everywhere in Marathi, Kannada, Tamil, Arabic, Turki, Malayalam, Portuguese. All of them left their mark somewhere on the landscape. Chapora and Anjuna are Portuguese rewritings of the Arabic Shahpur and Hanjun. Canacona, the southernmost province of Goa, derives from two Kannada words – Kannada being the language of the dynasty of the golden age, the Kadambas – meaning a forest full of bison. (And there are still bison, gaur, in the Cotigao wildlife sanctuary in Canacona.) Goa got its heterogeneity from inward migration, its great 'diversity in customs and manners' and versions of the mother tongue.

Because we roam, we change. Mario Cabral e Sa's *Great Goans* makes this clear. In their very different ways, his four heroes were all migrants. The Abbé Faria's father was an aggrieved émigré who always looked back. José Vaz – now a candidate for first Goan saint – left for Sri Lanka to follow his vocation of missionary. Lata Mangeshkar is India's most popular singer; her father Dinanath left Goa for Bombay to escape the stigma of *devadasi* origins. T. B. Cunha, fierce analyst of the Goan Christian 'cultural tragicomedy' and hero of decolonisation, left first for French Pondicherry, then for Paris, because

Portuguese Goa stifled him, and he became a socialist there. France was the hub of radicalism. An early Goan champion of Indian independence, F. L. Gomes, studied in Paris, befriending the writer Lamartine; the city set free the talents of Faria, and of Cunha, and inspired the liberal regime in Lisbon that in 1910 finally put an end to legal discrimination against Hindus in Goa.

'By now, we have a Goan diaspora.' Half the family of the author of *Great Goans* has emigrated, and he quotes a lugubrious Portuguese lyric about loss, but Goa's loss was Goa's gain: his heroes succeeded as they never could have done at home, and he writes of them with pride.

Portugal had created in Goa a moribund economy, a religiose and reactionary politics, that mirrored its own. One small country of persistent unemployment and emigration had created an even smaller one; but as compensation, it had enrolled people as members of an empire and a world religion. In the winter of 1997 the veteran cruise ship *Oriana* called into the port of Kochi (Cochin) in Kerala. Thirty percent of her crew were Goan, almost all of them from just two villages. 'The far-ranging Goan has a loyalty to his village you seldom find elsewhere. It seemed the first thing one Goan asked another – not in what city he worked, but from what village he came . . .'

Village solidarity was most obvious in Bombay, where the P&O liners took on crews, especially stewards, and where an entire community had grown up, supported by over three hundred 'village clubs' to help with accommodation, work and support. Anyone arriving from Goa, flush or broke, had a place to go.

Migration began in that first move – which left the new migrant between worlds, looking forward and back. Travel is voluntary; too often in the hard times migration was not, and it shows in the fierce displaced loyalties of the clubs, and in the stoical faces of long-lost relatives in old photos. Twenty years ago in Candolim I went to the travelling *tiatr*, paying a couple of rupees to sit up in the steep tiers of seats, as the hurricane lanterns were lit on the stage and a quartet tuned up in the wings. The performance was, as they say, 'housefull', and fully attentive. The backdrop, all grey and black, depicted the tenements of Bombay to a slow march on strings laden with vibrato and the lanterns turned down low; and no translation was needed to tell me that the play was a cautionary tale of innocent village folk lost in the wicked city.

The earliest migrants had been the Hindus and their temple deities fleeing Portuguese Goa during the iconoclasm of the 1560s. At the same time, though in much smaller numbers, servants and Goan assistant priests had begun accompanying European missionaries on their epic journeys through the new empire. Then, during the early nineteenth-century British occupation, Goans began to work for non-Portuguese speakers, and political refugees fled to the rising metropolis of Bombay. Mass emigration began mid-century, with serious economic decline being exploited by agents in the indentured-labour business right up into the first half of the twentieth century, and the sending of the luckless Kunbi tribesmen to Assam. Landless tenants emigrated. The coming of the telegraph, the train and the steamship – all properties of the British empire – extended opportunities to a small, inward place with too few ways of making a living.

By the turn of the twentieth century, Goan emigrants, mostly Christians from the Old Conquests, and uninhibited by caste rules about travel, food and association, had become indispensable. 'In Goa the British found this very interesting type: Westernised, Christian, reasonably educated, who knew Portuguese and quickly picked up English. It created such a wave of emigration that the population of Goa remained constant for seventy years.'

For the young, things British became fashionable. 'The Goans who have settled in British territory are striving hard to adopt English as their mother-tongue, just as they have Anglicised themselves in dress and customs.' The educated went into government service in Africa and India; in Allahabad my grandfather vied with his colleagues for the services of 'Goanese' cooks.

At home, a 'strikingly lax, inefficient and corrupt administration' brought even harder times. In the early 1920s, over-optimistic estimates of Goa's upcoming rice crop inspired customs duties on the rice that had always needed to be imported from India. The British retaliated with duties of their own, and the coconut trade – still, after twenty centuries, Goa's chief export to greater India – collapsed. Then came the depression of 1929–1933, and after it the war, during which British food control in India cut off rice imports to Goa altogether. Half the population 'managed to live on starvation rations, while the rest emigrated'. By the 1950s, Bombay was the biggest Goan city, with an émigré population of eighty thousand; the population of Panjim was a tenth of that.

After twenty years in Africa, FX came home to Goa to be a taxi driver. He arrived in 1947, the year of Indian independence, to find his village populated by 'aunties' and old men, and a few children sired in haste by fathers who returned immediately to Bombay. But he had his savings, and stayed – and soon the car would arrive. I first met him in 1983, when he was seventy-three, and the British prime minister, Margaret Thatcher, was coming to the Aguada Hotel up the road for a Commonwealth Heads of Government Meeting. The road was being widened, the bar had just lost its best mango tree and roadside shacks had been painted white; the joke was that everything not moving would be painted white.

This is my diary entry for November 1983:

FX is a long thin man. He claims that in his youth he was a great dancer – in a photograph from 1935 he looks quite the lad, all oiled hair and thin Latin moustache – and even now, dusting the car one more time, he has a great delicacy of movement. Occasionally he stops dusting and mops his bald brown head with a large handkerchief. The car is a rich dark green, and he has only to sit in it, he says, to be back in Mombasa. 'Give it up, FX!' his neighbour calls out from the next-door balcao. 'She's never coming along here.' FX does not answer. Both he and the Ford Popular will be looking their best – not out of vanity, though Mrs Thatcher will be unaware of that when she passes by, but in memory of the Captain.

It was the Captain (an elderly, passed-over captain by then, trembling with the first signs of Parkinson's) who sent the Ford to FX, from Mombasa to Bombay and on to Panjim. For twenty years FX had been the Captain's driver-factotum. No matter that there are no more parts for the car, or that FX's taxiing days are over. He calls himself FX as the Captain did ('Too damned many Francis Xaviers in Mombasa already, eh?'). The Captain will live again when the Iron Lady comes.

FX gives a final flick of the duster, fetches a ruined wicker chair, and stretches himself out in it with his long brown feet on the bumper. He can see strips of himself reflected in the radiator grille. He grins at the grille, and the grille grins back. The late afternoon sun is warm on his face. He takes a reviving nip of Honeybee from a hip-flask. 'FX,' calls out the neighbour, 'you fall asleep, man, they're going to paint you both white.'

The neighbour thinks FX is a bit cracked.

Most emigrants in the hard years had been men, fleeing from the absolutely unindustrialised and heavily populated Old Conquests. By 1947, the excess of women in Bardez was more than thirteen thousand. No attempt had ever been made by Lisbon to create employment, hydroelectric schemes for the Ghats, fish canning – or iron mining, despite persistent reports (the first from three hundred years before) of huge reserves on the midland plateau.

In Lisbon, the implications of Indian Independence created a sudden interest in Goan self-sufficiency. In 1947, fourteen tons of iron ore were excavated; three years later, it was seventy-two thousand. Things began to improve through the 1950s – as they had to, in order for Goa to be held up as the very model of the modern, happy colony. Still, FX found it an odd sort of place.

Until the Indian takeover in December 1961 there was no universal suffrage, no universal education, and medical provision was so primitive that the historian T. R. de Souza relates that he had to go all the way to Bombay to get his tonsillitis seen to. Coastal villages like Calangute depended on kerosene lamps until the coming of Indian electricity. A solitary metre-gauge railway ran up the Ghats to Castle Rock and the border with British India, little rutted roads ended at jetties – there was no bridge even over the Mandovi – and the deep-water port at Mormugao was undeveloped.

Goa lived on emigrant remittances (to everyone's rage, heavily taxed), on subsistence agriculture, fishing, and smuggling into India. With the free flow of imports from Lisbon, the latter had become a major industry. Very little was imported from India; and then the borders closed, and would stay closed until independence. Currying favour, the Portuguese sent in Mercedes Benzes and tools and clothes and shoes and food and drinks, Portuguese wine, French brandy, Scotch for thirteen rupees a bottle, German beer. So it was only on the morning after, as independence came, that it was realised how little manufacturing there was in Goa, how parasitical its economy had been allowed to become.

Many of the cheap imports, and of course gold for weddings, went straight over the Ghats to post-Independence, import-substituting India. It is interesting to note the vintage of certain celebrated smuggling methods, the gold being carried 'not in lorries but in the bodies of the smugglers themselves . . .'

The Portuguese dictator Salazar, since his accession in 1928 an ersatz Vasco, interminably presided over his antique and shrunken empire. His ascetic *caudillismo* reached far-off, colourful Goa as a kind of municipal glumness. By the 1950s, soldiers from Angola and Mozambique, bored to distraction, were guarding

Goan political prisoners in the Aguada jail when they weren't singing homesick songs to Africa in FX's local taverna.

Church harmonies, FX thought, were rather dull by comparison. Dutifully he drove to Mass. Soon would come the reforms of Vatican Two, the liturgy in Konkani in place of Latin, shirtsleeves instead of black suits; but now, in the rains, men still arrived from across the sodden fields in a loincloth, carrying on their head a clay pot containing the black suit and shoes. The service was interminable, featuring lachrymose sermons punctuated by reminders of upcoming saint's days which, excluding Christmas and Easter, numbered some thirty-two. (Perhaps to give the Christians as many holidays as the Hindus, FX thought.) The remains of Sunday he offered up to duty, visiting his once-rich *rentier* relatives in their crumbling mansion, where a row of wafer-thin aunties in black, doomed to spinsterhood, sat humbly in straight-backed chairs along one wall of a salon 'the size of a hangar'.

Panjim by then manifested 'a mellowed authoritarianism' under which the street lighting was turned off at ten and everyone had to go home. There were no nightclubs. There were 'no popular amusements beyond an occasional snake-charming and a well-censored cinema show'; the movies had finally reached Goa in 1932. The authorities, still trying to keep up standards in a manner recalling the sixteenth-century prohibition of the *dhoti*, had decided that a man going into town for any reason at all should go in a shirt and tie. T. R. de Souza remembers his grandfather, in 'the choicest vocabulary of bad words in Konkani and Konkanised Portuguese (though never in public)' fulminating against 'the pants-wearing class'. Goans still dress neatly, though not formally, to go into town, and every time you see some topless tourist taking his belly out to lunch in a Mapusa restaurant, Salazar gets your vote.

The Portuguese themselves were few. 'One can walk about all day in Goa,' Norman Lewis wrote, 'without seeing a white skin.'

Evelyn Waugh, staying in the Mandovi Hotel, or rather having it built round him ('noise absolutely infernal'), and waiting to attend the 1952 Exposition of the holy relics of St Francis Xavier, thought Europeans as rare as in the Amazon. Goans, he wrote, had no idea of 'the horrors of Hitler's or Stalin's regime and recount as a great cruelty the mild Portuguese rule of law'. Or rule of apathy. The law-enforcing was done by the local militia and police but strongly reinforced, you suspect, by boredom. At the Panjim riverside the statue of the Abbé Faria, immobile over his mesmerised patient, aroused in FX a particular empathy. 'Goa had stalled. Anyone with any go went to Bombay.'

But it had been much worse in the war. His friend and adviser Mr Naik, the cloth-shop proprietor, had only just got through it. 'He said it was dreadful,' FX told me. 'Money was too tight. But somehow he managed. War is a dirty business, Naik used to say, and people always need new shirts.'

Portugal stayed neutral, but took no chances. At the outbreak of hostilities in 1939 the government expatriated part of the national gold reserves to Goa for safety. So the Goa authorities made money there; and the Panjim finance-fiddlers and smugglers made money and threw parties, and bought Mr Naik's best white suiting. Around them formed a small champagne club, the same few dozen people meeting every week, thrilled to bits to see each other again, and wondering if there were any Turkish cigarettes or silk stockings to be had. Everyone outside this charmed circle wanted only that the war should end. Food was short, and every week people were leaving for Africa or Bombay or anywhere.

The champagne club included the Allied people who spied on the Portuguese and on the Axis people, and the Axis people who spied on the Allies and were careful to reward the Portuguese for their steadfast neutrality. In high places, Mr Naik told FX, schnapps was known to flow like water. A small corps of fixers moved discreetly between the better addresses.

But playing host to two giant adversaries was not always easy for the Goa administration. In December 1942, British agents abducted two Germans, Robert Koch and his wife, took them off to Belgaum and shot them, or perhaps only him. The event excited the champagne club tremendously. Koch had been quite charming but apparently a spy, and was said to have been making radio transmissions from one of the three German freighters, or perhaps the Italian one, which had sailed into Mormugao harbour at the outbreak of war and had been interned there ever since. It was not the first time this had happened: German ships had been interned in the first war, too. Now once more the authorities found themselves wishing they would disappear. Driven to distraction by years of confinement, sailors were deserting their ships, and several were living in Panjim – as they were entitled to do in a neutral state, though the British complained about it.

Then, three months after the abduction of Koch, a small coastal steamer entered Mormugao harbour at night. No one took much notice until armed men boarded a German freighter, the *Ehrenfels*, shot a sailor, and set the ship on fire. They swore in English, another sailor would testify at the hearing. There was an explosion and some shouting, Mr Naik's nephew Sanjay reported, and that was about it. Thirty-seven years later he met David Niven on the beach below the Aguada Hotel. A film was being made of the incident.

What was there to make a film of, Sanjay wanted to know. All that had happened afterwards was that the other two German ships and the Italian one were scuttled, and the crews were interned in the Aguada jail, where they became very expensive to feed in those straitened times. At the end of the war they went home. But a few Germans stayed on to live permanently in Panjim, some of those who had left their ships before the attack by the Sea Wolves, as the film would call the British irregulars. After the war they got hold of some money and lifting gear, salvaged their sunken ships, and settled in Goa on the proceeds. They married local girls, had children. In Panjim Sanjay met one of the German stayers-on, a quiet man who ran a watch-repair shop.

The British had said that multiethnic, multilingual India could never succeed as a unified nation state. Indian nationalists had argued that it could, that a composite nation could be made – if the demands of unity were not too crudely imposed on natural diversity. Unity had to defer to consent. Through the fourteen years that separated Indian decolonisation from Goan, the first Indian Prime Minister, Jawaharlal Nehru, made it clear that Goa was not to be tarred with the colonialist brush. When the colonial enclaves rejoined India, due account should be taken of their particularities. He would have preferred a peaceful transfer of power, the leader of the newly postcolonial nation being averse to sending in the gunboats.

He was unlucky in having to deal with Salazar, not a man content to let history take its course. 'We would be giving or selling the Portuguese of India, the land of Afonso de Albuquerque and our epic achievements in the Orient, the saints of the Church, our country's martyrs. And for how much? For how much?' Goa: a trophy of glories past but a trophy nevertheless, essential to nostalgia and self-esteem.

In 1950, upon India's demand for their return, Salazar had declared his country's possessions in India to be no longer colonies but overseas provinces of Portugal, 'Portugal outside Portugal', and therefore sovereign territory. Goan MPs sat in the Portuguese parliament. The timing of the declaration was a ploy to fend off action by a United Nations mandated to protect sovereign territory. Likewise announced at the UN was the enthusiasm of Goans for the colonial life. ('Nonsense,' FX told me. 'It was an enthusiasm for cheap imports.') It was all in vain. To India, Goa was not a foreign body. Geography was destiny. The imperial bolt was shot; it was all over.

The Portuguese and the *descendentes* began to dust off their suitcases. In 1952, as the crisis of Goan nationalism deepened, a newspaper editor had told Evelyn Waugh that the Hindus were 100 per cent in favour of union with India, Christians fifty-fifty, and the Goans in Africa, the 'Africanders', pro-Portuguese. The level of Christian support for the colonial power was 50 per cent

– and no more than that, in a population whose loyalty Lisbon took for granted. Ideas, which need no passports and go everywhere invisibly, are subversive migrants. As reunion with India approached, imperial authoritarianism was once again confronted by ideas of equality and justice filtered through religion, as it had been on every reformist occasion since the sixteenth century. 'Goa's culture is Christian,' Archbishop Gracias of Bombay famously declared, 'not Portuguese.'

Late in the nineteenth century, this struggle within Goan Christendom had been well illustrated in the hounding of one Father Alvares – an editor, writer and what we would now call a social worker. Alvares denounced the unholy alliance of Church and State, and denounced Europeans for distorting his religion, it having been 'in Asia that God's revelation had taken place first'. A religion born in the Middle East was entitled to assert its Asian self. In an attempt to humiliate this meddlesome priest, Alvares was driven through Panjim in his underwear by an army officer, and eventually excommunicated. His response, which was to join the Syrian Church as Mar Julius I, 'Bishop of Goa, India and Ceylon', did nothing to diminish his enormous popularity in Catholic Goa, and on his death a huge procession followed the cortège.

Alvares had the moral victory; but the fact was that all large-scale attempts at reform in Goa had so far failed. This discouraging record, complemented by pressure from the pulpit, persuaded most of the Christian laity to keep their aspirations to themselves and their heads well below the parapet. It was an opt-out already showing up in migration. The numerous critics of Christian passivity, led by T. B. Cunha, demanded more Old Testament thunderbolts and less New Testament lamb; but Church and State for generations had put much effort into teaching the virtues of suffering in silence. Nor is it surprising that a declining majority chose to 'hold onto nurse for fear of something worse'. By the 1950s fewer than 40 per cent of Goans were Christian, with numbers falling, as they have done ever since. Just over the Ghats, giant India, represented for generations as a pagan chaos, was waiting. 'At school,' I was told, 'we were taught to regard all Hindus as gentiles.'

Iron mining was soaking up unemployment by the mid-1950s, and the rest of the economy, much of it black, was financed and provisioned by Lisbon. Very little was spent on infrastructure and a great deal spent on inflating incomes, creating an artificial boom which could not last but was bound to be popular. Generally, people were not 'totally ecstatic about being liberated', and after Liberation – a term which the Communist takeover of Eastern Europe had recently made ironic – there were recriminations. The Portuguese had been the first Western imperial power to colonise a piece of India (albeit a tiny piece) and the last to leave. But it was not the inhabitants who evicted them: it was the Indian armed forces.

Imperialism had somehow survived the shortage of imperialists; the Portuguese had been in an absolute minority all along. Outside Panjim, the only Europeans most people ever saw were priests. Imperial defence sometimes had been farcical: one seventeenth-century fort on the Gulf had been reduced to defending itself with bows and arrows. In the mid-nineteenth century, Richard Burton had noted that the navy consisted of exactly one sloop of war. An early twentieth-century governor of Goa had been obliged to tour his northern enclaves of Daman and Diu in a British steamship.

By the late 1950s there were said to be only fifty Portuguese in Goa, and all FX would say about it was that everyone knew they were all leaving, and soon. The police and militia would desert at the first approach of the Indian Army, and then that would be that. And as Mr Naik of the cloth shop used to say, everyone was a Freedom Fighter at heart, but history taught caution. Gandhians – passive resistance activists – entering Goa in their thousands in 1955, had courted arrest, as they customarily did in British India, but had been shot at instead. Fifteen had been killed, which event convinced everyone attending the discussion group now covertly convening at the cloth shop every siesta that the success of passive resistance depended crucially on the behaviour of the opposition.

Having bought a couple of cases of green Portuguese wine and some Scotch for distress-sale prices and taken it home in the car, FX thought again and garaged the lot with a cousin in Pernem; then, having been told the Portuguese departure date by another cousin in the Telegraph Office, he discreetly bought an Indian flag from under the counter of the cloth shop. 'When it's all over,' Naik told him, 'sell the car. You'll make a fortune.'

'Never.'

'FX,' Naik said, 'it may be old, but it's foreign. It's duty-free. As soon as the border opens, this place is going to be one big shop. They can't get this stuff over there. For once in your life, make some real money.'

'Certainly not.'

Nehru had said that he would not tolerate the Portuguese even if the Goans wanted to keep them, and on 17 December 1961, Operation Vijay began. MiGs buzzed Panjim. It was rumoured that the Indian Army, thirty thousand strong, would come by train. To face them, Salazar had flown in three thousand Portuguese, who were billeted in the crumbling quarters of Old Goa and then flown out again; after which there was still only the obsolete frigate, and no aircraft or anti-aircraft defences whatsoever. Salazar's response to reality was to declare that there would be no victors or vanquished, only martyrs and heroes. 'Our soldiers and sailors must conquer or die.'

FX heard a little gunfire from Aguada, and was later told that there had been some casualties, but not too many. The little airport building was overwhelmed by luggage, the last official papers were incinerated and the last officials bade their retainers farewell. 'Don't be upset,' his departing employer told Sanjay, Mr Naik's nephew, who wasn't. 'It'll be Christmas soon.' Salazar ordered the torching of Panjim, and his commander there was pleased to be talked out of it by the Apostolic Patriarch.

At the last, the Governor-General opened the coffin of St Francis Xavier, and prayed for divine intercession over the holy relics. This had worked very well 278 years previously, when the Marathas, with the city of Goa at their mercy, had miraculously retreated – but it didn't work this time. (Nor the next. Ten months later, the Indian Military Governor of Goa would order another unsuccessful private exposition of Goa's saint on the occasion of India's border war with China.)

On 19 December, soldiers of the Punjab Regiment raised the tricolour over the Secretariat, the *Afonso de Albuquerque* sailed out to be holed by the Indian Navy, and Salazar wept on television. Thirteen years later, after forty-six years in power, he fell; and finally Portugal was free to say that Goa was gone.

10 VILLA PORTUGUESA

Modern times were coming, FX could feel it. His nephew came to stay, humming a tune called 'Telstar', and eventually left for Bombay to be a journalist.

'A what?' Hilaria asked. FX's sister Hilaria and her husband had tied the knot in Mozambique and honeymooned in Zanzibar – just before he went down with his ship, on duty in the First Class saloon. It was a tragedy of the too-extended family, of the war; he would never see his own son, nor had his wife's family ever set eyes on their son-in-law. Privately, FX disbelieved he had ever existed. When, through some inexplicable process of inheritance, Hilaria came by the mansion of the *rentier* relatives – who had gone *en masse* to Canada – FX drove her there in the Ford. All she had to say about her windfall was, 'Not by merit, Francis, but by His grace.' A year later she married the *rentier* relatives' lawyer, and then FX understood.

Her possessions filled only the back seat, and on arriving at the mansion she waited with them in the deep, dark porch that was the size of her old house, while FX toured the vast rooms in search of lurking rival claimants. In the salon, the wooden ceiling as high as the Candolim church's and thickly cobwebbed, the walls colour-washed in old yellow, he found an ancient couple, the family retainers, she holding the bamboo ladder, he precariously halfway up it, replacing the broken translucent seashells in the trellised windows, for something to do.

Old mansions such as this were bereft when their owners emigrated, taking their ivory icons and pictures and silverware and carved rosewood furniture with them. Unless they had big money, for most inheritors the traditional grand state was now unaffordable. These were nineteenth-century houses, with labyrinthine plumbing, a blackened kitchen at the rear of the house lit by a single, yellowed light bulb hanging in the gloom, and vast gardens waiting to join the jungle. So many hands were needed to clean the mouldings, the blue-and-white Portuguese tiles with their scenes of gesticulating conquistadors and transfixed martyrs. Someone had to polish the gilt in the family chapel and arrange the flowers; someone had to boil the water in the huge coppers for winter baths, and in summer sweep out the dust and hang the giant tarpaulin over the sea-facing balconies for when the monsoon came in.

Everything had to be done by hand, but the retainers were ageing with their masters, and the new help did not know the old ways. Nor were they so cheap. The great families had made their money from land, but – as had happened long ago in Portugal during 'the crisis of feudalism' – receipts had begun to shrink and had never recovered. Now this disaster was compounded by land reform, tenants' rights, socialism, public education and other daring innovations from India.

T. R. de Souza writes of today's '. . . strong and liturgically alert Christian minority in a state of economic and political lethargy'. This was already visible in the early 1960s. Christian dominance had vanished with the Portuguese. Christians of the upper castes tended go into the clerkish jobs, teaching, the Church, the more enterprising of them into the new professions – like journalism. Few were in the real new money, in the industries that India was looking to set up. Hindus had the mining, and they had always been the traders, wholesale and retail. Trade was beneath the sons of the grander Christian families. Indeed, many things were beneath them, and in 'Uncle Peregrine', Leslie de Noronha has left us a fine portrait of his eponymous hero, a man reduced to his manners, taking a stroll in the park, 'dressed as usual in his crisply ironed white linen suit, carefully removing his cream-coloured straw hat every time he passed a lady'.

In the same short-story collection, *Ferry Crossing,* we find the kind of house Hilaria inherited. They tend to be called 'Portuguese houses', though they were built by Goans for other Goans, for the Christian Brahmins, the first Asian elite to absorb the Western model of civilisation. The Portugueseness of these houses is in their unlikeness to the traditional Indian house looking inwards upon its central courtyard. The imported taste was for big windows and gardens and for verandahs, *balcaos* – a 'device for opening up to the outer world'.

'So the churches were built,' Lucio Miranda told me, 'and then the houses. All were designed and built in the European style; this outward orientation of life was one of the biggest transformations in the Christian society of Goa. And it was in the villages, radiating outwards from the principal church, that the transformation came about, this urbanisation process.'

The grandest mansions are in Salcete. In the façade of one house might be counted 'sixteen great windows in a row, and the salon was thirty-six paces long'. Even those mansions built this century were built in ancestral villages, like the replica of the royal palace of Zanzibar built by Zanzibari artisans in 1916 on the Anjuna–Vagator road for the ruler's esteemed Goan physician and awardee of the Golden Sword.

Building for the aristocracy began in the 1760s, Lucio explained. 'Under the Portuguese, the Christian Brahmins had become a sort of civil service. Very few of that class married the Portuguese. Those who did, married into the highest level, into a class much like their own. There wasn't even a colour barrier, because the Brahmins were light in colour.

'By the end of the church-building phase they had been culturally assimilated and Westernised, to an extent. So now they wanted houses. At that time there were no architects, but some of the Jesuits were trained master builders: there was the example of their ability in the great churches of Old Goa. And by then generations of Goan masons and craftsmen had been working there, and were masters of an acquired style. See that baroque angel in the cabinet there, made in Goa by an Indian artist who never saw Europe.

'There had to be climatic alterations made, and this wasn't appreciated at the beginning – the corrugated-iron rainshades that you see everywhere were tacked on later – but otherwise the earliest houses are as authentic as can be. The houses of my ancestors are Italian *palazzi*, designed by Italian Jesuits.

'Then came the nineteenth century. The aristocracy were still building in the grand style, but by this time the middle classes were building their own houses. These were the returned emigrants, once the tenants of the big landlords, with earnings from Africa. They bought plots from those landlords, and those are their houses that you see in Calangute, Candolim, everywhere. They sent money home, and came home on leave, and over thirty or forty years they built their houses and left them to their children.'

Like the émigré family living in Nairobi depicted by Hubert Ribeiro, the new middle class adorned their houses in the nineteenth-century way, with a confusion of treasures and bric-a-brac. 'There were Shiraz carpets, Chinese porcelain, water-buffalo skulls, Egyptian alabaster, polished turtle shells, Portuguese silver, African rawhide drums, hand-carved Kashmiri furniture, a jade Buddha, a bishop's throne and a Steinway piano.'

But there was none of this in Hilaria's mansion, nothing left at all, and when FX came back after the rains, she had already tired of her ghostly existence in the smallest of the great bedrooms, and had sold up and remarried and gone. Fifteen years later, once the roof tiles had come off and the rain had got in, the house became a depository for plastic chairs.

In 1964 Graham Greene came to Goa for Christmas, and in the cathedral in old Goa, sitting amongst a dozen people, felt that he was attending the last rites of Christianity. 'He was a convert – very keen,' I was told. 'Insisted on going to Midnight Mass. Then he came on to the party.' Where, at four in the morning, he was handed, 'as a matter of course', a Benzedrine tablet. 'Indeed,'

Greene wrote, 'there is more than a hint of the worldly Babylon which shocked Camoens . . . naked bathing parties take place at a secluded beach, and who sleeps with whom is known to all Panjim.'

Modern times were coming, FX could feel it, and he shrugged to see them come, but still, he didn't much like the new beach life. By which of course he did not mean the beach life of Greene's world, people coming down to Goa to be out of sight. He meant the summer season, when all Goa dressed up and took to the promenade. The sea's salinity is high in the hot evaporating months, the gluey, salty water ideal for easing blood pressure, aiding recovery from wounds, and relieving sprains. For the sake of their rheumatic legs, elderly visitors sat up to their waists in sand, and their saying was 'a week at Calangute and a week at the springs'.

Beachside, empty bungalows filled up with moneyed Bombay Goans and their servants, and Calangute fishermen moved their families into the back room to rent out the front room and the porch. April and May were the last chance for fishermen to make some cash before the fishless privations of the monsoon. In the south, in Colva, even the gentry from nearby Margao moved into fishermen's houses. Beach-shack lemonade refreshed the holiday crowds of relations pouring in from Bombay and Africa and Bangalore, and in the smart crowds on the beach matches were made and old acquaintances ne'er forgot. Hilaria came back the next year, from Mozambique, as before, but this time with her lawyer. They were moving to a posh suburb of Bangalore. 'Not by merit, Francis,' Hilaria said, 'but by His grace.'

FX's preferred viewing spot at Calangute had always been the wall near the Souza Lobo restaurant, where he could see the bandstand over the heads of the crowd. But lately he'd taken to sulking in the forecourt of the new Tourist Hotel. If you were going to listen to music in Goa it should be Goan music. Where else were you to hear it? *Fados* and *mandos* and *dulpods*, even

Konkani pop – not the Bombay show-offs' dance demonstrations and the clanging English numbers of the Simla Beat Contests. Unrequited love and village jiltings, the bawdy bawlings of the coconut pluckers. The old cheerful amateurism. The lady accordionists, the violin and drum. They were more his kind of thing than that Beatles racket.

He drove the Ford back and forth from the ferry wharf in Panjim, cleaning the sand out of it on Sunday evenings. This was his cash season, too, and when it ended, more or less in time with the rice planting at the end of May, he would be able to call in on old Naik. Soon the cloth-shop owner would be finally persuaded to retire, to spend his last days in comfortable contemplation by the temple near Ponda; but in the mid-1960s – FX forgot when, exactly – he was still at work. Leaning as ever on the old iron cashbox, pudgy in crisp whites and with one eye on the new tailor, he said to FX, 'They're back.'

'Is this a Portuguese joke?'

'A tourist joke. They come in here, not many, a few. Mostly in the winter. Western kids. Beatles types.'

'Good Lord.'

'Speaking of whom,' Naik said, a little smugly, 'they do seem to prefer temples to churches.'

'Protestants. The weaker vessel. Still, that's something,' said FX. 'Foreign tourists in Goa . . . They come in the winter, you say. What is there to do in the winter? And what kind of tourist goes to cloth shops? Why not just send someone from the hotel?'

'Ah,' old Naik said, and he smiled. 'But they're not that kind of tourist. They don't stay in hotels, they rent rooms from fishermen. They live on the beach, in huts, in bare feet and *lungis* – in the winter! – and you know what they wear on top? Velvet waistcoats.'

11 THE EMPIRE OF HIP

At six, an overture of whistlings, from mellifluous flute to strident referee, a spirited bird performance from next-door's tangled garden. At seven, a fanfare of cockerels and dogs, which dies away before the bicycle hooters of the bread boys. All over Goa they emerge from family-run and mostly still wood-fired local bakeries, hundreds of them, bike baskets filled with a variety of breads – soft rolls, hollow chewy spheres and butterfly shapes. They used to deliver by headload, as the bucket and mat peddlers still do.

The sea is limpid and a little misty. This is the time to see dolphins, but there are none today. The sun is just up behind the palms; the sand is not golden – as the brochures insist – but sand-coloured. A few people are sweeping up in front of their palm-leaf beach shacks. Men in shorts and baseball caps have hand lines out in the lightest of light surf. Perhaps it was they who left the empty bottles along the tide line. Some nocturnal fraternity sat here last night in a long row, admiring the phosphorescence and drinking Honeybee. The cool of the night is a relief. Perhaps the weather will change at the full moon, as it is often said to do; and when a ring is around it like last night, the locals say, the turtles come ashore to lay their eggs.

This is dog hour. They tussle peaceably along the tide line as the joggers come trotting past them in ones and twos and small packs, one madwoman bounding along ecstatically in a shift, three Baul musicians from Bengal strolling in saffron knee-length Indian shirts and white *lungis* and beards, long black hair done up in a bun.

To the south, Aguada in the last of the mist; to the north, the Baga headland. The joggers overtake me as I head north, but I will be going the farthest. I shall be calling into Calangute and then Baga, Anjuna and Vagator, and tomorrow I will take the ferry across the Chapora River and walk along the Mandrem–Morjim beach to Arambol. From there it is just one more beach to Terekhol fort where, in the shadow of a belching hilltop iron plant, Goa stops.

Walking is the way to do it. There are already too many travelogues called *In the Footsteps of –* , but in the case of the empire of Hip it is essential to walk in its footsteps. Its spoor is not so old, and it was the last empire to go along on foot. My historical hike will end in the early 1980s, with the coming of the motorcycle.

To recap: the Portuguese were expelled at the end of 1961, Goa rejoined India and soon – so soon – the foreigners were back. First in '66 to Colva in the south, where Mia Farrow would flee from the Beatles' ashram in Rishikesh, and where Dervla Murphy called in on her way to write *On a Shoestring to Coorg*. But soon Colva became an outpost. From the late sixties to the early eighties, it was these northern beaches stretching from Candolim to Arambol that were the heartland of the empire of Hip. As I set off, the sun begins to warm the sand, turning it to a brochure shade of gold.

The first monument on today's pilgrimage is a personal one. Six of us spent the winter of 1979 at the modest Candolim bungalow that is now a restaurant and shop fronted by red plastic chairs. Arriving blanched and bony from the privations of the mountain monsoon, we tore off our clothes and rushed into the sea. During my second swim I was stung on the back by a jellyfish. 'Piss on it!' cried the reclining Goa veterans. Our landlady took the pain out of the welts with vinegar.

Though these were hardly the huge, dilating deep-water Portuguese men-of-war you saw from the Bombay steamer, their sting could be severe. In Candolim once, a woman surfaced with a jellyfish on her head, and nearly lost her sight. They float just below the surface, when the sea is oily-calm; it was useful after an encounter to learn to scan the beach for the stranded jellyfish that indicated the presence of the gelatinous mass offshore. In fact there weren't so many, because there were more turtles then to eat them. Jellyfish are the turtles' favourite food.

The beach below our old bungalow is much busier these days. A Hero Honda motorcycle comes off the end of the path to bog down in the sand, loaded with cases of drinks, snacks and cigarettes, and boys come running up to stock a shack with the goods. Tourism is labour-intensive and most of its labourers are very badly paid. These are the sons of the fishermen who fish when their competitors the trawlers, whose fine-meshed nets catch everything, are elsewhere. The fishermen need long stretches of sand to dry their fish and repair their nets, but through the winter season the beach is taken up by sunbathers. So the fishermen wait for season's end, and during it, they diversify. On signs by their boats they paint 'Dolphin Trip (No Dolphin, No Pay)', 'Island Trip', 'Crocodile Trip', 'Fishing Trip', 'Fleamarket Trip'. But not 'Acid Trip'. This is Candolim, lately a province of the modern empire of Touristhan. A lady goes by advertising another of its possessions: her T-shirt says 'The Gambia – No Problem'.

Throughout the 1970s' empire of Hip, this long beach was a nature refuge and mystic shore, and now it is the seafront of the Candolim-Calangute-Baga suburban belt. People released for two or three weeks from the northern winter avidly embrace the sand. By mid-April they will all be gone, and though reminded of departed jollity by the plastic bottles winking from the bushes, the beach will give up being the seaside and go back to being immemorial. Up to a point. There used to be much more sand.

In the early seventies there were about twenty-six thousand motor vehicles in the whole of Goa. Now there are over two hundred thousand, and all over the state the old bullock carts prefer the car-free dead of night – especially the sand-stealers, creaking away from the beaches towards the construction sites and the glassworks. The dunes they dig by moonlight have been vanishing through the decades: sand excavation was licensed until the eighties, until villagers and environmentalists got it stopped. So now it is stolen instead, though not in such quantities.

Outside the Calangute restaurant, a billboard reads 'Lungi and Lacoste'. I stop off for coffee – real coffee – and a South Indian breakfast. The extending of Goa's culinary range by Indian tourists has ended the long and terrible tyranny of the fried egg.

By the early 1970s a languishing coastline inhabited by Indians, most of whom had been Christians for many generations, became the paradise of Western youth, most of them with countercultural tendencies and leanings toward Hinduism. This was an interesting twist in the postcolonial experience not necessarily apparent at the time. 'At last!' an old Christian lady is said to have exclaimed as the first foreigners arrived to meditate all day and take LSD in the nude. 'At last, someone to talk to.'

A prominent red sign stands by the ramp leading down to Calangute beach. Three tourist policemen are sitting beneath it, airing their feet and reading the newspaper. Most of the tourists will be going to the Wednesday fleamarket, and some are already gathering round their transport, a superannuated fishing boat flying the Union Jack; but on any other day they will be on their beach beds, and the policemen will be strolling amongst them to see that they are not mobbed by itinerant peddlers and beggars, whom they 'fine' if they can catch them before they reach the cover of the bushes.

The red sign reads 'Nudism is Prohibited'. Down by the sea, swimsuited matrons from Bombay are paddling, exchanging sisterly smiles with topless matrons from Manchester. Toplessness is now unremarkable. Behaviour once thought wildly bohemian has been absorbed by the mainstream. Now that everything is acceptable but full-frontal nudism, which isn't thought worth fighting for any more, the red sign is less a present warning than a memorial to the war fought so that torsos might be free. By the eighties, the flyers you were handed in Calangute headed 'Do's and Don'ts for Foreigners' said, among other things, 'Do not move stark naked on the beaches'. By then, only the starkness mattered. Today, even the most proper tourists wear the *cache-sexe*, tanga or thong worn on every beach on earth – and first invented here, in the late sixties, on Calangute beach. Or rather adapted, from the Goan fisherman's *casti* – but only for fear of the jellyfish.

In Sri Lanka in the fifties the American novelist Paul Bowles liked to go down every day to the beach. After a week he called in to see his travel agent. The man was alarmed to see that Bowles had a tan. 'Careful,' he said. 'You're losing your colour.'

I was walking down the Calangute ramp to the beach when a Goan friend asked me where I was going. I said: 'I'm going to lose my colour.'

'You can have some of mine if you want.'

One culture's therapy is another culture's torture, Bowles used to say. Until the early eighties, full-frontal nudism was practised by nearly all the foreigners here – nakedness invariably being called nudism by the press, as if it were a campaign, which in an unexpressed way, it was – while groups of men from Bombay and Pune and Bangalore in suits and shoes tramped along the beach like anthropologists, viewing the prone primitives in their state of nature, wondering at their lack of shame, at the taking of Indian hemp in the hot sun.

They asked the nudists why they were nude, and for their pains were shouted at and called voyeurs. Female nudists brandished sticks, foreign dogs were set on them. Patiently, they endured. The tramping through the sand in the midday sun was torture, the naked women (the silver band slung around the hips, the ankle bracelets) were torture, the curses of the nudists – as if nudism was normal – were torture, but the stories to be told afterwards made all the trouble and expense worth it.

Though much taken with Hinduism, nudists forgot that in India public nudity was usually encountered in the religious context only. On certain occasions, sadhus in procession dressed exclusively in ashes. To demonstrate yet more dramatically their indifference to the flesh, the sternest renunciates tormented with steel jockstraps and ropes and rocks their despised genitals – but here in Calangute could be seen the opposite, a genital boasting exhibition. A *tamasha*, a spectacle, and obviously intended to be so, since it was done in public. In Bombay, weekend tours were organised – one night on the bus, full board, another night on the bus home, all inclusive – and the more they were shouted at and called voyeurs, the more fully dressed men arrived, disembarked from buses in Calangute, and patiently set off along the beach.

We've got to get ourselves back to the Garden, the Woodstock song went. The identifying of nudism with obscenity bewildered the nude, who identified it with freedom and innocence. 'It's right to be naked in paradise, man,' a new arrival once said to my landlady. 'It's like Adam and Eve.'

'Quite so,' she replied, 'and look what happened to *them.*'

But for countercultural Westerners, if not for Latin Catholic Goans, nakedness as shame had vanished long ago. As a symbol of freedom and innocence, it first surfaced in the millennialist fourteenth century, with the Adamites, who in search of redemption went about as naked as the First Couple in Eden. But they were from Eastern Europe, and never went to the beach. Nor did anyone, for pleasure, and for countless centuries the beach was left to fishing and defecation. It became a scene of therapeutic bathing in the eighteenth century – but the pleasure-beach, where civilisation and restraint gave way to unfettered nature, was an invention of nineteenth-century urban romantics. Like the jungle, the beach could be seen as a place for forgetting, always its pure self, timelessly and endlessly self-renewing. Each day, yesterday was washed away and innocence reborn. In the 1920s the Germans reinvented nudism as sunbathing. The sixties took all its clothes off in public in this tradition, and brought it up to date, making nudism an advertisement for the sexual revolution, part of the revolt against repression and denial.

So the purest culture-outlaw territory was the beach, and the best place in India for the beach was Goa, which, despite the events of 1961, was Not India. This was a fateful discovery. Only a few years separated the Portuguese departure and the Hip arrival, but it was long enough to enable Goa to be 'discovered' by the West all over again. It was *our* Goa, full of European echoes, though all those churches were a bit much. It was a refuge and a hideaway, because India, despite its far more interesting religions, could be a bit much, too. In India you respected the local culture, and then you came to Goa to be your natural self – but here came the fully dressed men, tramping down the beach.

Nudism started a sort of tabloid panic in Goa quite devoid of the amiable relish of the fully dressed men. It was an echo of the tabloid panic in the West that you thought you had escaped. Goan columnists knew that a common view of Goa in greater India was that four centuries of European rule had turned the place into something attractive but naughty, a relative turned louche after too many foreign affairs. One went to Goa for a good bad time. The taverna-culture and other hints of wicked Europe made it the next best thing in India to a foreign holiday.

For those in Goa unable to laugh this off, it had been a long vexation, and sometimes the war against nudism became very shrill. Occasionally, even today, you come across something like this: 'They are mainly lower-class Europeans . . . with a decadent lifestyle. They come with their money to "freak" out on drugs, nudity and free sex.' The afterburn of a rage thirty years old, from a time when nudism was as bad as drugs, this piece in the language of the late sixties dates from 1993.

To save everyone's blushes it has since been dispersed, but throughout the period of the tabloid panic, some three thousand sex-workers of all ages and sexes continued to serve the public in the beach quarter of Baina, near the port of Vasco da Gama in south Goa. Meanwhile, far away in Calangute, you sat on the beach exuding the vegetable magnetism that came of negligent nutrition, reading *Autobiography of a Yogi*, and wondering where all the girls were. They were in Pune, at the ashram of the outrageous guru Rajneesh.

In the village, morality was of the old-fashioned kind and not made overmuch of. 'Why worry about our girls?' my landlady often said. 'They won't even look at the foreigners. The foreigners get married and unmarried every season. In India, marriage is forever.' You might stay away for years, but were never forgotten – and nor was your friend. When you came? Where were you staying? Same friend?

'Same.'

Clearly this was a relief, though a new friend would be made perfectly welcome. Next year you would be asked: 'Same friend?'

The coastal villages, of infertile soil, dependent on fishing and coconuts and the Bombay visitors in the summer, enjoyed the enjoyable parts of the foreigners' winter frolics and averted their eyes from the rest. My landlady thought nudism was vulgar, and said so, and left us to it. She took it *susegad*. That very Goan word (from the Portuguese *sossegado*, calm) carries many meanings. It is amiability and courtesy, balance and unworriedness, calm and unflappability, a sense of proportion. If the *balcao* is the junction of home and world, the heart of Goa, then its soul is *susegad*. But the word may also signify withdrawal, not getting involved, keeping one's head down, or, as a young Goan I met on a train put it, 'not protesting at outrages'. It was *susegad* that made the empire of Hip in Goa possible and gave it enough rope to hang itself with.

Villagers I knew read the press for the births, and the death anniversaries ('Month's Mind'), the political scandals and the football results, and ignored the rest. It was their villages the foreigners were living in, and they knew what went on and what did not. 'The Chief Minister told this journal that hippies were not the kind of tourist wanted in Goa.' My landlady glanced at the *Navhind Times*, and shrugged. 'He has to say that, doesn't he.' She thought his party would lose all along the northern coast if they threw the foreigners out. Emigration had emptied houses everywhere, and by the seventies, of Anjuna's population of nearly eight thousand, at least two thousand had emigrated. For years foreigners had been renting hundreds of houses that otherwise would have fallen to the white ants and monsoon rot. They kept the restaurants and bars open.

In the end, the villagers were more concerned that the nudist at the well did not drop the soap in it. The well was the one source of drinking water in those days, and where I stayed, soap-dropping was the only offence apart from violent madness able to truly upset *susegad*. Drug use did not bring down retribution if the local boys did not get involved, and if people did not 'have their name spoiled' by police raids. Far more than the foreigners and their habits, it was the temptations of Bombay that were feared, these being beyond village control. Village boys were vulnerable: the siren city was a constant theme of the Goan theatre, along with politics and corruption.

The ancient traditions of the village commune gave the village strength in present times. It was reinforced by the intense solidarity of fishermen, and by the family ties of neighbours. Uncles and aunties and cousins abounded. When a Christian died, Hindu friends called round to pay their last respects to the body laid out in the front room, and everyone wept regardless of religion. On one's birthday it was the custom to offer cakes to one's neighbours. Everyone avoided 'that family of robbers' who caterwauled and beat each other by night and let their goats out to eat decent people's gardens.

The police were never called. The madman who pissed in a well was tied to a palm tree in the traditional way, and beaten by the villagers. The lady protecting her coconut crop by fixing razor blades into the tree trunks carefully cleaned the slashes in the Swedish boy's feet, and told him that a thief had no right to be angry. When a foreign woman was attacked by a gang (fortunately mostly composed of overexcited little boys), a village deputation implored her not to call the police. The ringleaders were sent round to beg forgiveness; then they were banished to Dubai. Foreigners carrying towards a dry well another foreigner they had already beaten insensible for some drug deception were warned off by the local 'mafia'; this was their patch, and they didn't want the police on it.

At the end of this long beach lies Baga, once tranquil, now developing touristically both upwards and outwards. Never having lived there, I realise that for an account of Baga in the seventies I will have to walk in the footsteps of someone who did. Kim Morarji saw Baga for the first time in 1970, when he was twenty-three. He is from Mumbai (since 1981 the new name for Bombay), and like most visitors to Goa in those days, he came by sea: 'The road was not the way to go.'

'There weren't too many buses running between Bombay and Goa then, and the train journey was extremely convoluted, it took forever. So everyone came on the steamer. The coast was so attractive I could have jumped off the boat and swum ashore. You arrived off Goa sometime around dawn, seagulls escorting the boat along the beaches, empty beaches, with hardly a sign of urban existence anywhere apart from the tourist resort in Calangute. Otherwise it was all rich subtropical green, the palms and that long fringe of sand.

'There wouldn't be a bridge over the Mandovi for another year, so once ashore, we took the ferry over to the north, the Bardez side – a little car ferry, carrying mostly bicycles. Once there, we took a taxi, an Ambassador. The taxis were all Ambassadors and old Peugeots. The new Indian buses had yet to arrive, so all the buses were *caminhão*.'

The word means lorry, but in Goa it meant an antique little bus like a stretched old-style station-wagon with a long hood and decorated bodywork and maybe twenty seats jammed inside. With so few cars around they were the major form of transport, and their conductors prowled the bus stand, crying out their destinations. Their descendants do the same today, and their buses still stop on request, in the *caminhão* tradition.

'Where the Calangute temple stands now, there was a little shrine. The taxi stand is as it was – but there were only four taxis. The barber shop is still there, and it was a barber shop then. I remember a couple of juice bars and a few chaishops, but apart from the tourist resort there were only the old houses; no new ones, no hotels, no souvenir shops, no roadside stalls.'

Kim moved up to Baga, looking to rent a room in a family house. This was what everyone did, there being nowhere else to stay. The lady of the first house he came to had run a speakeasy in Bombay before retiring to Goa, and her husband had a little restaurant in Calangute. Kim ate there: 'Fish, Goan style, all the Goan dishes. Fish was almost free, and you bought it straight off the beach from the fishermen. I don't remember there being any tourist food: we were alternative tourists, the first wave.

'I settled in and from the first, I felt right at home. Bombay is a very Goan-influenced city: as a child I had a nanny called Maggie de Souza, from Mangalore, south of Goa. The Mangalorean and Goan cultures are very similar, both parts of the same expression. And I speak Marathi, sister to Konkani, so there was a language advantage. Nothing ever went wrong between us. If the posher landlady-types didn't care for Hindus, and you heard them say so, they were never anything but civil to me, because I was an educated Bombayite. Bombay was the Goans' second home.

'Goa was such a contrast to the urban life. Zero population pressure, and none of the poverty you'd see in the city. A land of plenty, with nature so bountiful. Walking through Baga, taking one of the paths that wound their way through the sand dunes, passing those old houses . . . Somewhere along the way, I heard about this small restaurant that had just opened, nearer the river. Tito's, when I got there, was a little house with a front porch. From immediately below the porch there began a long sweeping expanse of sand descending to the dunes, a pure beach, and then the blue ocean – a vast expanse of blue ocean all the way to the horizon. Nothing disturbed the eye.

'Tito's was very simple, there were pigs running about. I remember lots of animals. It was surrounded by sand. That little tar road ran down to the beach as it does now, but there were absolutely no modern constructions at all. Steps led up to the porch. I think there were six tables, or maybe eight, along it, and three doorways leading inside to where old man Tito stood behind the bar.'

It was Tito's first year back in Goa; he had just arrived with his family from Africa. In Baga he had found the house, leased it and eventually bought it, started the bar-and-restaurant. 'The bar was secondary. The restaurant was secondary, too. The real selling point was the view, which was so satisfying that people would simply sit there and sit there and allow themselves to expand, as it were. And the Titos were very nice.'

Baga – the name comes from *bagh*, a garden – begins again on the other side of its eponymous river, or tidal stream, and ends on the jungly slope of the promontory immediately behind it. Until the eighties you crossed the river in a canoe, or waded across it at low tide with your clothes on your head. Jungle Barry came to Goa for the first time in 1966. Then, he once told me, French bandits used to ambush people as they emerged dripping from the river, and if they found British Commonwealth or Irish passports, they carried them off. (Until 1984 these passports required no visa for India. The holder was entitled to stay in the country indefinitely.) A revenge raid on the bandits' lair unearthed about fifty passports, Barry said, which were dutifully sent off to their respective High Commissions in Delhi. After that, there were far fewer French bandits called Fred Smith and Mary O'Connor, though banditry itself did not entirely cease. There have been muggings in the new tunnel bridge.

In the fifties one Father Le Tellier, the Belgian Jesuit who began the Retreat House that stands on the tip of the promontory, planned a bridge; it is unlikely to have resembled the one that appeared thirty years later. The Baga Bridge is featured on postcards as the Baga Monster. By means of a steep and potholed ramp you enter a gloomy concrete tunnel with portholes, its walls hung with innards of pipes and wire. The function of a tunnel so remarkably ugly, of a tunnel at all, is a mystery; it squats on the banks of the pretty little river like a chunk of subway, a nightmare sent to remind holidaying urbanites of all they have escaped. Perhaps it was to have a restaurant on top; or an illegal hoard of cement had to be used up before the inspectors called; or it was a Baga Bridge of Sighs gone wrong. 'Perhaps,' writes a local historian, delicately, 'the planners of the bridge believe that there is beauty in dungeons too.'

The worn laterite path leading up through the light cashew jungle of the Baga hill was everyone's shortcut to Anjuna. Down there, on what I think of as the Other Side, there are trees painted in Day-Glo now, and motorcycles in ranks outside the bars, and the gaudy mansion called Orgasmic. But the dense green canopy of the palms prevents you from seeing them from up here. From the brow of the Baga hill, the panorama of Anjuna is the one I have been seeing since the mid-seventies, all palms and paddy fields in the arms of the sea and the dry domed hills.

In the unearthly moonlight you paused, a party pilgrim, by this sanctifying cross. The cashew bushes were silver and shadow. Through the stillness came the muffled thud of a generator, and a snatch of trumpet. From here on down I will walk in the footsteps of myself.

12 FROM UTOPIA TO ARCADIA

My first time in Goa was October 1976. I had arrived on a series of trains from north India, and was tired of trains and heat and distances. On the platform in Margao – or Madgaon, it had two names – were some French people. They lived nearby, in Colva, and wanted to know where I was going. I said north, to Anjuna. There followed a long pause in which that lovely name hung in the air like a confession; then one of them said, 'Ah, but that is definitely somewhere else.'

The bus going north was blue, and it was called *Mahalaxmi*. The name of the Hindu goddess was painted along the side in green italics, the down strokes picked out in white. I walked around the back, by the taillights red with dust, to ask the driver if he was going as far as Mapusa, and saw that along the other side of the bus was painted another name: *Mother Mary*.

Inside this bus blessed by two religions a tape boomed out odd music, a yearning soprano ballad, Indian quarter-tones over Iberian horns. As it ended, we left town for a landscape of monsoon electric-green paddy fields and terracotta earth. We passed a little wayside chapel freshly painted white and barred with iron, the tall roadside palms high above it leaning into an empty sky. I was sure that somewhere near would be the deeper blue of the sea, but then we turned inland. *Mahalaxmi/Mother Mary* traipsed around Goa for a while, stopping apparently at random, and eventually came to rest in Mapusa. I stayed the night, and the next day took another bus to the coast, getting down by a red and blue blockhouse of a bar called Starco's, the first bar I had seen since Park Street in Calcutta that didn't look ashamed of itself.

'Kingfisher', the beer billboard announced. 'Most Thrilling Chilled.'

I walked on through the village – a vast and unwalled village of old houses widely set apart – and halfway to the beach I found a place to rent. It was a little room with a porch, quite new, tacked on to the massive flank of a much older and quite decrepit mansion.

Staying in Anjuna a few years after the Portuguese departure, Graham Greene wrote that Goa would be transformed by India within a few years. But it took much longer. Salazar's retrograde regime had ruled Goa by gloom for nearly half a century, and in the mid-seventies, gloom lingered on. There were plenty of rooms for rent in big old houses (amongst the palms, within earshot of the sea and the exuberant birdlife) that shut out the sun and exuded tropical *tristesse*.

Crepuscular, with creaking four-poster beds that leaked ant-dust, with bottomless cane chairs and sepia prints of inter-ments – so many places were like this. The reliquary boxes and framed martyrs cast long shadows. My landlady's family were *rentiers* and small landowners reduced to genteel poverty. Several days a week they went to church or attended litanies at the wayside icons of patron saints. Their two men, one just back from Africa, the other a pensive unemployed uncle, wore Sunday suits. The boys were thoroughly starched; the girls and women wore flounced, frilled, multilayered, satiny dresses suggestive of Mexico. The widows went along in widows' weeds.

On the big saint's days I was invited to elaborate feasts, though the dull decades had made even these rather prim. I sensed standards being kept up in obligation to old protocol and the remonstrating pulpit. My neighbour Ratko had a grim landlord: outside on his *balcao* on St Sebastian's Day I once saw him sitting at table, sweating through his old black suit, gazing through the roast boar's ribcage like a prisoner. Long popular in Goa, Sebastian was a legendary martyr of the Romans, a centurion condemned for his faith. From the sixteenth century he was heavily promoted all over the empire as the exemplary suffering Christian soldier, with his eyes on heaven and his abdomen full of arrows, which he is said to have miraculously survived – whereupon the emperor had him clubbed to death.

My landlady's family occupied a house opposite and had interests in properties round about, but I never did find out if anybody actually lived in the decrepit mansion which abutted my little room. 'Hello,' my landlady would say, pocketing the rent money. 'Goodnight.' Then she would vanish round the corner into the dusk. There was no public lighting at all, but no villager ever needed the half-candle in the half-shell of coconut without which I was helpless on moonless nights. I understood why we foreigners loved the moon so much.

Where the back wall of my room met the side wall of the mansion, plaster had come off the laterite. Through several gaps between the weathered blocks could be seen a huge and derelict dining room-cum-kitchen, the tiled worktop, its decayed earthenware pots, and at the end of it, wood-barred windows – opening into what seemed to be another room with the same sagging wormy rafters and ant-ridden walls, cracking furniture and festoons of webs. Desiccation was universal, and bandicoots had tunnelled the floors. The walls of the nearest room had at some time been whitewashed as high as the painting-pole would reach, but above them hung a smoke-blackened ceiling of impossible altitude.

In my own room there was nothing at all but a bowed bed and a disembowelled suitcase and a graffito on the wall reading 'Spaceship Lenny Has Not Yet Landed'. I remember going outside to sit on the tiny white porch, and seeing the moon come up to silver the palms. The silence was absolute, until a dog barked, and then another, and then every dog in north Anjuna. All together they suddenly stopped, and through the silence came the generator thud.

In the Rose Garden I heard a man eating crab and talking about the Anjuna of five years earlier. This must have been the period Ratko called Early Hip. 'It didn't last long. The equality was a youth thing, and shared poverty kept it going. It vanished as soon as people started making money.' At which point the broke and the egalitarian had fled for Vagator and Arambol. This left Anjuna with the movers and shakers and a certain mystique. Its fame spread. Famous counterculture folk were said to go there. The movers and shakers began to appear all over the planet in silk, silver, brocades and exotic jewellery, telling tales so beguiling that by the mid-seventies Anjuna was being overwhelmed by its admirers.

Once upon a time there had been naked hermaphrodites to astound the fully dressed men. The mobile Californian commune called the Hog Farm had visited. There was at least one Family of unrelated adults; there were the Green People, each bearded patriarch marshalling his wives and babies. I saw Early Hip as the American discovery of Goa. America radiating from world-conquering California her visionaries, deft New World navigators of the modern flux, psychedelic conquistadors. In Anjuna in 1994 I met a man searching for the very spot where he had been spontaneously seduced by 'a nymphet' in 1972, on his way home from a party. He told me that spontaneity had been everything, openness had been everything, freedom had been everything, and now he was on Wall Street.

'Then there were the Italian Beautifuls,' Eve Green recalls, 'all walking on the beach naked except for the silver belt, the silver necklace. Super-poseurs, very elegant and in control, though I didn't know they were junkies until over the years they began to die off, and I asked what had become of them. When they wore anything it was white. Always white.'

There was nowhere like it; it was too rare to last. Anjuna in 1976 had an aggrieved air, like an artists' colony suddenly chosen to host a beer festival. There was the public Anjuna, the parties, the fleamarket, and within it another Anjuna that was not somewhere you went but something you joined.

Ratko had been there quite a while, but he was not a joiner. He was a gruff old wanderer from somewhere in Yugoslavia. His hair and beard were not long but disordered, he was obsessively book-ish, a sort of Gurdjieffian beatnik, and about forty years old: to me, ancient. To him, hippies were romantics yearning for a golden future or the golden past or both. Where he came from, the romantics had finished up endorsing communism, because com-munism itself yearned for those things.

And he worked. You didn't work in Goa, you *were*. Every evening he would retire early, and all night the big petromax lamps shone through the cracks in his door. He spent all night with his books and slept by day, except for every second Friday, when he would leave blearily in the morning for the Mapusa post office with a heavy parcel. When he had finished reading his books, he said, he sent them back. That night he would sleep. Late on Saturday morning, genial, he would invite me over for tea and a lecture, all the time fondling his latest tome, invariably a weighty hardback on something like Sanskrit prosody, or bio-chemistry.

He said he was too grim for parties. He didn't even read the Anjuna magazine, *The Stoned Pig*. Nevertheless, he got wind of everything. Anjuna came to him in emanations.

I would drink tea and he would talk. 'It's not that there are too many people. It's because they're the wrong *kind* of people.' Ratko's bony finger would shoot out and lock on to some guile-less youth tripping across the clearing. 'Begone, Bilbo Baggins! You will not last a week here! This jungle is too dark for you, it tolerates no *small* vices.

'In godless times,' he would continue, 'where does the poor Westerner go to find God? India. But he shouldn't go to Goa. Goa is not for truth-seeking, but for vision-seeking. Now the dull colonial time is over, this place has been reinvented as – of all things – a location for improbable dreams, an Eldorado. The new kings of the mild frontier – well, just look at them. Of course the moralists are enraged. They have never seen that kind of jungle craziness before.

'Raleigh died for Eldorado. Aguirre went mad in the jungle. Utopias were founded, and all of them failed. No perfect place has ever been found in the West, so in our time the vision-seekers came east. Here in Goa they found freedom. You know Grass?'

'From Thailand.'

'From West Germany. Günter Grass talks about "the freedom of the playground". That is the freedom you see here, against a backdrop of exotic scenery. Here there are no rules, no police, no pressure.

'So you get awesome displays of hubris, jungle craziness, an impressive casualty rate. Freedom means just that: you're free to live and free to die. It's accepted. A young girl swims out to sea – this happened a month ago – keeps on going and never comes back, and there's nothing to be said about it, apart from "She wanted to go beyond," or something metaphysical like that. What *does* get the vision-seekers in a rage, on the other hand, are the halfway hippies, the camp-followers, the bongo-players and god-botherers, the people with peace signs on their headbands. The mules. The legions of the uncool. You've heard it: "Loosen up, you uptight bitch, you're in Goa!"

'But these are democratic times. The legions of the uncool have the victory, and the old elites are in full retreat. These days, everyone has a right to everything, and access is universal. That rarest of experiences, visionary experience, is freely, democratically available – in pill form. The legions of the uncool have broken into this sacred grove, and are feasting on its bohemian delights – though one day, of course, they too will be outnumbered by new generations, the hordes to come.'

Then he would descend from the prophetic to the ordinary plane. It was Ratko who advised me never to ask anyone what they did for a living, and never to suggest the group photo. I never knew what was coming in my Saturday lecture. But one morning as I approached his *balcao* I saw a brand-new tin trunk on it; and coming out with the tea, he announced that he had decided to leave.

Because I didn't really know anyone else in north Anjuna, I decided to leave as well. He was off to Belgrade, and I thought I'd move to Vagator, where I had friends. After his customary week of sleepless nights he left one morning for the Bombay boat, labouring under the trunk. It was all books. 'Ratko,' I said, 'I hope you're going to be okay with that lot.'

'Lord, yes!' he exclaimed, in a sudden access of emotion. 'So do I.'

I start off up the long winding path that runs up and around the Vagator promontory. It begins at the Paraiso, the alfresco dance club owned by the grandson of the founder of Pakistan, over-looking the north Anjuna beach. I walk over the unspoiled hill, down to the twin coves of Vagator and their fine, silvery sand – and here are the remembered rocks, the terraces, the tall palms whose tops are twisted by the wind.

Both Utopia and Arcadia were states of perfection, Ratko had said, but there was a difference between them. Utopia was an ideal of the future, and Arcadia was an idyll of the past. The Lord of the Rings to Anjuna's Lord of the Flies, Vagator had been kept nicely idyllic by an extreme simplicity of life. The terraces climbed steeply up the cliff and there was no village to begin a civilisation in. It was palm-leaf huts, beach fires and bongos or nothing.

Of course Ratko had warned me that Arcadia was an illusion too. It hankered for the golden age – but we had all been evicted from the Garden too long ago, and there was no going back. The earthly paradise was not to be regained, especially not by befriending serpents. A well-known Vagator story underlines this: and here is a version of it.

'The guy had something on a leash. A turtle, was it? We came down on the boat from Bombay, you know how you used to group up on the boat, about ten or twelve of us, and this guy, he was Belgian, I think, young, one of those people you knew straightaway was an oddball, not the full shilling. He stayed in Vagator; we came down a few weeks later from Arambol to do the fleamarket, and saw him. He's into his metamorphosis. He's hit it. He's noticeably spaced out. He's got something on a string – it's either a lobster or a turtle. Maybe a tortoise. A shell creature.

'He'd got into an animal trip, he was communicating with the animals, that's what it seemed to be all about. Later we heard what happened to him.

'In Vagator there was a spring in the back of the jungle there, and a cobra used to come to this spring every morning at four o'clock – an hour before sunrise. Someone told the Belgian about this snake, so he goes to catch it. And he does catch it. He's caught this cobra, and it's bitten him. He decides he'd better go to the hospital, and he takes the snake with him: he's communicating with the animals. So he gets on the bus with the snake in a bag, but it gets him again a few times.

'In the hospital the snake escapes, and they have to clear the ward out. Then the guy dies. Do things like that happen now?'

Ratko had been right about Vagator. It was peopled by Arcadians. The tropical weather, the light breeze, the rhythmic sea, the primeval rocks, the pristine sand – all of these in concert put the inhabitants in mind of heaven. Heaven is a place, the song goes, where nothing ever happens. Events, even alarming ones, come and go against the backdrop of an apparently unchanging world. This enables those events to be seen as unimportant, and encourages an interest in metaphysics.

And in the tropics even an ascetic may live well. The Renouncer lived on a small terrace, high up the cliff. He was a small bearded man who wore the religious seeker's saffron *lungi* every day and strenuously practised yoga on the beach. By night, however, he abandoned self-denial and went about practising all the usual countercultural vices: and this had earned him his nickname, which he bore with an affronted dignity. After all, he had been careful to renounce only the things he would never do, like eating people or being judgmental.

Walking along, I look up towards my own small terrace, where once I lived with two friends in a palm-leaf hut called the Smack Hut, from its function of the season before. Now someone has built a toilet there; even Vagator has eventually tired of timelessness. Along the beach I count a small catamaran, a trampoline, a score of beach umbrellas and six or eight big restaurant shacks. The two shacks nearest the cliff have decorated it with little glaciers of garbage, which in the old days would have been cow food. But now a patrolling cow in search of paper bags (for the glucose, it is said) is disappointed, and goes down to the beach to stand ruminating by the sea, next to a juggler and a bikinied girl doing headstands.

'So not much changes,' the juggler says to me in conversation. 'Anjuna's still kind of precious, Candolim's the suburbs, and Chapora's where you go to see your dead friends.' He has no designation for Vagator. No one lives there: it's just a beach.

It isn't far to Chapora village, but I want to stay on the sand to the end of the beach and then climb up to the fort. My first day's walk will end there, high up on the curtain wall of laterite blocks warmed by the sun. You have to watch out for dozing snakes up there.

When Sambhaji's Maratha cavalry came down from the north and took the fort in 1683, they captured forty cannon and as many Portuguese, who were led away naked in chains. Thirty years later the fort was renovated and provided with escape tunnels to the river and the sea; but was promptly lost again, this time to clan raiders from Satari. After that the fort saw no more combat for 245 years – until a big techno party in the 1980s. The organisers had forgotten to square the police, so they stormed the fort at midnight, flailing at the fleeing partygoers with their bamboo staves. After that there were no more parties at the fort. Nor does the Archaeological Survey of India want its historic stones done up in Day-Glo.

139

In a cool breeze I walk along the beach, talking into my recording Walkman and deciding that if someone sees me and wonders what on earth I'm doing, I will hold it up to my eye and pretend it's a camera. In the mid-seventies a camera would have been an object of suspicion, but to be seen walking along the beach talking to it, or to nothing in particular, would not. The beach was the promenade of the mad. In 1976 a woman meticulously made up as the goddess Kali – black body, black tongue and necklace of skulls and all – imperiously paraded along here, tearing up her travellers' cheques and throwing them into the sea. I watched this theatre of renunciation in the company of a man on vacation from his sex commune in California, and another from, as I recall, Brazil, who was wearing a costume composed entirely of feathers. Someone once said that Surrealism was not a movement but a prediction.

NEW CONQUESTS

13 THE NEW FRONTIER

'Coffin Cross Maker and Modern Picture-Frame Maker.' Siolim modernises, but with an eye to the past. There is no beach, and thus no tourism. It is a classic sprawling Goan village with beautiful old houses in open space, and nothing obstructs its view westwards towards the estuary, the fort, and the sea. At the congested landing-stage on the Chapora River, the River Navigation Department's ferry sets off, loaded with people (fare: half a rupee) and two-wheelers and a couple of cars. Minutes later, she is easing round the feet of the new bridge. The bridge is being very slowly but solidly built, and the price of land on the Pernem side is beginning to rise in anticipation.

Near the sandy spit that points across the estuary to the fort, our ladies of the oysters are at work. Shoulder-deep at low tide, fisherwomen cowled like nuns against the sun pluck shellfish from the riverbed with their toes. When the Chapora canoe men on their narrow river-strand beneath the fort began to inflate their rates for the short paddle across the estuary, even the foot traffic went upstream to the ferry. From Chopdem, the ferry village on the other side, you could take a little old bus back down to the river mouth, passing inscrutable buildings and ancient groves, duck ponds, pig wallows, and hamlets where old men dozed on chairs by the roadside. Wakened, they sold petrol in bottles, but not often: this was bicycle country, as if Chapora, a mere motorcycle rumble away on the other side, did not exist. As if the river were still a border. For nearly three hundred years, it was. Until the Portuguese takeover of 1778 this was the frontier of an unchanged Hindu Goa; people on this bank watched those on the Chapora side becoming inhabitants of a foreign country.

In a copse by the road, just off the sandy spit, there is a little juice bar. The two old men always there on the wooden porch would turn to look me over, a fairly rare foreigner, with friendly curiosity. This was my picture of riverside Goa: two old fishermen on the porch in faded khaki shorts, a whiff of mangrove and shellfish and mud, a couple of beached skiffs, peeling paint on clapboard walls, a slow river threading off through the jungle towards crumbling old forts up in the Ghats. If little had changed here, upstream it was immemorial. Narrow up-country roads glimpsed from a canoe veered off inland to places the maps forgot. They touched the river by mildewed old houses with boats up on stocks, skirted the fortress-grey river wall of Colvale church, and ended at wooden jetties. In his book *Goa*, J. M. Richards writes of these narrow roads ending at rivers, the numberless rivers and rivulets and creeks that run down from the Ghats to the sea, slicing Goa into thin segments of dry land.

In the juice bar there was no juice, no bar, and no refrigerator, just limes for lime sodas, chipped glasses, and piled cases of dusty soda bottles. These were mostly the old refillable kind, stubby and thick-walled, with marble stoppers to hold in the pressure. Survivals like this made Pernem about as different from Bardez as it had been in the time of the Marathas.

Like most Pernem people, the juice bar man was Hindu. His calendars came from old-fashioned general stores; they had the gods on them for auspiciousness, and were written up in English and Marathi. There never had been much Portugal here.

'Where you from?' he would ask each time I turned up. 'German?'

'No, I'm . . .'

'Good! Good! What you do in German?'

The fort on the point looks too strong to be taken. One escarpment drops down into the sea, the other into the river, and inland, the promontory sloping up to the curtain walls is rough and rocky. This defensive cornerstone of Portuguese Goa commanded the Chapora estuary and the north-western frontier, and to strengthen the force of Goan militiamen it was manned by the forty doomed Portuguese and their cannon. In 1683 Sambhaji the Maratha was camped at the foot of the promontory with his cavalry, the best in India, but was short of siege engines – unless you count the *ghorpad* as a siege engine.

In the villages they say that to drink its blood is to become a Hercules. It is fast and agile, carnivorous, with a forked tongue and wicked claws and recurved teeth. It is a swimmer, diving for fish, and it climbs trees after roosting bats. The *ghorpad* lives in a hole in the mango tree, and if you see one you shouldn't tell, the older people say, or the boys will kill it for sport. I did see one once, one September in Candolim. The bus ahead of me stopped suddenly on an apparently empty road, so I passed it on my bicycle to see what was up. The *ghorpad* was perhaps a metre and a half long, and was across the road and into the undergrowth very quickly for its stump-legged bulk. The dark glittering body and thick tail switched from side to side behind the heavy, scaled shoulders, and I saw its implacable lizard eye.

What makes this monitor lizard truly remarkable is its ability to climb and hold fast, despite its weight and size. While drawing water from his garden well at six in the morning after a party, a friend of mine saw the armoured head of a monitor, tongue flickering, suddenly appear over the three-metre wall above him, and he fainted. In Ximer I was told that the *ghorpad* cannot be prised from its hole, even if the strongest man in the village gets a rope round it. It will jam itself into a crevice and inflate, and starve rather than let go. 'The stories of monitor lizards being used to scale the walls of forts could be true,' writes J. C. Daniel in *The Book of Indian Reptiles*, 'as a large monitor, once it is wedged in a hole, can very well support a person of light weight for a short time.' There are stories of the

Marathas' *ghorpads* scaling enemy walls with a boy soldier and his grappling hook on a rope.

As I leave the juice bar on the far bank for the two-and-a-half-hour beach walk to Arambol, *El Cid* – the old Hollywood epic – comes to mind: the penultimate scene, in which the black-clad Moorish legions march along the beach towards Charlton Heston's Spanish castle.

The Marathas, though, were an army of horsemen. It is likely that they did ride along the beach at low tide towards Chapora fort from their own stronghold of Terekhol at the far north end – but then, to lesser cinematic effect, turned upriver short of the sandy spit in search of an easier crossing. Sambhaji took the Chapora fort unresisted, but from the landward side, it being impossible to cross the estuary under the Portuguese guns. This accounts for the building of the Colvale and Tivim forts inland. Attacks into Bardez, the Portuguese front line, came from inland.

After the Portuguese departure it was proposed to rename the port of Vasco da Gama after Shivaji, founder of the Maratha power. Richard Burton had written in the 1840s that the Marathas had 'a well-defined idea of what patriotism means', and today Shivaji is a hero of Indian unification. But there is little evidence that in Goa at least the Marathas were much interested in anything but loot, despite nearly driving the Portuguese into the sea, twice.

Solidarity, frugality and equality gave the Marathas strength. Unburdened by baggage trains heaped with courtly paraphernalia or by crowds of dawdling and gun-shy camp-followers, they moved fast and struck hard. And unimpeded by the shibboleths of caste, heroes ascended through the ranks. Born a Dhangar, a nomad, Malhar Rao Holkar rose from general to duke to king.

In 1664, Maratha cavalry led by Shivaji himself were halfway into Goa, with 1600 Bardezi captives in the bag, and the Portuguese on the run, when a fortuitous Mughal attack took them in the rear. The Bardezis used the respite to build the Colvale fort and to defoliate the hills between Anjuna and Vagator, to deny cover to the next attackers – and to predatory animals, chiefly the crop-ravaging wild boar and the big cats that preyed on them (the name Vagator derives from *vagh*, tiger).

History is irony. Halfway through the campaign twenty years later in which Sambhaji, Shivaji's son, was poised to take the island city itself, having taken Chapora fort and Bardez, the Marathas were once more taken in the rear by the Mughals. But even if notable enough in Bardez to earn itself a title – The Great Invasion of Thieves – this campaign was otherwise not unique, and attacks continued to come at regular intervals for the next fifty years. Finally, the Marathas were bought off with the gift of Bassein, a once rich but now defenceless trading enclave near Bombay.

After the Marathas would come the Bhonsle and Rane clan raids that helped to further refine Bardez' defensive strategy. The populace would flee for the forts (whose defenders were by now practised in prompt yet dignified surrender for purposes of ransom), while the invaders galloped around the countryside, looting and pillaging. Between raids the Franciscan father made his rounds – it is said, without zeal, but there had been zeal enough. In the island city the inquisitors were still racking the faithless, should there be anyone well enough to rack: cholera and malaria raged on. And from the still zealous south, socially displaced persons came seeking refuge amongst the tolerant, if besieged, Christians of Bardez. (As late as 1964, Franciscan Bardez might still be called 'a poorer but surely a happier region' than Jesuit Salcete.)

Warfare permitting, the villages, Portuguesed into *communidades*, went doggedly on as before, auctioning off the fields to the highest bidder, tending the palms, growing the rice and spices, farming the fish. Here was self-sufficiency: fish, curry and rice, to this day the Goan national dish, followed by a *digestif*, betel nut, from the village's areca palms.

A version of the vertical order of fealty – villein to vassal to lord – that we call feudalism had been first imposed on the village communes of the coast by the Adil Shah at the end of the fifteenth century. Removed by Albuquerque from his portion of Goa, the system continued in the territories beyond right into the eighteenth century, to the advantage of rising local clans like the Ranes of Satari in the east. They settled into a long series of raids and counter-raids into the Portuguese enclave. Secret treaties and connivings made for treacherous times in which disaffected feudal underlings of the Ranes were tempted into intrigues with Portuguese who might be their enemy's enemy one week, and their enemy's friend the next.

In this confusing world, Bhonsle clansmen joined in the attacks – as ever, on Bardez – in 1705 and were repelled by one Don Lourençio de Lisboa, Christian son of the Hindu clan chief Mucund Rane. The Bhonsle response was to occupy the whole of Bardez for two years, right up to the Aguada and Reis Magos forts on the Mandovi River, their arrival on the banks so panicking the surviving citizens of the island city that in the rush south to Salcete they forgot the remains of St Francis Xavier. Parts of him had been despatched around Christendom as relics, the rest remaining miraculously incorrupt. Little else did in that pestilential burg of abandoned mansions and forsaken quarters whose population might now be counted in mere hundreds. The viceroy and the wise were all gone to the coast.

In the end, the elders of Bardez paid the Bhonsles a huge ransom. They left, leaving the citizenry to wonder how, in that same year of 1740, the French enclave of Pondicherry on the opposite coast of India had managed to fight off the very same Bhonsles and pay them nothing. The borders of the Old Conquests were too long, and as porous as the laterite beneath. Especially in indefensible areas like Anjuna, the better houses of the time had to be furnished not only with rosewood furniture, Portuguese tiles and ancestral portraits, but with priest's holes and concealed attic stairs and trapdoors leading down to the crypt. One way to identify a house of the early to mid-eighteenth century is by the little citadel with musket ports, set into the angle of an unscalable garden wall.

As the century wore on, Bardez learned to relax. An expedition captured two Bhonsle forts in the jungly badlands high up the Chapora River. Finally it had been decided that good fences made good neighbours, and that buffer zones made better ones. A deal – protection in return for suzerainty – was made with a local ruler for his territories to the south and south-east of the Old Conquests, and another for turbulent Bicholim and Satari in the east and north-east. With the taking of the Marathas' old Terekhol fort in the far north-west in 1776, and a deal for the rest of Pernem two years later, the protective circle was complete. In 1952, Evelyn Waugh would visit the palace of 'the Raja of Suridem, pensionary'. Overlordship had passed to the Portuguese Crown, though not necessarily ownership: the Viscount Deshprabhu still owns most of Pernem.

While republicans in North America celebrated their independence from the young British empire, in India the old Portuguese empire bought itself more territory, three thousand square kilometres of it, and for the sake of morale called it the New Conquests. In reality that old empire was dead, but it wouldn't lie down. This reminds me of the last scene of *El Cid*. Charlton Heston is killed fighting off the Moors, but his aides keep quiet about it, and lash his corpse to the saddle to rally the troops for one more charge.

Now was a time for peace, of a kind. The New Conquests were now the new frontiers, and they would retain certain frontierish qualities. Only somewhat interrupted by the Portuguese takeover of Satari, raids and reprisals dragged on into the nineteenth century and through it and into the next. The last clan attack on the Portuguese took place in 1912. And through the fifties the new borders would continue to prove as porous as the old, letting thousands of nationalist demonstrators in, and thousands of smugglers out.

14 THE CHAISHOP YEARS

A Hindu fisherman would never eat or sell a turtle. He would perform a *puja* in his house, a blessing ceremony, and then ceremoniously bear the creature back to the sea. 'Would you ever sell the gods you worship?'

Perhaps the story is true. In P. Naik's moral tale *The Turtle*, a fisherman does sell the turtle he has caught, but only because his family are starving. (The moral is that he gets only two rupees for it.) In better times it would be pointless to kill the goose that laid so many golden eggs – and so it is difficult to understand why the turtles are disappearing from the Mandrem–Morjim beach. For the forty-odd days until they hatch, the few caches of eggs are having to be guarded by the villagers who once had their share of them.

Just as they are blamed for the overfishing that sends patently undersized pomfrets to the market, it is the little trawlers with their catch-all nets which are blamed for the turtle deficit. There are something like 850 of these inshore boats, unrefrigerated and too small for the deep-sea fishery, and far too many for Goa's 105 kilometres of coastline. The Goa fishery still employs about forty or fifty thousand people, but the men working the same waters in catamarans (direct descendants, apart from the outboard motors, of those sketched by travellers in the sixteenth century) are catching less and less.

Twenty or twenty-five men make up a fishing team, each with its fishing licence, boats, nets and onshore shelters held in common, a kind of natural communism to be found among fishermen everywhere. The women in their hitched-up saris come running down the beach with wicker baskets to carry away the catch, which will be mostly mackerel and sardines, the cheapest and most popular fish; some of which will still be dried at the onset of the monsoon to feed the villages through the time of impossible seas. The sandy beachside soil needs to be enriched for fertility, and leftover fish is mixed with the drying salt and added to a mulch of quicklime, shells, ashes and rotted foliage to feed the coconut trees.

The villagers, never wealthy, were always fishers and coconut growers. The Konkani word for landowner, *bhatkar*, comes from a word meaning a coconut grove. A big village will own about twenty thousand palms, and around the ubiquitous slim brown trunk village football has developed – football like pinball, in which a rebound off a palm suddenly sends the game off in a new direction. The coconut's presence was first recorded in the first century CE and now the industry is believed to support one-sixth of the population of Goa. Under the Ghats, vast plantations boost the venerable nut's fabulous statistics. In Goa there are around 4,800,000 coconut palms in three varieties, each tree producing twenty-eight nuts or so per year: in total, 134,400,000 nuts.

Here the Jesuits deserve honourable mention. Before introducing the Central American cashew (in Goa correctly called *caju*, from the original Tupi), and grafting the local mangoes to produce paragons like the Alfonso, they compiled the *Arte Palmarica*, the coconut bible. That was soon after their arrival in 1640. Twenty-three years later, Ralph Fitch, soon to escape Goa through the plantations the Jesuits had planted, wrote: 'The tree is called the palm: which is the most profitable tree in the world: it doth always bear fruit, and doth yield wine, oil, jaggery sugar, vinegar, cords, coals, of the leaves are made thatch for the houses, sails for ships, mats to sit or lie on: of the branches they make their houses, and brooms to sweep, of the tree, wood for ships.' Fitch doesn't say so, but Hindu scriptures were inscribed on treated palm leaves.

An enterprising restaurateur has built a good little thatched eatery on the low headland overlooking Morjim beach, and I break my long walk from the estuary to lunch there with a friend. 'God help Goa,' the waiter says under his breath at the band of government undersecretaries at the next table; they are uproariously but appropriately drinking a whisky called Whitehall. We fancy something more local, and stepping down from the restaurant and on to the beach, we walk along to a neat grove of young palms.

For the fifteen or twenty years before first fruiting, coconut palms are known as toddy trees, because only in that protracted youth do they produce toddy, the sap of the trunk. A good palm will give four hundred litres a year – which means that every year Goa produces something in excess of nineteen million litres of toddy, all of it tapped by one agile man or another from the six thousand-strong AGTTA – the All Goa Toddy-Tappers Association.

His method is little changed since Fitch's time. 'The wine doth issue out of the top of the tree. They cut a branch of a bough and bind it hard, and hang an earthen pot upon it, which they empty every morning and every evening, and still it . . . and it becometh very strong wine in short time.' The pot is more likely to be plastic nowadays. The 'wine' is called *feni*, and before it ferments and is distilled, the toddy is drunk for health and strength, reputedly fending off bad fevers and gonorrhoea.

Behind the toddy palms lie groves of shade trees, mango and jackfruit, little patches of market-gardening, the village, the road. The green belt of coastal Pernem is narrow. Immediately above the road the plateau begins, the realm of the cashew. The gnarled evergreen bushes, tenacious but fiercely territorial, allowing nothing to grow under them, were introduced in the first instance to hold down the thin, dusty topsoil. The boiling of the poisonous nut to make its kernel edible and the pressing of the fruit for the odoriferous *caju feni* were much later ideas. Some years ago, returning on the little local bus from Terekhol – meaning a steep downward path, which it is – to Pernem town, I saw men trampling the soft apple-like fruit in a square pit dug in a courtyard by the road. We waited to take on passengers in the heavy sweet smell: it was like being soused in Southern Comfort.

A huge acreage of cashew has been planted in Goa, but the nut remains expensive. It is expensive to produce, as it cannot be mechanically harvested from the obdurate dense bushes and has to be picked by hand. Also, the bush is not prolific: each of its few fruits yields only the one nut, sticking out of the soft flesh like a sore thumb.

'When the Aryan colonizers came down to Konkan,' wrote V. P. Chavan in 1924, 'their first question, when studying the habits of the aborigines was: "What is this intoxicating drug?" ' Chavan's theory was that the name for the Konkan coast, whose etymology is obscure, was derived from a Sanskrit word meaning a drug or seed used in fermentation. The Konkan indeed ferments – in the spring, when the *urrak*, the lighter first *feni* distillation, appears. At the second distillation, *feni* aficionados will disdain the bottle shop; they prefer to visit their uncle, who will most likely be from Pernem in the far north, or Palolem in the far south.

Feni from the red coconut is said to be superior to that from the green. Palolem is noted for both. We arrived there one early evening to find the big village somnolent: crows sat on prone pigs, local men in baseball caps sat on walls, tourists sat on the beach. On a rock face at the far end, someone had written in billboard-scale lettering 'No Topless, No Nudism, No Cocaine'. A warning, or a lament.

Our guesthouse belonged to a toddy-tapper. Without delay and for less than a dollar we bought an old rum bottle full of backyard coconut *feni*, squeezing green limes into it and remembering just in time to offer some to the Dutchman next door. He hadn't been in India for twenty-six years. Through his long exile he had never forgotten how to survive the Goa of 1971, only to return in 1997 to supermarkets, pollution, techno and traffic. 'Now I must learn to survive all the new things.' He didn't think Uncle's home-made *feni* was going to be one of them. 'I'm not drinking that,' he said, sniffing it. 'I don't want to be blind in the morning.' Sour fellow. This *feni* had the dawn tang of the toddy still on it. We

153

drained it to the dregs, and bought another bottle for the next day. In Agonda you probably couldn't get stuff like this.

You couldn't, for a fact. In Agonda the next evening, we presented the bottle to the proprietor of our guesthouse. He was big and vigorous, a healthy man, but at the sight of our *feni* he paled. Quickly he reached under the bar and came up with a bottle of clear liquid. 'This is *feni*,' he said. 'My uncle's. And *yours* is what they sell to the junglies. It's super-cheap. It's super-strong. The junglies drink it, and they beat their chests' – here he beat his chest – 'and they say "Woo! I am strong now!" But soon they become weak. And then they go blind, because this stuff – which is really minimum *feni*, maximum water – is cranked up with battery acid. But as long as you don't drink it, you don't go blind.'

That night I dreamed of battery *feni*, of a little battery lying in our bottle of cloudy liquid like the worm in tequila.

The coconut cutter – in Goa, a plucker – gazes upward. Goan palms are very tall, and slow to fruit. The stumpy midget palms of Kerala mature much earlier, nutting in a mere three years, but they live for less than half the Goan palm's seventy years, and the coconut-robber never has to leave the ground. Muttering perhaps the mantra against tree snakes, stepping over the shoes or the skull hung on the tree against the Evil Eye, the plucker begins his ascent. Halfway up, he is already looking down upon the world and, in these days of multistorey houses, into upstairs windows – and thus his traditional role as town crier of the local scandals is enhanced by modernity.

From the top the old-time plucker hollered tributes to the village harlot. The crown of the palm is another kind of margin or boundary, a frontier of the village, the top end of town, as it were. There the other world begins, and the usual rules do not apply. All along the Konkan coast it was believed that witches in animal form carried people off to the palm tops. In Anjuna, Graham Greene heard tales of supernatural abductions: '. . . she should have been praying for the evil spirits to pass. She was carried right away over the rocks by the seashore, and put up a coconut palm.'

A coconut falling by chance will never fell the innocent. It has eyes, and can see. Once on the ground, in Calangute at least, if you get to it first it is yours; in Salcete it belongs to the *vaddo*, the ward. The point is to send for a plucker before the nuts are over-ripe and the stems get brittle. From the palm top he cries a warning and lets the cut nuts go. The chickens flee, the plucker descends with the machete and is paid, at least in Arambol when I was there, with 10 per cent of the crop. Auntie, my landlady, would come out and complain that half the nuts were unripe. Pedru, as small and lean and dark as the plucker, and by then quite old, would come out to divvy up the coconuts and put Auntie's under the lean-to.

Pedru was a Mhar. He did the labouring jobs around the compound that Auntie's orphaned and rather slow nephew Vitus couldn't or wouldn't do, and doubled as sexton-cum-gravedigger at the church. Most weekday afternoons he would pass my room on his way to the cemetery, potter round there for a while, and then go off to the paddy fields of north Arambol to sit with his own auntie, the lady with the healing touch. It was Auntie's phrase. 'By Grace of God, she has the healing touch.'

Arambol people were different, Bardez people said; old fashioned. Arambol was still a very agricultural sort of resort. Before the motorcycle era that began in the early 1980s you arrived there by way of the ferry and the bus, to rent rooms in compound-cum-farmyards with undeclared *feni* stills in the shed. Auntie's place was like this, and Auntie herself was respectable in the local way, going to church often, herself in a black dress and Vitus in a tight suit, afterwards to return and change back, she into the Goan hitched-up sari, he into tattered shorts.

Straightening up after leaving the pig toilet which stood outside the compound (a pukka pigloo, three sides of laterite, the sky above, a palm-leaf door and a shy pig), I encountered Auntie one Sunday before lunch, a cheroot clamped between her teeth like Popeye, sari hitched a little further up, standing pissing into the sand. For his part, Vitus would usually spend the hours of leisure roaming the compound with a sick chicken in his arms. There was always a sick chicken. Its fierce eye would glare into Vitus's dim one while Auntie, grinding coconut masala in a stone mortar the size of a bucket, gazed fondly upon her nephew.

This was where the healing touch came in. Vitus was a victim of the Evil Eye – as, less gravely, were the chickens. I never discovered if the Evil Eye belonged to an evil person, or was disembodied and purely supernatural; as a good Christian, Auntie wasn't saying. All she would say was that Pedru had offered his auntie's services, and by the Grace of God she had the healing touch.

Nor could I discover how the healing touch healed. Chillies were thrown in the fire, or perhaps salt was flung around the compound. If Vitus' appetite failed or his stomach griped, if the buffalo gave no milk or the eggs were off, if Auntie had the ague or Pedru the flu, then the Evil Eye was about. Time for the healing touch, though Auntie insisted on denying it other kinds of supernatural work. A theological rift had evidently opened between Auntie and Pedru. Auntie was pious and officially disbelieved in magic. 'Local custom,' she said, when I saw her hanging beads around the buffalo's neck against the Evil Eye. Local custom also explained why she crossed herself fervently at the cry of the owl or the sight of the bat, why she thought that a crow cawing near the house meant good news, that a wailing dog foretold of an untimely death, and that birdshit on your head was good luck.

Pedru, on the other hand, was superstitious. It was he who knew where the exorcist, the *ghadi*, lived, and called him in to paint the Eye of Providence on the fishing boats. 'To stare down the Evil Eye, surely,' I said to Auntie.

'Tchee. It's bad luck to mention. No, he even calls the *ghadi* to drive the spirits from the beach when the fishing begins. The *ghadi* sacrifices a coconut. In front of *Christian* fishermen.'

The sea was both essential to life and casual in taking it. It was unpredictable and had to be appeased. Fishermen believed that the sea was owed for the catch: symbolic heads, coconuts, had always been sacrificed. And it was owed a life for the lives it spared; by custom the drowning were not rescued, for fear the rescuer would one day be drowned himself.

Auntie's reasoning was that Pedru had been insufficiently catechised in his youth, and had a weakness for folklore. This put Vitus at risk. If a snake appeared, even a useful rat snake in the woodpile, Auntie would drive it off before Pedru could profane the place by sending for the *ghadi*. She was convinced that Pedru had at some point given up on the Evil Eye theory and now believed Vitus to be demonically possessed by a spirit-serpent. The healing touch would be far too light to deal with this, and Auntie was certain she would return from Mass one day to find the compound full of scrawled incantations, foul emetics and peacock feathers, and Vitus coiled up on the ground, hissing.

I didn't know Konkani and couldn't ask Pedru about the spirit-possession story. Auntie herself flatly refused to say any more. I persisted in my questions, and after that she refused to speak to me – beyond saying hello, goodnight – in any place but the front room. It was kept for company and funerals, and I knew I'd get nothing out of her there, straight-backed in a wooden chair under her shelf of saints. At a slight angle nearby hung a gold-framed Byzantine Madonna and her manly Child.

I was in the front room one morning, drinking tea and vainly trying to pass Auntie some torn bills with the rent money, when terrible throaty roarings from outside suddenly drowned us out. Auntie calmly went back to winnowing the notes while I rushed out to the *balcao* to see the hunt I had heard so often but had never seen close up. It was the huge sow from next-door's pigloo. The butcher's dogs, coming from behind to avoid the teeth, not to mention the breath, had taken her by the ears and capsized her in the dust. A moment later the butcher's boys came running up with a rope and a bicycle. The sow shut up. Only when she was lashed to the carrier like a fat grey-brown sack, her big head dragging on the ground, did she begin the throaty roaring again, like a throttled vacuum-cleaner. The boys wheeled her away. No more evening summons – *yea yea yea yea yea* – to the trough of vegetable and fruit peels and rice-water.

Hindu houses never kept pigs. They were a Christian matter entirely, Christendom from its earliest days having been encouraged into the swine-husbandry that emphasised the distance from Judaism (and later from Islam). Auntie's house piglets – in Goa, 'piglings' – were born edible, and before they could move on to faecal food they were discreetly killed by Pedru out the back. Such bristles as grew on the tiny pale hides he burned off in a fire of dry palm leaves, before gutting the carcasses and halving them lengthways for market, or impaling them whole on sharpened branches for later, if there was a feast coming up.

Squads of the living went on skittering about the yard like plump platoons in double time. If allowed to, they grew up very quickly. Neither your Western farm pig (a barrel on stumps) nor your Indian wild pig (a barrel on stilts), this was a wily hybrid, an altogether trimmer beast. By the end of the season it was adolescent, hairy, eyeing you sideways, poised to go jinking away through the red dust.

The village was mostly animals and very clean. Scavengers in order of size processed round the house, and after a decent interval for the arrival of scraps from the kitchen window, round they came again. I would sit on the step outside my room, reading – as I remember, the second half of a sensational novel about India called *Gates of Fire,* the first half of which had been eaten by a pig. Oddly enough, at the end of the book the villain, while unconscious on Anjuna beach, has his privates devoured by a pig.

It was too dark to read inside. Besides, when reading palled, round came the procession. First, pigs. Then hairless identical dogs, timorous, with pointed snouts, a far cry from the butcher's professionals. Then chickens oppressed by cockerels, miniature cats, evasive rodents, roaches and teams of ants, and back to pigs again. Then on their way home at five the cows would make a galumphing appearance, and stop the show.

15 SUSPECT WITH A SONG

Right outside the village chaishop the dogs dug yodelling pits, for coolness. Occasionally they would rise to yodel at nothing, then collapse contentedly back into the pit. Inside the chaishop, long seasons went by. Life was so simple it seemed perfect. For beast and man, these were the chaishop years, and it comes as a shock to remember that my own season in Arambol took place in what I think of as modern times, in the fall of 1981.

Modern times had arrived elsewhere and were on their way, had been sighted over the river and would be here soon enough – but in Arambol in 1981 the sole modernity I can recall was the name of one of its buses, *Reagan Baba*.

The bus itself was unmoved by this touch of the up-to-date: facing its resigned passengers from the back of the driver's cabin was a sign reading 'Not Responsible For Non-Functioning Of'. The function that did always work was the bus's successful distancing of Arambol from places no distance away. It was only thirty-five kilometres to the shops of Mapusa, but this could be made to last all day. Once there, you bought cigarettes and spices, candles and plastic buckets, coconut oil, coconut cake, and coconut-fibre rope for keeping your clothes off the floor; if you went to Mapusa and let them lie there, the bandicoots came and ate the crotch out of your underwear.

'You got sick of the world, you went to India. You got sick of India, you went to Goa. You got sick of Goa, you went to Arambol.' It was a refuge, a retreat. One morning I climbed the little headland at the north end of the lake beach to walk to Terekhol on the long deserted strand that slopes sharply up from the sea to a fringe of wind-bent pines. The only thing upright was a lone man approaching through the haze. I saw he was Japanese, a modern Basho, a wandering monk poet with spotless loincloth and stout staff. He, dignified, nodded. Then he saw my Nikon, and scowled horribly.

Keeping itself to itself, Arambol was nevertheless well known and visited, an open secret, not a closed secret like Gokarn or Hampi, in Karnataka. The connoisseurs of secret India had gone to a lot of trouble to find the way to those extraordinary places, and only fledgling connoisseurs were let into the secret, not people who wore peace signs on their headbands. To be told of Gokarn and Hampi was to arrive.

In Arambol in the chaishop years you went to see the three-master dhows from Muscat cruise along the horizon. At six they would be in silhouette against the orange sunset, and the place to see them was the lake beach.

It is a small lake, a big pond by the sea. Only a narrow isthmus of beach separates it from the high tide, but its water is kept fresh by a stream running down the hill behind. Kingfishers wait there. The slope is rough and jungly. A narrow path runs up towards the low plateau where in the early 1990s the Japanese government planned to build settlements for its aged citizens, as it had done in other 'relatively cheap, sunny . . . places such as Australia and Mediterranean Europe'. Goa guidebooks talked of a sheltered retirement village, a gated community of six hundred cottages in three hundred hectares, with, of course, golf. Trained staff would have to be brought in, and there were protests at this latest example of 'enclave development', another self-contained island of wealth and/or tourism depending on the outside only for supplies and the humblest grades of labour.

If the retirees ever arrive, they are advised to make straight for the therapeutic mud of the Arambol lake. Goa is rich in curative springs and wells for the relief of rheumatism, arthritis, ailments of the intestine and the eye. Arambol lake mud is balm for the skin. The most famous springs have names: Manora cures snake, mouse, spider and scorpion bites; Vell in Caisua restores the appetite; Bimbol, Fatorpa and Raidor are sulphurous; Pernem town itself has a famous spring with which the Mandrekars, folk-doctors, cured snakebite. Ambora is iron-bearing and also good for bad skin, as is the lower of the two springs at Aguada. In 1900 an English priest had his skin condition cured there, and in gratitude founded a school.

In 1994 I wrote in my diary: 'On the banks of the lake, people coated all over except for eyes. Mud dries to a yellow-orange crust. Tandoori tourists sunning on the grass are photographed by friends, then wash off. One naked poseur immediately nicknamed the Member for Arambol. Another man, amiable, immensely short and wide, with a clump of hair. Equilibrium is not for him, and he knows it. Approaches the lake, topples in, heaves himself out to lie wallowing on the grass.'

The path up the hill branches off to a banyan – the most generous of trees, as the poet Tagore said, offering its shade far beyond itself. This one is vast and beautiful. Butterflies love banyans. They flutter around the buttresses of the mother-trunk and the far-flung air roots that join branches to ground to become trees themselves, members of the banyan's extended family. In the clearing below the canopy's giant parasol you are cool in any heat. Travelling holy men, locals and foreigners sit reading, chatting, eating, smoking, knitting and thinking amongst the snake-god stones propped against the mother-trunk.

Around Christmas 1982 I ran into the Renouncer there. I hadn't seen him for years. Now he was wordlessly at peace in his saffron *lungi*, polishing a half coconut into a black shining bowl. I asked him where he was staying. He pointed up through the branches to a man-sized nest. After several minutes of silence, he said: 'This is my paradise,' and smiled.

It made the third lead on the front page. '*Triplo assassinio no paraiso dos hippies em Arambol.*' In 1983, the *Herald – O Heraldo* – was still in Portuguese.

It was a day late, beaten to it on 8 January by the *Navhind Times*, which had the story as 'Bloodshed in Hippy Haven'. The story concluded with the formula follow-up: 'The alleged assailant is absconding.' In the early hours of the day before, three men – an Indian, Ram Swarup, a Frenchman, Alain Georges, and an Armenian, Rouben Filian – had been killed, in that order and within about twenty minutes of each other, by a man with a knife. On reaching the little police station in Arambol village, a witness the paper called 'Miss Brenda' had named the killer as Thomas Gross, 'a Czech with a West German passport, thirty-two years of age, well over six feet, and 115 kilos in weight' (253 pounds or eighteen stone – surely an exaggeration). He was said to be an expert mountaineer and swimmer. A few days later there was a photo, a faded picture of a smiling big bearded man holding a small guitar. The caption read 'Suspect with a Song'. That was the angle to go for in a musical place like Goa.

There wasn't much to go on. The police station was a long way round the headland from the lake, and in the dark 'Miss Brenda' had taken a long time to get there. In any case, nothing could be done until daylight, by which time the trail was cold. It took all that day to find the murder weapon, which turned out to be scarcely a knife, but a coconut-plucker's standard short-handled chopper with a honed blade a foot long. Armed reinforcements were immediately sent for.

That night a woman living in Arambol village had thirty people staying on her *balcao*. All of them were foreigners from the lake beach, where on the fatal night they had been asleep in the jungle in little huts, under the banyan or on the beach itself in sleeping bags. That was how the Frenchman died; he was asleep on the beach when Gross fell over him. By that time Ram Swarup was already dead, killed in Gross's hut.

'At the south end of the beach there is a little spring, and that was where the hut stood.' This version of events was told to a friend of mine by a friend of hers who was there that night. 'They all took acid. Then Gross came back into the hut and threatened them, my friend and Brenda and Ram, and then he went down to the beach. Dancing. He was dancing, doing some kind of ceremony. My friend went off tripping and Brenda went out too, and when she came back it was all over.'

Another version has the drug as datura. *Datura stramonium*, thorn apple, the lowly jimson weed on which the cattle feed. The famous old poison had enjoyed something of a vogue back in the seventies, and previously at odd intervals throughout Goa's history. In the sixteenth century it was the preferred husband-stupefier of philandering wives. In the mid-nineteenth, Richard Burton's time, love and datura were still happy together. In his tale of the thwarted abduction from the nunnery, the lightly fictionalised Burton enlists a confederate, of all things a professor of Latin, who mixes up 'a little datura seed with the tobacco served out to the guards that evening'. By the 1970s, a time intent on visions, datura had been promoted from sedative to radical psychedelic, from enabler of amours to dictator of alternative realities. Datura's effects crucially depend on dosage. The results could be merely bizarre, as they were for the woman who found herself sitting in a chaishop clad only in a pair of red knickers and with no idea how she'd got there; or fatal, as they were for the man seen reading Carlos Castaneda one day and found floating in the bay the next.

Campfires were lit on the beach every night, but by the early hours most of them would have burned out. People slept on, unaware that murder was afoot only metres away from them. And in any case, at any hour, antic behaviour was not unusual. Between murders Gross attacked another person, without the chopper, and was driven off; assumed to be 'just another flip out', he was allowed to rage and run away into the dark. Then he went to Rouben Filian's hut at the edge of the jungle. Filian was a karate expert: his body was found in the morning hacked about the wrists, chained about the neck and drowned in the lake.

Parties of police began to search the jungle for the absconding suspect. Sensibly, they began by asking the locals if a huge bearded white man had been that way lately, and the locals asked their friends further up the jungle, who knew someone going up to the road, who questioned passing bus and truck drivers. By now, people had seen the papers. The killer was still out there somewhere. Out of the velvet tropical night might step the man with the machete, his frenzy unspent – and his motive a mystery. The day after the search began, my landlady in Candolim was round to ask me if I'd vouch for the big bearded foreigner staying next door, before the boys tied him to a palm tree.

It was a small bearded foreigner: the Renouncer. On a visit to the ground from his nest in the banyan he had been arrested on suspicion of being Gross. Released, he had found the vibe terrible. The night after the killings there had been a blood-red sunset, and fishermen had flocked to the beach. To them a red sunset meant mackerel; to the Renouncer it meant goodbye.

All that week the search went on and it was reported that at least three more 'hippies having similar looks' to Gross had been captured, only to be identified and released. Then, one late afternoon, just as they were about to give up for the day, a police party happened upon a hooch den deep in the jungle. Inside, all alone, sat a big bearded white man slightly the worse for drink and apparently without possessions. The police took him under armed guard to Arambol police station. 'Splendid, chaps,' the inspector is said to have said as they led the chained suspect in for interrogation. 'You've caught Jungle Barry.'

16 SPEED

The police gave Barry an official certificate to say he wasn't the wanted man, and went back to searching for Thomas Gross. They never found him, dead or alive. The jungle remained imperturbable, and dispassionate tides had already cleaned the beach. Gross had once lectured at the Himalaya Club of India, and his expertise in survival techniques may explain how this very large white person was able to enter the jungle, with its population of smallish brown people, and simply vanish. Ten days after the murders the *Navhind Times* was asking 'Has Gross Got Away?' Rumour, circling outwards from the lake of Arambol, saw him in Bombay airport, and in a cave in the mountains.

Goa now had its very own hip murderer, a Mansonesque embarrassment. Having to say things like, 'You can do what you like, but you can't do that,' was making life difficult for the unjudgmental. 'Call me old-fashioned, but I think murder is a bad thing,' the Renouncer said, after some thought. 'Time to quit,' he announced, just before leaving for Gokarn. 'Goa is finished.'

To the authorities, the horrors had been waiting to happen. In Arambol, an amoral paradise of nudism and drugs, a crazed foreigner had killed three people. Something must be done – if not about the murders, the perpetrator being gone, then at least about the amoral paradise. The world had long seen Goa as a holiday destination, a frivolous place. For at least a decade now it had seen it as a hippie hangout. And after this, what?

That same year of 1983, on a train descending the Ghats from Castle Rock, I met a civil servant, a development specialist from Delhi seconded to the Goa government. He pointed out the

Dudhsagar waterfall to our left spilling down into the jungle. Goa was beautiful, was it not, but undeveloped; of course, India had only been in charge since 1961. Of 383 Goan villages, the Portuguese had electrified three. India had electrified the rest and built schools and hospitals, but there was still much work to do. Most of the state still lived with colonial infrastructure. There was no coastal railway. The Zuari bridge had been under construction since 1971, and people going to Panjim from the south still had to cross the river on ferries. The power supply 'fluctuated'. There was rural poverty. And sometime – this was most important – the iron would run out. But Goa was beautiful, was it not? A potential tourist paradise.

At this point the tea came round, and the civil servant said, 'What tourist would drink this?' When I said that I would, he thought he'd offended me, and said, 'I didn't mean budget tourists', and thought he'd offended me again. Embarrassed, he foraged for a packet of biscuits. It was time to move the conversation on. We had a biscuit. Where, I asked him, were the proper tourists, the hard-currency tourists? My lot, I said, to relieve his embarrassment, had no currency to speak of. The civil servant relaxed. He knew the figures: the tourist people estimated a yearly total of over fifty thousand Indian and four thousand foreign tourists – in a state with, officially, only 450 hotel beds. Where were these thousands staying? On the beach? The World Tourist Organisation, a UN agency, prophesied a big future of 2.5 million tourists in Goa, twice the entire population of the state.

The UN plan had been around since 1967, but in this year of 1983 it was going into operation. Development men like himself, he said wryly, were going to be too busy. As the train pulled into Margao, he showed me his Delhi newspaper. Goa was about to be taken seriously. The political heads of the Commonwealth – prime ministers, premiers, colonels, dictators – met every two years, and this year they were coming here. A porter came to take the civil servant's suitcase. We shook hands. 'Welcome to Goa,' he said.

On the platform I bought a local paper. It was true. Work on the Zuari bridge was about to begin, bullock-cart roads and telecommunications were to be modernised and the Dabolim airport, still a naval air station, spruced up. Money was pouring in from Delhi for everything from river cruise boats to power-station upgrades. The Taj Hotel at Aguada had completed its posh Hermitage. Infrastructure was coming. Mrs Thatcher was coming. Seriousness was coming. The freedom of the play-ground was over.

In the mid-eighties, an Anjuna veteran told me, 'it was as if everyone suddenly woke up and said: "I know who I really am, now. Time to go make a buck." ' The rebellion of the civilised against their civilisation was over.

After a few worries about selling out, it was soon okay to wear trousers, even shorts. Now, as the Renouncer pointed out, unexpectedly appearing at the fleamarket at happy hour, you couldn't get into the better parties in a *lungi* any more. Gandhian homespun was too self-effacing for the new world of glitter personified by the super-confident Thatcher and Reagan regimes; and, in any case, a new Gandhi, the technocratic Rajiv, was on his way up.

The Renouncer had found Gokarn unexciting. Down there, the last seekers of the golden age sat on the beach polishing coconut bowls and watching the income gap. Up here, a newly prosperous bohemia flowed as happily along with the mainstream as it did in the West, where power-dressed professionals took drugs, Eric Clapton was Muzak in the supermarket, and earrings and long hair were worn by bank clerks of both sexes.

Flasks of imported moisturiser began to appear. Nothing symbolises the fading of the old mind-culture into the new body-culture like moisturiser. Or cocaine. Both required mirrors and appeared to slow the ageing process. Youth lost to the chaishop years was magicked back to life and baptised in rivers of booze. The Renouncer, in silk shirt and tasteful ponytail, took to appearing at the better parties with a startlingly young girl-friend and vocabulary, the latter having lost the word 'laid-back' and gained the word 'attitude'.

Right through the seventies, in a world ravenous for new destinations, Goa the potential tourist paradise had remained a refuge for Us. That is why, to me at least, that time belongs in Part One, *Old Conquests*. The seventies preceded modernity. The famous parties were psychotropically advanced but musically backward, and while the rest of the seventies resounded to punk, radical reggae, early electronic music and New Wave, in Goa the top tune was Steve Miller's psychedelic chestnut 'Fly Like an Eagle'. On Planet Goa the news was always late. The post office slumbered, local telephony was so bad that the Goan musician Remo wrote a satirical song about it, and the one place you could make an international call was O Coqueiro, a restaurant miles away on the Porvorim plateau.

'Speed is the form of ecstasy the technical revolution has bestowed on man.' Speed came with modernity: they are twinned. The history of travel between Bombay and Goa tells us that in the mid-nineteenth century, Richard Burton's sailing pattimar took three days. A century later, the steamer took twenty-four hours. Today, the new Konkan Railway is timetabled to take eight hours, and the plane takes forty minutes.

If there was one hinge year, it was 1983. In January, Thomas Gross murdered sleep. He closed the curtains on the chaishop years, on one age, as it were, and in November Mrs Thatcher arrived to whisk them open on another. The hinge that swung Goa open to modernity and the coming of Touristhan was oiled by speed, by the quickening ecstasy of the technical revolution. Its emblem was the motorcycle.

At Andrew's Bar in Calangute market German George was saying, 'Get a bike, man. Get a bike. You can go to Arambol for the afternoon and be back for a beer in Chapora by sunset. And in the worst heat you get that cool breeze' – and then I saw the big bandage sagging down from the grated mince-red length of George's thigh. There was grit still in it. 'Nothing,' George said. 'Exhaust burn.'

'A pig,' said Afghan Aziz, disgusted. 'It was a pig.' He threw the paper down on the table and called for another peg of *feni* and a cold soda. ' "Goa to Host Commonwealth VIP Meet", it says. So this is why they make the road like autobahn, so the pigs can play chicken.'

The news that the world was coming to Goa thrilled Panjim and then eddied and broke along the northern beaches, creating a kind of nausea and in some quarters, panic. I ran into the Renouncer, just back from the Osho ashram in Pune. His girl-friend had run off with a Rebirther, but it was all part of the flux; the city suited him, he was smoothly shaven and thinking of leaving Goa for good. 'Western life is a nightmare you used to come to Goa to escape,' he said, ordering another vodka and tonic. 'Ice and lemon, please. And a pack of Marlboros. And then *she* turns up.'

The apparition of Mrs Thatcher caused houses, freshly white-washed for the season, to be left empty 'until afterwards', and people to talk darkly about surveillance, the SAS, deportations and raids at dawn. People who never read the papers wrung their hands over gloating articles about the coming of real tourism. One recitation of the Foreign Currency mantra, and beloved, seedy villages were levelled for resorts. Fishermen became flunkeys; prawn curries became prawn cocktails. Goans buttonholed in bars by agitated foreigners tended to laugh at the prospect of real tourism, but many of the agitated had seen what had happened to the coast of Spain.

German George's mantra was: 'Spain is only Spain, but *this* is paradise.' Come November, he and Aziz left it for Hampi, as the forecourt of the Calangute police station filled up with khaki tents. Important roads were walled with gaily coloured cloth to conceal what the paper called 'buffalo dairies'. The Zuari bridge opened.

The Candolim road was torn up, widened at the cost of four hundred trees, relaid and beaten flat with wooden billets by hundreds of women from Karnataka in threadbare saris. As the Commonwealth Heads of Government Meet impended – 'Goa Awaits Golden Weekend' – I met FX by his polished Ford. Border Security Force troops no longer played football on the beach with village children; the kids were shooed off home, and the troops began to trudge the dunes. The Heads duly met. Canada's Prime Minister Trudeau was briefly arrested as a frogman-spy during his early-morning swim off the Aguada beach, but there were no deportations, no raids at dawn.

17 THE RISE OF TOURISTHAN

Two years later, in 1985, I arrived in Goa by taxi from Karnataka
with three friends and a Tibetan monk. Candolim was not much
like the monk's cloister; he had been surveying the sybaritic
scene with furrowed brow, and as we strolled onto the beach he
said: 'I suppose you think this is paradise.'

If he meant an earthly paradise with no claims on Nirvana, then
yes – but only if he was speaking of years past. All wintertime,
with the stars above and the phosphorescence below, it had been
a paradise; but now the beach wasn't safe by moonlight any more.
People who had seen Thailand and Bali lately thought Goa a paradise
still, but here we were unused to any development at all. Now half
the pine grove had gone missing, a hotel was rising by the beach,
and cherished old habits were under attack. I showed the monk
the Government advice sheet titled 'Do's and Don'ts for
Foreigners'.

'You are advised as the following in the general interest of all
including your welfare', the flyer began, before moving on to the
welfare of your valuables, and briefly touching on nudism.
Another item suggested you inform the police if offered drugs.
Mysteriously, there was no mention of the new Narcotics Act,
with its minimum six-month jail sentence. Many people still
thought things to be as they'd been in the balmy days before the
Arambol murders, when drugs and nudism were equal and
appeared in the press, and in court, yoked together – as if going
naked on the beach was of the same order of offence as possessing, say, a bag of heroin. A typical day in court in those days
might see a man convicted under the old Narcotics Act of 1964

getting two days in jail and a 500-rupee fine – and another arrested for 'moving about nude' getting only one day inside, but a fine of 700 rupees.

No fewer than three more Don'ts concerned visa regulations. Do not overstay. 'Do not keep your passport in the custody of undesirable persons.' 'Do not tamper with writings in your passport.' Nudism, drugs, visa-fiddling: plainly, it was out with the old and in with the new model tourist.

Beyond the Foreigners Registration Office in Panjim, where at the end of 1985 applicants for visa extensions were having their palms checked for hashish stains, official scrutiny was focused on the rising language 'agitation', as protest movements tend to be called in India. Agitation was high; policemen were being readied for demonstration duty.

Goa's status was unclear. She had never been a full state of the Union. In company with the enclaves of Daman and Diu, she was that lesser entity, a Union Territory, whose policy was made in Delhi. An intense conflict of interest had simmered since the Portuguese time between those who believed Goa to have a right to full statehood and official recognition of her language, and those who believed her to be a colonial creation unnaturally separated from the rest of the Konkan coast and therefore due to return to Maharashtra and/or Karnataka when she was once again part of India.

This was unfinished historical business, an old argument over Goan identity: praiseworthy multicultural composite or unworthy hybrid? Increasingly, the argument was bearing down on the language question. It was language that sustained and expressed whatever that Goan identity was. The choice of Marathi would lead on to unity with Maharashtra; the choice of Konkani, towards full statehood.

Konkani was split by history. It was the vernacular, the daily language of Goa, but having no script of its own it could be claimed by partisans of Marathi as a dialect. Goan Hindus used the Marathi script and a Marathi-based vocabulary. The vocabulary of the Christian community, on the other hand, was 10 per cent Portuguese, and it used the Roman script, the legacy of a long-gone imperial attempt to get rid of Konkani altogether.

Maharashtrian claims had been rejected in the 1950s by Nehru, and again in 1967, with Goa's absorption into Maharashtra being rejected by plebiscite. But the argument went on. Politicians keen to connect with one or the other of the competing populist causes still had plenty of room for manoeuvre. In November 1985, forty thousand people demonstrated in Panjim against the adoption of Marathi as Goa's official language. There was violence, and a few days later, another demonstration and more violence in Margao. Differences at home being intractable, it became Delhi's problem.

The old Nehru argument – the right to regional singularity – won again. He had even said that Goa might keep her liberal alcohol licensing laws in a rapidly drying India. Two years after the riots, Goa was granted full statehood (1987 was the year of the first charter flights from Europe, so statehood and Touristhan got off the mark together). Konkani was given constitutional recognition, which was nothing if not a recognition of its staying power.

The colonial power had tried to replace one culture and identity with another, by replacing one language with another. Language was the key. But the Portuguese had never succeeded in this, one of their oldest and smallest possessions, as they had elsewhere in their empire, in enormous Brazil and in the five Lusophone nations of Africa. Shortly before Portugal's precipitate departure from Angola in 1973, teachers were still trying to replace the 'forbidden' local languages with Portuguese. It was an effort they had given up in Goa three hundred years before.

Scripts aside, a tenacious and most various language attached Goans at home and abroad to each other and to their most various state.

On an unseasonably hot evening in the early spring of 1998 I am in the bar, waiting for Paul, who is said to have a story for me about the serial killer Charles Sobhraj. Sobhraj was in Goa back in 1986, but I wasn't. I have been reduced to reading the newspaper reports of his visit. The story lacks something – the real presence of the man, actuality.

The cool, dry sound of the shells in the wind-chimes above my head is a tonic in this heat. It is early, just an hour after sunset, and the only other people at the big table besides myself are two young tourists from Calcutta. Someone comes down the drive – not Paul, though, but a bronzed, shaven-headed, imposingly roman-nosed man in a black loincloth, carrying a newspaper. He may well have been here in the mid-eighties, but I am not going to broach the subject of Sobhraj with him. I avoid his beady eye as he decides where to sit: he is said to be mad, and is clearly in search of an audience. He sits opposite the young Indians, and evidently having decided to share with them his deep knowledge of their history, he remarks: 'Nehru's memoirs are out. It says in the paper.'

'But Nehru died in 1964. His memoirs have been out for decades.'

The bald man bridles. 'It says in the paper.'

'Can't be his memoirs, then. A biography? Letters?'

'Same thing.'

'Nonsense. What are these "memoirs" called?'

'*Nice Guys Finish Second.*'

'Pandit Nehru, first Prime Minister of India, writes his memoirs thirty-four years after his own death and calls it *Nice Guys Finish Second*? Are you mad?'

Abruptly the bronzed man stands up and departs, revealing on one buttock a monkey tattoo, and leaving his paper behind. I scan the reviews: the memoir-writer turns out to be another Nehru altogether. Then Paul comes in, and yes, he does have a Sobhraj story. 'I met the guy. At Rocky's.' At this point I realise with dismay that I have left my tape recorder at home.

'Rocky's was at the back of Anjuna. He'd been working in the Gulf, had money, set up this place where you could watch videos.

He had a cupboard: all the Western bottles, out they came. The power was very bad that night, the lights were low, there were two guys next to me I didn't recognise, couldn't see properly. I left my drink and went out for a pee. Came back, the lights were up bright – and it was Charles Sobhraj sitting next to me with some English guy next to him.

'Unmistakable – the face, the Vietnamese eyes. I was outside again *immediately,* two fingers down my throat, went over the way for a glass of salt water, drank it down and threw it up. Sobhraj the poisoner. They caught him two days later. Of course he set it up – to pre-empt his extradition to Thailand, where they would've shot him.'

It was 5 April 1986. Sobhraj had last been in Goa ten years before, when he had drugged and robbed three Frenchmen but failed to kill them. Indian-Vietnamese by birth, his fluency in French and his knowledge of India enabled him to get close to the French abroad, and a few months later he was caught in a Delhi hotel in the act of drugging a sixty-strong tour group. Since 1978 he had been in Tihar jail for that crime, as well as for passport fraud and impersonation and for a culpable homicide in Delhi. And in Thailand and Nepal and India there had been other deaths – since 1975, eight murders following the trademark druggings and robbings.

These were still under investigation when Richard Neville and Julie Clarke wrote their book on Sobhraj in 1979. They were pre-scient. 'It will be on one of those lazy tropical afternoons when interest in the case has waned, and the flies buzz and the guards doze in the heat, that Charles Sobhraj will make his move.' With six others, all Indians, he escaped Tihar on 16 March 1986, by drugging the warders with doctored sweets. David Hall, an accomplice on the outside, drove the getaway car south while back at the jail people were being fired for accepting sweets from, of all people, Charles Sobhraj. A 25,000-rupee reward was posted. In Mumbai a week later one of the fugitives was arrested, and it was probably he who told the police that the great escaper was already in Goa.

Goa had changed. Sobhraj had a friend in Baga, but he would have to find him first: that beachside idyll had fallen to Touristhan, and was no more. Or, in construction terms, much more.

Sobhraj and Hall had arrived five days after the breakout, and in Parra, near Mapusa, they immediately rented a house, but never stayed in it. It is not known where they did stay. In the seventeen days before his rearrest, little is known of Sobhraj's activities except for his visit to a certain Panjim hotel whose manager knew him, having once testified against him in court. It was important to Sobhraj that someone identify him. Newspaper reports quoting 'the Delhi police grapevine' support Paul's suggestion that Sobhraj set up his own recapture, further charges and consequent return to Tihar rather than to Thailand.

There was one sighting of him on a blue Rajdoot motorcycle by the Mapusa police. While they and the contingent of Mumbai sleuths already in town waited for him to surface again, Sobhraj presumably called into Baga, where an old confederate of his had been living for some ten years. This was probably the man of many aliases whose passport in the name of Ajay Chowdury had been discovered in Thailand at the time of the 'bikini murders' that first made Sobhraj's name.

On 5 April Sobhraj and Hall went to Rocky's in Anjuna. Then, on the evening of the seventh, they rode the blue Rajdoot up to the restaurant and telephone rendezvous on the Porvorim hill called O Coqueiro – and were followed, the honour of arrest having been accorded to the Mumbai squad. It was led by a Sobhraj specialist, a chief inspector who fifteen years previously had arrested him for attempting a jewel heist.

The *Navhind Times* reported that Sobhraj and Hall, sitting at a table, offered no resistance when 'nabbed by two dummy waiters dressed in *lungis*', though Sobhraj had a gun in his bag. 'When the twosome were arrested there was a wedding reception in progress . . . and it was utter confusion when the police swooped on the alleged criminal.' Hall was arrested too, though the *Times* did not explain why someone who must have known of Sobhraj's rearrest plan would be there to be rearrested with him, being under no threat of extradition himself. Perhaps he didn't want to spoil the party: it was Sobhraj's forty-second birthday.

It came as no surprise to the authorities that a hipster-gangster like Sobhraj should be drawn to Goa. For twenty years it had been an 'abode of hippies'; there were even postcards thus titled. Tour agencies in Mumbai promised sightings of naked blondes, and prurient, shaming articles appeared every year in foreign magazines. Where was Goa to find a better class of tourist?

The planning people knew that the best, most profitable tourism was measured by quality, not quantity. Not arriving in tribes, but in short queues with deep wallets. Golfers. Everyone in the business knew there were forty million golfers in the West – and how many more in golf-crazed Japan? – and that golfers meant money; even a few dozen of them would be much better than hordes of backpackers with no money. The planning people – and developers looking to buy up likely sites – knew that whole forests in Sumatra had been felled for golf courses. Plans for golf in Goa were on the anvil, as the phrase went, but costs were prohibitive and there would be wrath from the environmentalists, in Goa a tough and practised bunch who knew how thirsty a pastime golf would be in this water-poor state. The average golf course soaked up something like three thousand cubic metres of water every day.

And in other respects the tourism resistance was not to be trifled with. While happy to replace the sinful, broke hippies with proper, moneyed tourists, it would deny sin to them, too. Goa closed at eleven sharp. They would have early nights and be saved from casinos, marinas, discos and nightclubs, from imported booze and slinky hostesses. Instead they would be offered folk-dancing and stuffed pomfrets.

Rich people used to getting what they wanted did not take their pleasures in such extreme moderation, and so they would go elsewhere. Virtue would be preserved, yes – but still Goa would need tourism. How else was she to make a living? The mining was purely extractive, there had never been much industrial spin-off. The new clean hi-tech industries would first have to be attracted, and even then they would hardly provide enough employment.

Given the resources available, which type of tourist might be attracted to Goa? Not the culturati. There were baroque cathedrals enough in Europe. And the Hindu temples, which were newish – fourteenth-century Muslims and sixteenth-century Christians having razed most of the old ones – were themselves baroque-looking, their builders having long been employed by the Church. The colonial cultural cleansing had succeeded in erasing the ancient Hindu centres of pilgrimage and much of their splendid world of festivals, of elephants and processions and great bazaars. Now, the very snake-charmers came from Karnataka.

Indians visited Goa in much greater numbers than foreigners ever would. Still, tourism from the West to the tropics had quadrupled in ten years. It was tourists from the rich and frozen nations who would fuel the throbbing generator of foreign exchange every winter.

Those guaranteed to come in their thousands could be found in a sociological summary called Cohen's Tourist Purposes. Among these purposes were Experimental ('modern pilgrim looking for authenticity'), Experimental 2 ('going further, experimenting with other lifestyles') and Existential ('actually acquiring a new spiritual centre as a result of the travel experience'). Goa had seen quite enough of that kind of thing, the tourism planner might well think – but at last, at the very end of the list, came Recreational. In another summary, Smith's Categories, it was baldly called Mass Tourism. Package-deal travel to a relaxation destination: it even rhymed. And what did Goa unquestionably have in plenty? Beaches.

The air age had been symbolically inaugurated back in 1985 when the Pope, *Pap Saib*, had flown in. The airport was attract-ing more and more traffic, and trafficking too: in 1986, shortly before the arrival of Charles Sobhraj, 255 pounds of hashish were seized there. People were beginning to fly to and fro in numbers, connecting Goa to the modern world. Change had always come to Goa from the sea, and sea-changes were slow. Now, change was sudden: at the beginning of the 1987 season, Touristhan abruptly arrived in the form of the inaugural Condor charter flight from Frankfurt.

In India, the journalists' term for flying somewhere urgently (and hence glamorously) is 'airdashing'. Visiting India perhaps for the first time, the tourist airdashed over various geographies of green and brown, leaping all the barriers that had for so long made Goa a place apart, and eventually came to a halt on a lat-erite-red plateau. Suddenly Goa was easy to get to. This was an advantage that people coming from a different environment could find most disorientating. The first Condor flight taxied to a halt on the Dabolim airstrip, a hatch opened on the blue and blazing Goan day, and the very first charter tourist to Goa, a frail and elderly man, appeared at the top of the steps. At which point a volley of cowflop struck the plane and an activist of the Vigilant Goans' Army roared: 'Don't think we're providing prostitutes for you!'

As if everyone had the sense of an ending, the Mumbai steamer was packed. I got on somehow, carrying a magazine and a minor football injury, but too late to find any room on deck for that night. There was nothing for it: the chicken coop stood empty, and it was big enough. If I had known that the next morning (clambering out with dignity, removing feathers) would be the end of my final Mumbai boat trip, I would have spent the money on a cabin. A year later, in 1989, the boat and its sister ship would be requisitioned for Indian Army transport from Sri Lanka. Neither ship would ever return, and some years later an expensive and unromantic hydrofoil appeared in their stead.

I crawled into the chicken shack and swept the floor and settled down to read the football results. Dempo, Sesa Goa,

179

Salgaocar – mining company-sponsored teams; Churchill Brothers . . . I was trying to remember who my neighbour Elvis played for. My own modest, and last, football season had just ended. In Candolim I had kept goal in a sweat-drenched tracksuit, kneepads and elbow bandages, hoping I wouldn't have to dive on to the red gravel that grated flesh like cheese. After motorcycle skids on that gravel, people spent long irritable days in deckchairs, covered in ointment.

But it went well enough, we lost to a team from Mapusa, and they bought the beers. Our German fullback said Otto was a very German name for an African, and Otto the Mapusa midfielder laughed and said he wasn't really African. His family were from Canacona, on the southernmost border of Goa, and his father, a footballer himself in his time, had named him after the famous Ottolino.

Ottolino was a football legend on this part of the coast, and an account of his finest hour appears in Carmo de Souza's Calangute memoir *In Search of Sands*. Like his young namesake, Ottolino had been of African and Goan descent, and notably played barefoot, never fearing 'to defy even the strongest-booted European'.

On the day (not specified, but sometime in the late fifties) that made him famous, his Calangute team were to face formidable opposition at the Mapusa ground – the top team of the Portuguese military. Ottolino had to be in Panjim until shortly before kick-off, which would be at five, after the heat; but he let everyone know he'd be back from Panjim in plenty of time. At Betim, the ferry village, he'd catch the Mapusa *caminhão*.

Ottolino was not to know that the Portuguese had 'persuaded' the *caminhão* drivers to take a detour that day. He duly arrived on the ferry and walked to the bus stop in Betim but the *caminhão* never came. Perhaps he saw the trick, because he tore off his city shirt and tie and began to run. Without stopping, he ran the ten kilometres from Betim to Mapusa, to arrive just as the military men were exulting at the sight of his cringing substitute taking the field. An improved version of this story has the ferrymasters being bribed too, obliging Ottolino to begin his marathon by swimming the Mandovi. In any case, upon his dramatic arrival the Calangute team were moved to heroism. 'The match witnessed galore of goals from the bootless Ottolino.'

Young Otto's family had been Goan forever, he told me. They were Christians and had Portuguese surnames. There were several Afro-Indian villages along the south Goa–Karnataka border: Christian, Hindu and Muslim. Beyond that, the subject didn't much interest him, so I followed up the Afro-Indian story for myself.

It is probable that Otto's African ancestors originally came to Goa as slaves of the Portuguese, and escaped, or their descendants did, sometime in the seventeenth century. Canacona was well outside Portuguese jurisdiction then. It is impossible to know where in Africa they came from, though it may have been the west coast; their settling in the Ghats, where they hunted, fished, and grew vegetables, suggests the West African immunity to malaria.

Goa's southern border marks the inside edge of a zone of Afro-Indian settlement that extends from Hubli, Supa and Yellapur in inland Karnataka to Karwar and Ankola on the coast. Well off the beaten track in the back country once, the son of a friend of mine was astonished to find himself 'in an African village'.

Employment opportunities in neighbouring Muslim states were at their height in the seventeenth century. There was far less prejudice amongst Muslims (Indian or Arab) towards black Africans, slave or free, and this inspired an endless stream of escapes from Goa. The Portuguese offered big rewards for the recapture of slaves, and deals were struck with Muslim rulers for their return, or for compensation if they did not. Laws were passed against harbouring runaway slaves; bounty-hunters were hired.

The southern route was popular with escapees, down to Karwar on the coast or south-east across the Ghats and on to the Deccan; Otto's ancestors followed that route. Heading north, the fortunate or ambitious escapee might find service with the Siddis of Janjira. In the seventeenth century, the Siddis – originally meaning Islamised black Africans, and later, any African settled in India – controlled the island fortress of Janjira off the Maharashtra coast to the south of Bombay. Siddi power was felt in Gujarat and the Deccan, where Africans rose to the highest rank. Malik Ambar, a general consistently successful against the Mughals, began as a slave and ended as strategist to the rulers of the Deccan Sultanates.

The runaway slaves of the Portuguese were not the only source of descent for Afro-Goans. Slavery in India long predates the European arrival, and though they were to become for a time the biggest, the Portuguese were never the only slaveholders. From the sixth century, Arab merchants along the Konkan and Malabar coasts traded in black African slaves, and in the next century slaves are known to have lived in Goa's Arab settlements. Anjuna – Hanjun – may have been one of these. Thousands of Africans were serving in armies, navies and civil administrations all along the coast when Vasco da Gama arrived.

Black stone statues of saints in Goan churches may have been sculpted by African freemen: the Church encouraged the freeing of slaves, including its own, on conversion, and was especially keen to release those women it feared had been working too intimately with the clergy. Despite the colour bar, the Church's insistence on the moral life necessarily made her an engine of social mobility: a Portuguese soldier with a child by his African slave might marry her and give the child his name. Empires are great miscegenators. In the village of Chandor, according to Olivinho Gomes, there live 'some negroid elements called "mulatos" . . . believed to be the offspring of the liaison some men might have had with black women servants . . .' – who presumably had accompanied Goan émigrés returning from Africa. From the 1930s, troops were brought in from Angola and Mozambique by the Portuguese, and some of them stayed on.

The Portuguese power in Goa was underpinned by slavery until the late seventeenth century, when it was made redundant by the shrinking of the European population and the standing army. After that, trade to Asia steeply declined in favour of the accessible and profitable Americas: in her long career as a slave destination, Brazil would receive millions of slaves.

A Goa trader's letter of 1800 regrets the lack of demand for guns for runaway-hunting, and in another fifty years there would be no more than one hundred slaves left. Richard Burton saw few Africans in Panjim. But here and there, variant forms of servitude remained. In the late nineteenth century, D. D. Kosambi's Goan grandfather moved to the village of Sancoale with two 'slaves', though 'slavery was not a recognised institution, and nothing except tradition held the slaves to the decayed feudal household.' Poverty preserves the ties that bind. The writer of *Slavery in Portuguese India* says that some people in Otto's borderland belt of settlement are 'even today employed as bonded labourers'.

18 THE GULF

In September 1990 I met Otto again, in Calangute. He'd been offered a construction job in Kuwait, but the Iraqi invasion had put paid to that. He shrugged. 'Goodbye money.' He was going fishing with his uncle in Mangalore. With everyone coming back from the Gulf, no one in Goa was hiring.

Remittances were drying up as Goans in their thousands were repatriated before the coming desert storm. So heavy was dependence on the Gulf that demonstrators marched in Panjim – the most prosperous-looking demonstrators anyone in Goa had ever seen. It was worse for the coastal districts that depended on the charter flights which used the cheap route through the Gulf. Before the charters came there had been perhaps four or five thousand foreigners in Goa every winter; now there were ten times that number, but no one knew if any would come this year. Even Sunny the publican was worried. Bars never went bust, but his had recently become a charter-tourist bar.

Before the boom his bar had been kept going by his deftness at the cash register and by the head waiter, who tried to corner all the tips by being the only waiter. But the tips were too few – most of the clientele were locals on cheap *feni* – and the service grew too slow. Inside there was hardly room to sit down, but the *feni* crowd preferred it to sitting outside, perhaps because of the stained-glass effects of the multicoloured shelves of liquors, from Grand Old Nun to Old Monk, that towered to the ceiling. Even so, the clientele began to complain at the waiting, and in the end Sunny came up with Melwyn.

Melwyn was perfect: he had only one arm. He helped Sunny

with the locals inside while the head waiter saw to the foreigners outside and got all the tips. Thereafter the bar went along smoothly, until the head waiter's day off. Then Melwyn had to do it all, and they took to calling him Sunny's Right Hand Man.

Someone would order a beer. In hopes of a change of mind, Melwyn would repeat, 'Beer?'

'Afraid so, Melwyn.'

In his other life Melwyn was a professional mourner. Now he would scale the three steps and disappear into the sanctified gloom of the bar, to return after some time with a tepid Kingfisher.

'A cold one, Melwyn.'

'No cold.' Refrigeration in those days was very less, as Sunny would say. The beer would be accepted, and Melwyn would scale the steps again. In time he would return with a glass in his one hand and set it down. Then he would climb the steps again, for the opener, and by the time he returned, the drinker would have prised the cap off with his teeth.

Sunny said bar management was a matter of coming back from the Gulf while still young and fresh. You never let anyone but your wife near the till, kept your wage bill down and social conscience up by hiring the disabled, and that way you made a living. Not through daring investments and saturation advertising, but by attrition, by opening every day. And by providing everything. More foreigners came every year – though perhaps not this year – and in addition to drinking copiously, they were used to having everything.

Foreign brands were coming to town – and when they didn't, Sunny revealed, fake brands did. Cheery Nigerians cut Glenfiddich with what was called Country Liquor, and decanted tinted hooch into Johnny Walker bottles. Wide boys from Mumbai bought empty gin bottles for a few rupees and filled them with water. The Russian vodka too was water. Every delivery day, Sunny suffered for his drinkers. Not that he thought of them as drinkers, but as children, and he the father watching over them. He couldn't be too careful. The white rum was oily water, the dark rum dirty water, the advocaat watered mustard, the bourbon paraffin. Only last week some Europeans had sold him four cognac bottles full of soup. It had been a thin, brandy-coloured soup, and it was a marvel how the caps had been resealed. At this point someone came in, and Sunny broke off to cry out a greeting.

He had learned affability tending bar for oilmen in the Gulf. Sunny's is a story of modern migration. In the past, when you emigrated on a ship, with the streamers falling into the sea and the handkerchiefs of your loved ones shrinking and shrinking to a distant white flurry on the quay, you really left. A door closed. It's not like that at the airport. The plane that takes you in two or three hours to the Gulf can, if necessary, bring you quickly back again. Leaving is not the end any more; and now that Goa is not so poor, you may not have to leave home at all.

By November 1990 this was a bitter joke, as rising expectations and incomes in the villages went into free fall. Gulf returnees had been coming back rich, like tourists. They had reproached the stay-at-homes with their urban dress, duty free hi-fi, Reeboks and English slang, and with their money. Because of the money there had been a village consumer boom. *Feni* drinkers had gone over to Scotch, there was a bike on the porch, a little white Maruti car parked in the sand, a satellite dish on the roof and a fridge in the kitchen.

They had carried back to Goa the modern world as their returnee ancestors had carried back the old one. You could hear it in the names of the new babies. Older men might still like their sons to be called Elvis, but there were few Bismarks and Victorias and Adolphus any more. The new world was giving birth to Denzil, Loretta, Rex, Georgie, Iris, Romeo, Gaylene, Dylan.

Locally, the Gulf was so pervasive a presence as to be almost local itself. It was the people's destination, with so many coming and going now that it had ceased to be interesting. Nobody questioned you about your time there. And so a mechanic I knew got away with pretending to have been in Dubai for two years, when all the time he was living down south in Margao with his girl-friend. He and Philomena were both from Bardez. Her guardian – she was an orphan – never moved from his village near Calangute, he would never find them out, but it was he who at some point would have to be persuaded to let them marry. It was not going to be easy. Philomena was a convent girl; the mechanic, a poor boy from a Gauda village.

Over the centuries, Christian Goa added extra pieces to the jigsaw of famously composite India. As nowhere else in the subcontinent, in Goa the missionaries converted right through society from top to bottom. This preserved the hereditary order. For Hindus, caste remained intact; and now they were joined by a parallel hierarchy of Christians, though slimmed-down to three castes.

The Gauda exemplify this very Goan complexity and take it further. They are a caste of two separate religions, Christian and Hindu – and of both; a third branch consists of once-Christian reconverts to Hinduism. The Gauda were the original Goans, the mechanic said, an ancient community, but being original didn't help. In his village they hadn't been Christian for nearly as long as Philomena's family, who had the second-biggest house in their village, and had been Christian for seventeen generations.

Seventeen-generation Christians tended to suspect the newer Christians of not knowing their place, especially in matters of acute caste-sensitivity like marriage, and 'interdining', for whom you ate with also mattered. The very bounds of religion were broken when Christian and Hindu Gauda married. All this seriously blurred the borders of identity, and seventeen-generation Christians had until recently – in the lifetime of the mechanic's own father – retaliated against their low-caste co-religionists by refusing to accept food or water from them.

Non-interdining was acceptable in Hinduism, among the caste-conscious, but to the professedly egalitarian Church, caste barriers were a severe embarrassment. Eventually the Church managed to get interdining going again, but by the late 1920s the damage had been done. In despair at encountering in their new religion the divisions of the old, some fifty thousand Christian Gauda returned to Hinduism.

Bridging the religions earned them no thanks. Ceremonially purified they might be, and officially titled New Hindus, but to the old Hindu community they didn't quite know their place, especially in caste-sensitive areas like marriage.

'We'll marry the New Hindus but the Hindus don't like to as yet,' the mechanic said. 'Marriage is such a problem.' Fortunately, Philomena and he were modern people. They'd sort their own problem out.

By the time I ran into him again, he was coming to the end of his fictional time in Dubai. Soon he would have to seek permission to marry. His plan was to turn up at Philomena's guardian's house wearing a shiny Middle Eastern suit, with some Scotch in a duty-free bag. All of it available right here in Candolim. And if the old man's caste scruples stuck? They'd elope. To where?

'There's always Dubai.'

By December the price of petrol from the Gulf was up 25 per cent and availability down 10 per cent. The village was full of bored men pretending to be home for Christmas, scanning the airwaves for news of Kuwait. There was little else for them to do. Farmers who had left their fields fallow for the crop of apartments that would save them from farming forever sat waiting for the developers, but development had stopped. Foreign tourism had also ceased, the most obvious consequence being serious overmanning in the casual trades. Boy waiters already on the very minimum wage were sent home. 'Pilots', motorcycle-taxi drivers who had once been fishermen, sat in doleful ranks in Calangute. Squads of indefatigable Kashmiri salesmen with briefcases scoured the empty beach, though it was well known by now that few of the charter flights would be coming. They couldn't get insurance for the Gulf route.

One night a girl was mugged for her purse; her attacker was a pilot. In this season of misrule, men poked long hooked sticks through window-gratings by night and carried off Walkmans and wallets. Houses were rented for the quality of their roofs, because a 'tourist place' with a cheap single layer of tiles and only a few laths beneath it would let the burglars in. Locally, the rash of burglaries was blamed on rising expectations grown unreasonable in people not long out of poverty, on a poor man's frenzy of get-rich-quick. Financial dishonesty had the same cause: some people had simply gone too quickly from tilling the soil to soiling the till. And they were 'from out of state', always. Sometimes they really were. Tourism drew them. When a sozzled retiree was rolled one evening for his wallet, he wasn't surprised. 'This is a tourist resort now. When there aren't any tourists, some people will resort to anything.'

Some 30 per cent of the population now came from out of state, chiefly to take up the jobs left behind by Goans off to the Gulf. In the old days the only emigrants in the money had been the professional classes. Then democratically the Gulf had begun to take everyone, drivers, clerks, cooks, musicians, teachers, domestics. Wages for all were good. Many Gulf emigrants now were women, and now they too might have expectations of money and freedom. Modernity shook society up; no one knew their place any more.

I was used to thinking of Christmas simply as a big winter party, so the appearance of the Nativity in the sand just off my porch was a shock. The children had set up the toy crib, the stable, Mary expectant, Joseph at the door, and approaching across the sand the ox, the ass, a dinosaur, a gorilla and, from the other direction, three plastic kings. The first was the one you would expect, with a crown, and the children had given him a tiny box of incense. The second king was a cowboy in a golden stetson, and the third a hunched but beefy figure, swathed in bandoliers and weaponry, that you would have to call a Schwarzenegger.

Christmas Day. Like generals at play, the children had plotted their advance across the sand day by day, and now the Holy Family, three kings, farm animals, dinosaur, gorilla and all stood clustered round the crib. Finally the Babe was installed in the manger, and we all had lunch.

Next morning the story went into reverse. Every day, according to some inscrutable order of precedence, one personage was removed from the Nativity tableau until somewhere round New Year the children themselves lost interest. By then the only figures left on the sand were the gorilla, the cowboy and the Schwarzenegger.

As the United Nations deadline approached, men arrived to install a satellite dish on the palm-thatched roof of the beach shack. CNN appeared, dim and frantic. We turned to face the Gulf, three flying hours away, and ordered large brandies; on Anjuna beach, they meditated for peace. It was 10.29 in the morning of 16 January 1991, wartime, and the third week of Visit India Year.

19 GÉNÉRATION TECHNO

It is from the sea that the jail is best seen, standing in odd relation to its neighbours. It is old and Portuguese and sits at the foot of the Aguada headland, just inside the mouth of the Mandovi River and around the point from the Taj Hotel complex and its Hermitage. Next upriver stands the opulent modernist mansion known as 'the palace'. A discreet and glowing pile of wealth with a golden dome and a gatehouse flanked by guardian statues, it intimates a quite different world of sun and sea, of eccentric Mediterranean glamour, a touch of Gaudí or the Emperor Tiberius.

On the headland above squats the Aguada fort, not picturesque, but blocky and purposeful. Down below at the entrance to the jail stands the statue of a distraught man bearing a dead child. It commemorates the jail's role as an incarcerator of Freedom Fighters: the indomitable T. B. Cunha was once imprisoned here by the Portuguese. An inmate of more recent times, a European entrepreneur, is said to have bought up all the jail's old colonial furniture piece by piece and had it shipped home for sale so he'd have money when he got out. For others, tedium was relieved by gambling. Someone would catch one of the jail's flying cock-roaches and thrust a match up its rear, while everyone bet on the creature's likely trajectory. Then the perpetrator would light the match.

A more painful pastime, for the prisoners at least, was gazing through the bars at the boats floating on the blue Mandovi, or across at Panjim where the lawyer action was. Once I arrived at my guesthouse to find some prisoners' families in residence.

They were in Goa to check on the appeals process, their sons having been inside for nearly two years.

Dinnertime was disputatious, and during a lull a young man nodded apologies over to my table. 'Politics.' I knew that. The row was in Hebrew and unintelligible to me, but unmistakably political. On the Left, youth, body-pierced and tattooed; on the Right, age, massive and crewcut. He had the firepower. He listened to the arguments, shaking his head, and then spoke at some length, prodding the table with one big blunt finger. Soon the Left left for their rooms and turned up the techno.

The Right was the father of an incarceree. 'You know this jail.'

'From the outside. It's the one with the statue.'

'The statue! Ah, that is how they come out! But he is a good boy. Paratrooper. Like me.' Every day he wasn't allowed a jail visit he sat on his porch drinking black tea and fretting. This snail's progress of affidavits and advocates was not his kind of action.

The new Drugs and Psychotropic Narcotics Act of 1985 was made draconian in 1989. Now anything more than five grams of hashish – a piece the size of a sugar cube – gets the possessor ten years inside and a huge fine; a larger haul, or a harder drug, gets him or her jailed for even longer. It is a 'non-bailable offence': once you're inside, you stay there unless the eventual trial proves you innocent. The younger paratrooper had been in possession of twenty grams and not enough money. 'Wish You a Super Vacation', read the posters and the limited-edition and most collectable T-shirts. '. . . Drugs Can Land You in Jail for up to Twenty Years'.

We were playing beach tennis – volleying a racquet ball back and forth with wooden bats – when a woman lying on the sand nearby got up and came down to the tide line to whisper urgently to my partner. Here was an opportunity between practice strokes – the swipe, the lunge, the miss – to wonder why Indian tourists almost invariably collected and threw back an errant ball and foreign tourists did not, unless it landed next to them. A mystery not entirely explained by the Indian love of cricket. Then my partner motioned me down the beach. What had the woman said? Our play had been disturbing her. She was trying to sleep. If we had been so slothful as to miss a party, then we should at least consider the needs of someone who hadn't.

Since the Portuguese departure, the Western art form in Goa has been the party. They matter most of all to *génération techno*, who may go to several every week – until the spring, when Anjuna parties are halted out of consideration for the school exams. But parties also matter to faraway Panjim, where politicians weigh in on the side of the people who don't need the parties and would have them banned, who accuse 'drug lords' of financing them to provide themselves with customers. Opposing politicians weigh in on the side of the people who do need the parties, who make a living from them. And parties matter to the police who, it is said, also make a living from them, by issuing pricey party permits.

In short, there is a highly developed party politics, and the only way to escape it is to go to one.

The ragged ranks of bikes, hopeful taxis and private cars wait just off the road. Higher up, overlooking the little Vagator cove and the sea, and overlooked by one bare hill and one crowned with a new hotel, is a small dry plateau crisscrossed by little crevices. At one in the morning, the earliest civilised hour for partygoing, there don't seem to be nearly enough dancers for all that transport until you realise that at any one time half the party is sitting cross-legged on the straw mats of the chai ladies. A large portion of the plateau has become an alfresco snackery and chill-out zone. The massed kerosene lanterns turn the night yellow and send smoke gusting across the hairy old laterite towards the cliff edge, which is marked a few feet in by strings of coloured bulbs and UV strip lights.

The palms on the terraces descending the cliff are tinted silver by the moon. From the bare hillside above (defoliated in the eighteenth century against attackers) you can watch the advance of the Anjuna bikes, a long wobbly procession of one-eyed creatures drawn by sound and light. Walking up from the transport park into the ambit of the black light, their riders grow werewolf eyes – and, if they have just used fluoride toothpaste, green teeth. They are dressed for the practicalities, with jackets for the fresh night breeze, baggy pants, clever footwear. All bright: the fleamarket is nothing if not a vast party-clothes emporium.

The dance floor is one of the few unfissured flat bits. Stacks of speakers on either side are wired to the transparent plastic tepee at the back where the DJs work. The moon is full now, high and clear, and the music is coming up to peak; a soundtrack for the tropics. Tonight it's techno with a sense of place. On other nights it has felt like being repeatedly kicked in the stomach by a sound engineer.

The atmosphere is psychedelia Lite. No one is exhibiting symptoms of transcendence. People don't believe those old transformational claims any more, and Ecstasy simulates not transcendence but sociability.

Towards dawn the moon turns yellow and finally a rich mustard. It falls into the cliffside palms and then into the sea, as people go climbing the hill to see the sun come up. Then at the end, or at the beginning, the sunglasses go on, the bikes start up, the trippers come down and the party becomes fully visible. People leave the plateau to heat and dust. A boy comes past, kicking plastic bottles over the edge of the cliff.

Just as people in the sixties eased the pressure on their subcultural pleasures by leaving the country, so they did in the eighties – but this time they went to Ibiza, and only then to points east. In Ibiza Ecstasy became an avant-garde taste, just as LSD had been twenty years before in California, before mass hippiedom took hold.

A friend of mine once described techno as 'the soundtrack for Ecstasy'. In Goa by the mid-eighties the new music had risen to dance dominance; and soon any techno music suggesting a kind of tropicalised ambience was being filed under Goa Trance. The artwork on covers and flyers portrays Indo-exotica, as albums like Jimi Hendrix's *Axis Bold as Love* did thirty years ago, but this time it is done on computers. In Goa now you see more Day-Glo and tie-dye, bellbottoms and beads, UV and strobe lights than ever before. Always hospitable to nostalgia, Goa is hostess to psychedelia revisited. It is in the new technologies that the originality lies – in miniaturisation, portability, sampling and editing capability, sound quality.

By the second 'Summer of Love' of 1987, two decades after the first, Goa was a notable stop on an international rave tour where the same sophisticated equipment was available in jungles everywhere. That year the direct flights started. Now the music played in London clubs could be in Goa the same day, and so could the clubbers.

The Nine Bar is a big concrete blockhouse. The dance floor is outside, and has the surface of a village football pitch, as they all do. The DJ sets up quickly: two Minidisc players into a compact mixer, the mixer into a big PA amplifier, the amp into big boxy speakers. It's all he needs. Digital has the victory. The stage belongs to the DJ – the conductor – and his machines. It starts, and you wonder if there is any way for those who ride the mighty techno flow ever to find their way back. Especially from here. In the West, techno is dance music. In Goa, it is all the music.

The portentous stage has been demolished and replaced by a tableful of equipment. The sweating rock band in sagging tights has been displaced by a cool figure in baggy pants, the lone DJ. The balance of power has gone to the dance floor. 'Techno brought out in people the dance again. It's open to freedom: everyone out there has their own ballet and is consumed by it.' When the Nine Bar closes, the Primrose is the place, the waiting room for Party Central. The lane is jammed with idling transport, drivers, hangers-on. Inside the compound, people are sitting around drinking and talking but really waiting to go somewhere and dance. Many of them have been dancing in Goan sand for decades, and their knees are invulnerable. No live band, supposing they wanted to dance to one, could possibly keep up with them.

'Goa is a major venue now. It's a big draw for the top DJs, and nobody expects to get paid. From India and all over the world people gather for this sound. The parties are absolutely together with nature. A party in the jungle at night – you see these strange fluorescent floating Shivas, costumes, lighted trees . . .

'The sheer joy of the music, the people you get involved with – these are your people, that's what you feel . . . And you've got to say about India that it has allowed a freedom that no other country does. You can be very expressive of yourself. People find something they never knew was inside themselves, because of that freedom. India opens another kind of door and for a lot of people the very best comes out of them.'

Somehow hippiedom survived – in the sense that *génération techno* are understood to be hippies themselves. In Goa 'hippie' is a kind of tribal designation applied to anyone of perceived bohemian tendencies. It is the locals who decide what you are. The neat sociological distinctions made in the West ('nothing points up the difference between the youth cultures of the sixties and nineties like body-piercing') are pretty sharp, but irrelevant to the bangle-seller deciding whether to trudge down to the beach towards the mob of tourists in the haze.

If they wear tattoos, and studs in their tongues and boots on the beach, or if they wear big hats and shades and moisturiser and their knees creak as they arise from the sand, if they are fifteen or fifty, it is of no concern to a Lamani woman trying to make a sale in the midday heat. Only charter tourists buy big, and so she will make the crucial distinction. 'Hippilog?' – hippie people? – she will ask, pointing at the distant foreigners. 'Or charterlog?'

20 In Touristhan

A bus pulls up to the gates of the resort, and Europeans fresh from the airport disembark. The resort is long and narrow, looking small from the road but running deeply back into the palm groves behind. In blocks three stories high, with squares of grass and a swimming pool, it looks like the modest estate of apartments it is. Far fewer official permissions are required to build apartments than to build hotels, and the blocks have been already sold off flat by flat, to be leased back by the builder as a three-star charter tourist hotel. Further savings have been made. In 1998 three such apartment-hotels along the Candolim road were reported to have been caught bypassing their electricity meters. But in one respect the three-stars do resemble the plusher establishments they are modelled on: they too are examples of self-reliant enclave development. With its shops, moneychanger, generator, swimming pool, restaurant and in-house transport, even the most modest resort may reassure the tourist here for a fortnight or so that there will be nothing to do but relax. That is the promise of Touristhan.

There is nothing to fear. On the bus from the airport, the tour company's rep has told his charges that the resort's restaurant menus are extensive and its prices competitive with anywhere in Goa – not to mention back home. The trouble with eating 'outside' is that two weeks doesn't allow enough time for bacillary dysentery, gastro-enteritis, salmonella. So confident is the resort of its standards that it offers a big discount to guests paying for all their fortnight's food and drink in advance.

Off the bus, into the room, shower and change. A beer, dinner by the pool, a little resort music – Elvis and the Beatles, the Everlys, Del Shannon – by a band in purple jackets.

On the beach next morning, other people from the flight are already prone, slick with suntan lotion, and watching the show. The boys from the shack bring cold drinks down to the beach beds – there are lots of shacks, the nearest being *Rover's Return* and *Tipsy*, and lots of beach beds, beach umbrellas, beach towels. Tankers sit way out on the horizon in the haze, trawlers are near, and just beyond the surf line surge the jet boats, the waterskiers, another boat with two parasailing girls high in the sky. The sea is busy with transport, like a road. The waterline is the sidewalk, a promenade of joggers, paddlers, pairs of girls, oglers, muscle boys, tourist police. Mid-beach is the idling area, a kilometre or so of Coca-Cola umbrellas like an endless pavement café attended by waiters, traders in hand-drums, masseurs, hawkers of fruit, small boys with cigarettes in plastic sacks, sellers of semi-precious stones, *lungis* and saffron. The young tourists from Mumbai strolling in their moccasins and jeans and polo shirts have it about right: they are dressed for the street. The waves loom up, hang, and fall, a scenic backdrop for this urban beach.

The first day in a new place you always get the same conversations. People on their first tropical package say things like, 'Oh, we're not worried about malaria, we've had Indian food before.' The more experienced are too kind to laugh. They ask, 'What's been the worst thing so far?' and the new people say, 'The drive from the airport.'

But there's more. It's not dull here. If you keep your eyes open you'll see all kinds of things the reps don't tell you about. Behind the shacks, people have been offered tiger skins, smallish ones, for 5000 rupees. And government workers have been seen spraying the roadside ditches against malaria. But the worst thing *is* the driving, it's true. You see two people driving along side by side, chatting. You see people drive out of side roads into the traffic without looking. Rear-vision mirrors are for brushing your hair in. You see people driving on both sides of the road at once. It's all in the papers. 'At nights, some drivers switch off the headlights of their vehicles and resort to drunken driving.' Walk on the verge facing the oncoming traffic, as you should, and you're asking to be run over from behind by a Tempo on the wrong side of the road. It's much safer and less unnerving to take the resort minibus everywhere, to Mapusa, Old Goa, the fleamarket. At the fleamarket you will see things you don't want to see, people with no legs, no arms, crawling on the ground. All kinds of weirdoes, street people, hustlers – but it's not a bad day out if you always know where the minibus is.

Touristhan soothes anxieties. The minibus will charge 200 rupees for the return trip to Mapusa market when the local bus charges five, but it has no ruffianly conductors or screaming music, it drops you off at the entrance, and when you return, the driver will be smiling by the door with an identity card clipped to his pocket.

The potholes will be filled in by Christmas week. Along the edge of the road file this week's new arrivals, pale, brightly clad, middle-aged and more accustomed to sidewalks. The taxi drivers watch and wait, hanging out in and out of the little white Maruti vans that surround the gates of every resort.

A driver hands me a flyer with a price list on it and this message: 'Our taxis are very cheap compared to lousy coaches, who rip off your purses.' A price list! Unheard of. Taxi fares have always been a haggling matter, with concealed tourist-specific surcharges. It's always been the responsibility of the tourist to pay like one – but now the taxi trade is hurting, and the price list is an attempt at public relations. The trade has always lived on its wits, haggling, cutting corners, improvising in the old, casual way, but now Touristhan is here. Touristhan is a system, and does not need improvisation. The taxi driver is an employee on a percentage; his job requires an ability to drive, nothing more, no local knowledge, no investment, and so every man drawn by tourist glamour does it. Stories of sudden wealth abound. A carpet can cost thousands of rupees: 10 per cent from the carpet emporium for each tourist he takes there and who buys a carpet will keep his taxi waiting at the gates of Touristhan forever.

For the same reason that there are too many taxis, there are too many beach shacks. They too belong to the old days, are run by people from fishing villages, and improvise everything from their electricity supply to their garbage disposal. The government would like to tax them; the hotels would like to get rid of the All Goa Shack Owners Association, do the shacks up and put their staff in proper uniforms to serve drinks for 600 rupees a month, about fifteen American dollars.

For most of the 1997–8 season the big hotels did manage to get the shacks closed down. Then they opened again. They inhabit the same territory as the taxis, the fleamarket, the parties: rackety, street-level, they all live together in the informal economy. They have their supporting politicians, and so does the formal economy; that is, Touristhan, the five-star hotels, the corporate and high-toned. During the shack shutdown, the Shack Association staged a hunger strike, a Fast Unto Death. At the same time, the hotels happened to be hosting a Food Festival, a feast unto death. No one died, at least not at the hunger strike.

The old Anjuna fleamarket has grown monstrous, more sprawling and unkempt as each year passes. Inevitably, an alternative flea-market has appeared elsewhere, smaller, smarter, a sort of Flea Upmarket modelled on the way Anjuna used to be. The old market has been left to the rag trade and Touristhan, but profits are up and now the beggars arrive for their day's work in a Tempo van from Mapusa.

The van park is one of the best places to see resort minibuses and taxis together in the wild. Hundreds of them graze amicably all day in the dry paddy fields while their passengers browse the stalls. Bric-a-brac from all over India, bedspreads, Tibetan and Kashmiri souvenirs, incense sticks and wooden elephants abound.

I eat pizza and drink espresso while the dust swirls around my knees, and I eavesdrop. 'You think I don't know what things cost in India?' The ragged child flourishes his bunch of flutes and grins up at the speaker, gazing up at a world where wanting something is merely a prelude to having it. The voice is familiar. It is the Renouncer, down from his Pune ashram, where he is an adept of something he won't talk about, beyond giving it a name. 'Finance.'

He tosses away the remains of his pizza. When the sun goes down, cows will ruminate on the crusts, the trashed clothing and cigarette packets. The fleamarket is a bit rough-and-ready for Touristhan but still essential as a simulacrum of India, a pretend bazaar in a state with few of the Indian tourist attractions. It is as essential as Old Goa, the licensing laws, beaches, and crocodile-spotting. Touristhan is travel aspiring to the condition of television; sensation as leisure, with all its teeth removed. 'Croc-a-doo-dle-doo!' crows the tour firm's poster, suggesting that the saurian menace is chicken. And the descendants of the crocodiles who defended Portuguese Goa in the sixteenth century can do no more than gnash their rows of teeth in vain from the banks of their immemorial habitat, the inlet, now the Cumbarjua Canal, as the boatloads of Touristhanis go snapping by.

At Liberation the bars were liberated too. In the village of Chandor, according to Olivinho Gomes, there were seven tavernas in 1961. Now there are at least twenty, plus illegal 'holes' in private houses. In the 1980s there were reported to be more than 4300 Country Liquor shops and bars in Goa, or one such establishment per square kilometre. This figure does not include the posher IMFL (Indian Made Foreign Liquor) shops and bars, where the tourists go.

Kim Morarji left Goa in 1971. On his return in the early eighties he went back to Baga, and to Tito's restaurant-bar. 'Tito's hadn't got bigger, though the inner room now had seating in it.

Tito himself had become an alcoholic and his health was deteriorating, but his place had become the focal point of Baga and that part of north Goa. There was more activity at night, music . . . And the crowd had changed. By that time, the first travellers had moved out to Anjuna and further north. Other, more affluent Westerners (but of broadly the same counterculture) were moving in. Tito's was their nightspot. Alcohol was proliferating, much more than I remember from the seventies. In the seventies, people didn't really drink.

'Through the eighties I saw the place grow outwards from the front porch towards the unparalleled expansion you have now. Finally Tito's sons took it over and turned it into a club, a disco, a venue for product promotions, for live music. It has become the most popular place in Goa for kids from Mumbai, and is also extremely popular with British charter youth. By now, alcohol has become the drug of choice, as it were. Police pressure has definitely had a deterrent effect. But Tito's son has often said to me that with alcohol now so pervasive, there have been all kinds of drink-culture problems. Every season they have their fair share of violent episodes.'

Most Goan bars remain very Indo-Lusitanian, hospitable to locals and foreigners alike, and free of tweeness. But just off the Candolim road there is a bar with a rebuilt *caminhão* outside. It isn't a piece of history: there's no explanation and no context. There are restaurants called Mughal Heritage and Victorian Heritage, and the old bus is Heritage too. She just stands there, a dignified grandmother hoping her old-time charm will give that tatty side street a bit of class.

Heritage Goa is not a new idea – the Taj Group positioned their hotel complex behind the old Aguada sea walls in the 1970s, designing part of it to resemble a traditional village – but now everyone is doing it. Goans coming home to retire may not find much of their past left to look at, but they have their heritage. Indian tourists get something Euro-exotic, and Europeans get something Euro-familiar. Most of the Portuguese remains – churches, monuments, forts – are owned by institutions with no great interest in tourism, but the beauty of heritage, or of the heritage business, which is privately run and very interested in tourism, is that it doesn't really depend on the past at all.

Heritage is history without tragedy: a simple re-creation (or recreation) of history's fun bits, the banquets and minstrels; concrete baroque like the model of Vasco da Gama's flagship on Cavelossim beach, Portugoa refurbished. But Goa is Indian now. The heritage industry creates an optical illusion: the less Portuguese Goa gets, the more Portuguese it looks.

'In the first half of the twentieth century there was still plenty of time, and so you got what we call in architecture an organic development.' In the second half, Benetton and Nike shops from city malls have been deposited on the Candolim roadside, and as night falls they glow extra-terrestrially, as if hoping to be beamed up again. The current growth springing up is inorganic, an unquarantined import, not acclimatised. The ecstasy of speed rushes new worlds into existence, and they end up sharing with the old world the same space and time, but little else. The village behind Benetton is wholly unacquainted with designer knitwear. The village kids admire the Nike display, then buy their shoes in the Arson Shoe Mart.

As Touristhan dispenses novelties exhausted elsewhere to its furthest-flung regions, a Tex-Mex restaurant appears near the Candolim iceworks. When questioned, the off-duty waiters are unsure where Tex-Mex is, and go on deftly spooning up fish curry with their fingers. They are ushers in the aisles of Touristhan's global theatre. The audience itself is assured of getting the same cheap seats wherever it goes, and the same comforts, or versions of them, in the same variety available at home. This impoverished idea of travel is successful, within an impoverished idea of success, and it employs people. Giggling at his reflection, the waiter dons his sombrero.

Around four hundred million people travel between continents every year. One kind of human encounter among the many possible is hospitality – which includes being hospitable to new ways of thinking about and doing things, so perhaps the Indo-Tex-Mex restaurant should be given another chance. But before hospitality was an industry, it was personal, and the mark of civilisation. In Goa, much hospitality has survived the industry. If you have never been there, time and space are made for you; if you have been there before, you are remembered. When this old-style hospitality fails because the arrival of fifty thousand charter tourists every season makes impersonality inevitable, the faces changing every fortnight, and you complain that the smiles are only for your wallet, it is because the old hospitality has been overwhelmed by Touristhan, where warmth is professional.

Worlds collide. A European couple in Goa for their winter-sun fortnight have been invited by an old school friend to a party in a village some way from the resort. They have never been in a Goan village before, and so get lost, arriving very late and apologetic; they hope dinner hasn't been delayed for them. 'No problem,' their friend, the hostess, says. 'It isn't a dinner party.' They realise there is nothing to eat at all, and the restaurants are long closed. By four the party is near peaking, they are famished, and when someone proposes going on to somewhere else they go along with her. There may be food there. But in the dark the houses all look the same, they can't find the one they're looking for, and the couple succumb to inanition. They slump down under a tree.

Their guide says: 'Tell me what you're on. I can help you, I can, but you have to tell me what you're on.'

One collapsee manages a word. 'Food.'

The guide hurries back for their friend the hostess. 'They're ill. They say it's the food, but it can't be, there wasn't any.'

The hostess arrives at a trot, bends over the stricken pair. 'I can help you, I can. *But you have to tell me what you're on.*'

When the beach shacks were closed down for most of the winter of 1997–98 one solution to the loss of income was for villagers to invite their shack regulars, all charter tourists, home for dinner. Most had never spent any time in the village, though they had been through it, commuting between the resort and the beach every day.

Bored by eating poolside every night, the visitors find life outside quite congenial. People appear to live normally, with motorcycles and satellite dishes. There don't seem to be too many local customs or arcane rules of acceptance. If you are civil, paying your bills and not spoiling the village name, it is enough. Soon it is all quite affable around the table in the sandy garden, and people begin to speak their minds.

'I wish they'd do something about the dogs.' A mutter of assent goes around. 'The state of them.' There are dogs under the table even now, inbred, untrained, devouring your dinner with their eyes. By night, packs of them circle the resort, their cries clearly audible in the bedrooms. But in the village, the lady of the house explains, they are the patrolmen, the night watchmen. Next door to my own guesthouse lives a lady who keeps ten dogs, because her husband is away in the Gulf and her neighbour is troublesome. One night he came and threw stones at the house, later explaining that it was impossible to get properly drunk with the dogs making all that noise.

My own landlord does not object to it, irksome as guests find the midnight din, because in their roamings the dogs are defending his compound too. He prefers to take it *susegad*. When one of his guests, a light sleeper, demanded that he do something about the noise, my landlord retorted that life was a matter of live and let live: every creature, including humans, had to put up with every other, including dogs.

In the village there is an extreme reluctance to take dogs' lives, even the rabid being allowed to live until they become dangerous. In desperation during the thin time of the monsoon, dogs eat dried fish, and it is said that this makes them mad. Undoubtedly from time to time there has been hydrophobia. 'Dog is sick,' its owner may observe, regretfully, as the doomed animal gnaws frothing at the rope, eventually escaping and running amuck through the village, only to be hunted down and beaten to death by the boys, or pursued by the licensed dog-shooter from the Candolim market.

The dog-shooter is always the least favourite option. His cartridges cost ten rupees each and once his discharge at a mad dog went clean through the village and a roadside shack, finally embedding itself in the side of the passing Calangute bus, the *Rocket*.

Round the table in the garden the charter guests are on to dessert. Pigs and chickens and dogs come and go, there is a distant row, a big Gulf stereo can be heard playing a medley of Christmas carols. The reassurances of the resort are missing, the discipline, and in the absence of uniforms it is difficult to tell who the waiters are; but everyone is very nice, and the family have hung strings of coloured bulbs from the trees. The toilet is blessedly clean.

The flush toilet is taken for granted. It isn't to be spoken of at dinner, but the children of the house are dying to ask the guests if they've ever been in a pigloo. In the eighties it was decreed that everyone renting out rooms must install a WC and septic tank, but these were not always installed by experts. Eating at a restaurant once, I noticed that the tank only a few feet away had no venting pipe; it might one day erupt, a faecal Pompeii. Most likely it was not a tank at all but a soakpit, the contents leaking gradually away into the laterite and eventually into the nearest well. In any case the tank signalled the end of the pigloo, and the disappearance of the pig as a feature of the landscape once as familiar in Goa as reindeer in Lapland. In the future, villages will be as pigless and pristine as the model village at Aguada.

Modernity has been around for no longer than a decade or so, not yet long enough for the people of the fishing villages, sustained by centuries of solidarity, to begin worrying that it will lead to social breakdown. When the most popular young man in Ximer died in a road accident, Christmas was immediately cancelled without debate, the illuminated Stars of Bethlehem were taken down from the doorways, and several days' mourning were observed throughout the village. The shock of this sad but not unprecedented event was dealt with in the traditional way, by the whole community; it remains to be seen how the same people will deal with truly unprecedented events.

'In Baga I lived in the fishermen's houses,' Kim Morarji says. 'I stayed with all of them along there at one time or another. Back in 1970 the beach was nudity and fishermen pulling in nets. The fishermen didn't bat an eyelash. It's only recently, since the early nineties, that they've got into the frenzy of tourism. I suppose they observed the growing prosperity around them and wanted a piece of it. So now they have more money, of course, but the change has been more radical than that. This is the first time they've ever known a cash economy.'

Their expectant mood contrasted sharply with that of their neighbours the coconut farmers. The slow rhythm of the coconut year, the predictability of it all, inclined farmers towards the percentage view of life. This was very different from the unpredictable world of fishing, where the prospect of a huge catch under a red mackerel sky – if not today, then tomorrow, perhaps – made fishermen by nature optimistic. And old poverty made them relish the new rich times.

'But prosperity is expensive. A better life costs more. And mass tourism has increased prices to the extent that during the winter season, Goans can't afford the fish they've always eaten. I'm more or less a local resident now, and I see that during the rest of the year fish is plentiful and cheap, especially after monsoon. During those three or four tourist months, it is not.

'There are so many more tourists now. The pressure on traditional life is pervasive. The people you once knew no longer have the same time for you; there's a distance. They're more preoccupied than in the old, easy days.'

21 A Good Place to End Up In

Now there were fourteen charter flights arriving every week; now Goa knew what mass tourism was. 'It's tourism by the masses,' an embittered journalist on cashew *feni* told me. 'Goa used to be a cheap six months for hippies, and now it's a cheap two weeks for' – pause for effect – 'Brits.'

He had been at Arrivals when they first appeared, tall, stylish people, cheerfully chatting to the Customs men in their clear English. These were the Dutch. Then the UK flight landed, and out lurched the first three: Bleary, Weary and Beery. Now, the journalist said, 'everyone knew' the Brits lost their consonants and wore purple shell suits and football outfits. Many brought less than the 'expected' £200 per holiday fortnight. They had less money than the hippies. Tickets had been sold to people who clearly were not gentlemen, to ravers in Day-Glo Doc Marten boots, to shaven-headed men with incomprehensible accents and tattooed necks.

A week later the journalist had interviewed some amiable fifty-ish couples who'd arrived on that flight, and it seemed to him that they were quite satisfied, but with alarmingly little. They'd done Old Goa and Mapusa. They'd done the crocodiles. Wednesdays they'd giggled round the fleamarket – 'a circus' – and of an evening gamely applauded the resort band's renditions of 'Viva España' and the big sixties hits. For the rest of their two weeks they went belly-up on the beach.

They're coming back next year – if that's what the travel advice on the Teletext recommends. They can order a complete holiday in Goa, *the* price-watcher's winter-sun destination, without getting up from the sofa. You can't go any further for less, and these winter-sun veterans have been everywhere. Goa is much nicer than the Dominican Republic and the Gambia, safer than Egypt and cheaper than Tunisia. The people are very nice. 'We've sung "Viva España" in Tunisia, too, Don.'

'And in the bloody Dominican.'

The journalist said that at least they didn't clamour for strip clubs or wet T-shirt contests; he was a bit sniffy about class, as if beach shacks in Goa were where one expected to meet the aristocracy. And he hadn't noticed that once the charter tourists sampled the world beyond the resort, they enjoyed it. They were curious about local life. They were invited home, and thought they might even rent the flat upstairs next year. In the shacks they learned Konkani nursery rhymes from the children, and the next year they brought them football outfits, magazines and Barbie dolls, and hand cream for the girls in the kitchen.

For their part, the villagers were intrigued to meet foreigners who actually worked. 'People want to get on. I don't think most Goans ever did identify with people trying to escape materialism. Goan working people appear to have more points of contact with the charter tourists than they ever had with the hippie Raj. After all, they have all the normal things in common, sports, family, jobs, money, cars, clothes, food. All the things hippies didn't have.'

My landlord gave Goa a few more years as a charter destination, no more. Touristhan was the industrialisation of travel. It was tourism on the conveyor belt. When it went, it really went. When it stopped, as it had for the Gulf War in 1991 and for the (brief and highly localised) bubonic plague in Surat, in 1994, it really stopped. Charter companies worked to tight margins; when it got cheaper elsewhere, elsewhere was where they went.

Fortunately, an Indian beach culture was developing. More well-found urbanites than ever before were being drawn to the sea air, Goan food, the sunset promenade and seaside civilisation. The literal meaning of the word 'civilisation' is city culture – but in

Goa, the bringing of civilisation to village culture had turned urban into urbane. City people enjoyed this. Tourism was diversifying.

In the bar the radio is playing Goa FM, an amiable burble of DJs and their playlist of American guitar ballads with big choruses, one after the other. '. . . And this one is for Mina and Carole from Saligao, Sanjay from Cuncolim and Gil from Anjuna. Sanjay says Hi to everyone at the Medical College, Bambolim.' Later the playlist will go Konkani, for their parents. Konkani pop swings from the smooth and lounge-like to the rude and rollicking, relishing its escape from folk and classical music while remaining a cheerful bastard of both. It also helps that the zest of its Indian parent has taken some of the syrup out of its Latin one.

I am reading a magazine in which Charles Sobhraj is being interviewed in Delhi on the occasion of his removal to Paris. The interviewer calls Sobhraj 'Charles', in the way that interviewers have with celebrities. Interviewer: 'Charles, do you plan to continue crime?' Charles: 'Certainly not. I hope to collaborate on books and films about my life.' Celebrity is shame-proof.

It's late, the traffic has thinned out, and as the radio fades you can hear music coming from the north somewhere. From just down the road or from miles away, it is impossible to tell; it floats on the wind and is bounced around by the trees. Candolim dogs can be heard wailing between tracks. In Anjuna the dogs have techno nightly. They wouldn't even stir for this. It's resort music: 'Ticket to Ride'. The Beatles arrived, the Portuguese left, and for his generation everything changed, a Goan musician told me. Youth and freedom arrived together. The Beatles gave the song new, inventive life; and so techno, instrumental music without song form, when it came along, caught on with Goan dancers but not with musicians, the makers of songs.

The few, the most talented, move on up. The others make a modest living playing hotels and weddings, dances and feasts, the Carnival in March, Saturdays at this or that venue, charter resorts in the winter. An interesting side effect of resort work, this musician told me, is that the players learn or re-learn their own traditional music for a foreign audience who want to hear something Goan. And Goan audiences of a certain age in Mumbai and the Gulf are nostalgic for the old tunes. They bring back the old Goa, unchanged.

Next to me an elderly drinker is demonstrating the art of sitting at the wrong table. He is reliving the Second World War: 'We're legless, aren't we, on bathtub gin, when they come in and tell us the Germans are only two hours away.' But now the Germans are only two seats away, drinking peach schnapps and pretending not to notice. One makes a wry face at the red-haired woman facing her across the table.

'And as for you,' the red-haired woman says to the man next to her, who is trying to hide his expensive Turkish cigarettes, 'what happened to your new lady friend?'

'I brought her in here once. Once was enough.'

After a moment I recognise the Renouncer, his pigtail gone grey, his face now beefy, his beard a tuft at the point of the chin. It's been a while. He half-knows me, nods. 'This bar is social death, no? Worse than not knowing what cocaine is. Thing is, she's got a jeep and a flat and a mobile phone and an air-conditioner and plays tennis at the Taj and gets her legs waxed every fortnight and her horoscope done. You meet these people now . . . She knows everyone and hasn't been here a month. She was making me feel like Rip van Winkle.'

'East and West,' says the man next to him, abruptly. 'East and West just aren't so different any more,' and he turns back to his audience of two. Sharply citified behind their Marlboros, lighters, bike keys and vodka tonics, they are charter lads from London, and have been a challenge from the start. His first question to them was: 'What are you doing in India?'

'India?'

'Goa.'

'Goa? It was ten quid cheaper than the Gambia.'

And ever since, he has been trying to dent their awful urban armour. They have not seen it all. They don't know what goes on here. He goes straight back into the firework story. 'Anyway, it was the guy's birthday. He wanted to share it with everyone, so we got permission for a massive fireworks display, a party for the village.

'We spent 40,000 rupees – getting on for a thousand American dollars – in Mapusa and filled a taxi. We had four bandoliers with ten thousand crackers on each bandolier, and all these rockets – rockets like cannon shells, about ten inches long. You line up ten in a row, pour petrol on the fuses and throw a match and whammo! A salvo! We had Golden Fountains, and five thousand bangers all together in a big bag with the common fuse sticking out, and these things called Atom Bombs, the size of tennis balls, wrapped up in glue and string, very dangerous. Very short fuses. And Dada Big Bangs. And the Firework Baba made us up some very big fireworks. He makes fireworks in clay pots, they're very good. He doesn't have many fingers left, but he makes very good fireworks.

'The birthday boy set out the bandoliers of crackers in the shape of a star. We lit sparklers – and on the count of three ignited the Golden Fountain things. Showers of sparks landed all over the star, and with just that one hit we set off the forty thousand crackers. They went off with such a roar that the spectators all fell over, people fled through the bushes and were impaled on cactuses, kids were screaming, dogs howling, it got worse and worse and worse. The explosions went on for minutes! Like hundreds of people firing machine guns. Clouds of smoke and dust.

'First, this local guy arrives from one end of the village with a posse of henchmen. I knew he was a real heavy, but I didn't find out till the next day that he was reputed to have killed two of his relatives and thrown them down a well. Anyway, he arrives – and up from the beach shack comes the shack lady with *her* posse of henchmen; and from the other way come the police, with rifles, creeping through the bushes. Some in plain clothes, and at least four with rifles. In the morning, when the smoke had lifted, we found a hole about a metre deep where the star had been.'

Two men with gold-chained wrists and heavy tanned faces are

sitting impassively in an alcove facing the door. Their table is littered with imported lager cans and lobster shells. Their eyes play restlessly over the tables. The London lads are at least grinning at the story; but if all the fireworks went off again, right now, these particular tourists would narrow their eyes a little, and no more.

Evidently, tourism is diversifying. A British police inspector on holiday drinks here on Fridays. The man in the Hemingway hat and beard has bought a jeep. The retired couple coming down the drive have rented a house with a real lawn in front of it, and have adopted a dog with mange. 'The first characteristic of travellers who have been more than tourists has been that they have not found what . . . they were looking for.' Curiosity will outreach Touristhan. In the resort they are asking to hear Goan music, to see Indian dance. And as the pigloos disappear and Goa modernises, a new kind of foreigner sees possibilities in Goa. Goans from Liverpool are hosting friends from Kuwait; the Belgian business partners of a Mumbai family borrow their holiday home in Sinquerim. A Dutch couple in Goa for the third time have rented an apartment long-term, in the new estate, and are thinking of buying it. The other day my neighbour saw the wife on the beach in her bikini taking long calls on her mobile phone.

Some days later in the bar the Renouncer fully recognises me. Over a beer, we catch up. He's given up on Pune, it's not for him; he missed the sea air. There are opportunities here. He has to see someone, he has to be somewhere, and after that there's a party. His taxi is waiting. 'Bike's at the mechanic's. Awful, this going back to public transport. This taxi driver asks me if it's my first time in Goa, sir. Well, I know we all look the same, but do I look like a charter tourist?' He is sweating a little into his retro tie-dye T-shirt.

He looks around as he talks, scanning the place as if he's never been here before. He takes in the decorative pots on brick stands, the works of art on black velvet, the drink ads and drug warnings, the calendars and travel ads; the turtle shells and electric fans, the portrait of Jungle Barry and the kitsch clay busts; the weaver-bird nests, the tropical plants and the macramé lampshades.

'A good place to end up in. Listless before another bloody sunset, in one of those grubby white suits, clutching a warm pink gin in one shaking hand. A tropical pub of character. I say pub because in the gents there is a sign reading "Pass Urine Only".' The Renouncer is not having his first drink. 'But aspiring to be more than just another one of those tepid-beer and slice-of-shark places.' He orders and drains a Glenfiddich – 'Cut, for a certainty' – and orders another. 'A jungle watering hole where the different species drink but don't mingle. Look at that! Two Scotsmen drinking Royal Stag. Two Austrians drinking Beck's beer. Two Goans drinking *feni*. It's like Noah's Ark.' His eye falls on two pale men fitfully dozing in a corner. For them, paradise is a pharmacy in Mapusa. The Renouncer gazes thoughtfully at them for a moment, as if trying to remember what paradise was to him.

Then gathering up his bumbag, he rises from the table and, grimacing, straightens up. I notice that under his exuberant T-shirt he is wearing a pair of exuberant tights. 'Should be the best party all season,' he says. 'So they say. See you there, maybe.'

22 Most Dangerous Animal

Wrapped in mist at dawn, Seema is a gaunt ruin on a jungled hillside. Beating back the bushes, you emerge into overgrown gardens to discover a massive building with a fine view of the beach half a mile away. At the rear, three storeys of blank windows survey the ramp which begins at the tangled approach road and ends in a dungeon. Inside, the walls are mildewed. At the far end, a grand staircase leads upwards, ending in mid-air on the next floor. There is a way through to the sea-view side, where a terrace of cottages is being strangled, wooden shutters dragged askew, cast-iron balconies torn off by vines. The vines are the jungle's muscle, scaling the walls like giant lizards, entering by the window spaces, writhing round the little rooms and bursting out into the air again through tiled roofs. Broken tiles lie everywhere.

The swimming pool is a Sargasso mass of algae. 'Visit the monkey hotel,' we had been told: the Seema Resort at Agonda, nearly finished, only to be abandoned to lower primates than expected. The dungeon, for parking, never held a car, and rusting pipes hang creaking in the atrium.

Back down the path to the sea, the No Entry sign reads 'High Court, Bombay, 1991'. Legal action is popular with environmental activists. In a small, picturesque state where heavy-industrial plants, placed on hilltops to free up fertile valley land, loom like the castles of ogres, environmental activism is high profile. Where the polluting of water and air by anything big – mining, resorts – threatens everyone's backyard, Stay Orders stall projects and overrule bureaucracies notoriously subservient to vested interests.

Nine years in the building, the Seema Resort got its Stay Order and joined the list of Goa's ruins, not as the biggest or most romantic, but as one of the most expensive and certainly the most modern. Its posh cottages of laterite and wood will one day ecologically and poetically return to dust, but the reinforced-concrete main building will resist the jungle to the end, tropicalised, moulding in the monsoon, cracking, crumbling at the edges, but never giving up. Concrete never dies.

The land had been bought for a pittance from absentee landlords, the opponents of Seema said, and huge investments made – until under the Tenancy Acts the local 'cultivators', presumably the toddy-tappers of the palms down by the beach, were granted ownership rights, and the environmentalists backing them won their case. But the stalling of Seema didn't satisfy everyone. A big project that could have boosted local business and employment was now wasted. I heard other accounts of its fall; that the enormous investment in the project had attracted envy, and during the building, sabotage had been threatened and protection money demanded. Threats had appeared on a seaside rockface: 'Your tourists will never be safe in Agonda'. It was said that the toddy-tapper plaintiffs had been hired from elsewhere; there had only ever been one tenant on this unused, unprofitable land, and he had been bought off long ago. Other versions had it that the plaintiffs had been cowed by developers' 'goons' and dogs; the shareholders had fallen out; the foreign investors had pulled out because there was no golf course and the hotel was too far from the beach.

Certainly, the hotel was not too near the beach. Goan beaches may well have only been saved from hotel ribbon-development by Indira Gandhi's 500-metre-line law of 1981: nothing substantial may be built within 500 metres of the high-tide line, and though this has sometimes been 200 metres or ninety, the coastline is not Miami, even if it would like to be.

Heading home to Touristhan, we join the main highway heading north. It is flanked by billboards advertising the purchasable beauties of Goa, the big new multistorey clusters on the edge of town with grand names, gates and garaging, security, a pool, shops. Goa is sold as a languid lifestyle, tourism in perpetuity, laidbackness, the old hippie dream coming true for immigrants from the polluted and overpopulated cities. And for the contemplative: real estate is available, I read, in 'a rustic setting of ever-busy fisher folks toiling all day long . . . It's a place to set the mind at rest.'

In the mid-seventies my favourite ad, to be seen everywhere in that first age of billboard erection, was the forthright 'Panama is a Good Cigarette', though the example at the top of the Chapora hill had been graffitoed into 'Panama is a Banana Republic'. The new generation of signs is more subtle, and environmentally aware: 'Goa is Beautiful, Keep it Clean'. Some billboards announce environmental initiatives; between them can be seen glimpses of the environment.

There are no signs any more publicising the bullfight, the *dhirio*, outside this Margao football ground. A few days before the event, boys would go round sticking the flimsy posters to power poles. On them the combatants – Rambo, Ringo, Bruce Lee, White King – were listed in order of appearance and accompanied by blurred portraits of themselves and their stiff, white-shirted owners, men who were ruined when the bullfight was banned in 1996. A good bull, bought for 12,000 rupees, or a water buffalo worth 18,000, was trained only to fight, and was expensive to feed.

For all their meat and muscle, they posed for the camera as peaceably as any old bull you might meet on the street. *Dhirio* comes from a word meaning 'a close lock'. Never the Spanish death-sport, the animals fought each other in the Portuguese way, the padded horns locked together in a trial of pure strength.

The matador, a man in a T-shirt and shorts, hovered like a circus ringmaster, unarmed but for a stick with which he futilely leathered the huge hindquarters whenever the contest looked to be tied. This was often. The bulls heaved away like sumo wrestlers, not charging but trying to unbalance each other, circling in swirls of dust until one broke away and fled. In this arena, size was everything, and David never beat Goliath. At one fight I attended, a small hairy buffalo eyed his approaching rival and turned tail and galloped off between the goalposts and across the waste ground, with half the boys of the crowd ('Goal! Goal!') in pursuit. The older aficionados mopped their foreheads and fanned themselves with newspapers and hats and grumbled and got their wallets out.

It was a betting sport, a Sunday and feast-day entertainment, like football and the Konkani theatre. Prizes were small, but bets were big. The unconquerable Pele from Dovandam, home of the great bulls, might attract 60,000 rupees or well over a thousand American dollars in bets for every fight. On Sundays you went to church and then home for a big lunch. In the late afternoon you went to the bullfight, at sunset strolled *en famille* on the beach, dined well or badly according to your winnings, and afterwards went to the theatre.

The cool weather was still overdue, but by the early evening a little breeze had come up. In next door's compound it blew the dead leaves around. Coconuts had fallen with no one to pick them up: the family hadn't arrived from Pune yet and their big place with its wide, dusty *balcao* was that familiar thing, the shut-up Goan house. The garden was home to nothing but one monkey, a wild and solitary black-faced langur.

'Chickens are crying,' my landlord observed. The chicken is said to have been first domesticated in India, and they fear the call of the wild. In this climate, nature can never be defeated. If the humans give up, their habitation immediately becomes a monkey hotel. Bandicoots tunnel the floors. Frogs invade the house and sit on your forehead. So there has to be a deal, a civilised deal between humanity and nature.

But in the shade of the banyan, dreaming by his car, watching the women builders, the developer sees grander things. He sees thrusting human aspiration, bulldozers and teamwork, towers rising from the green, transformation. Forwards! So much that is called picturesque is the past preserved by poverty. And that old life – call it by its name, poverty – was so boring. Not the God-given fate of the resigned and the religious, not the simple life so admired, in comfort, by the sentimental – just boring. Progress ennobles. Goa is the second most literate state in the country. Per capita income is amongst the highest. Life expectancy is high, expectations are high, house and car ownership are growing.

'Today Goa is pulsating, vibrant . . . Roads are trundling with cars . . . villages are revelling in two and three-storey marble-floored houses . . . Every economy has to adjust to new realities in this fast changing world . . .' The writer of this magazine article is enthusiastic about a report of 1992 which thought Goa the best site in India for a free port, an enterprise zone something like the ones in China. Where better to site a free-for-all with the new global economic order than Goa? Nowhere in Asia had a longer continuous connection with the West. And few Indian states in recent years had been so notably entrepreneurial, directed by mining and hospitality industries with far more practice at running things than the politicians whose experience of government had begun with statehood in 1987.

But in the night the developer awakes. Power cut. The air-conditioner has died, and his room is a sweatbox. Transforming the tropics, it seems to him, as he struggles with the window latch, is a thankless struggle of under-resourced visionaries against wretched infrastructure and the bureaucrats and defeatists and their implacable ally, nature. The developer thinks nature is the aggressor; his opponents think it is all of us. Theirs is the view accepted in the museum of the Cotigao wildlife reserve. On one wall, above a picture-sized curtain, a notice reads 'Lift to See Most Dangerous Animal'. Approaching it, you pass sloughed snake-skins, a row of predatory teeth, the photographed pad prints of big cats. You lift the curtain – and there, of course, is the mirror.

October 1997 had been the hottest on record, and November had been as hot as April. At least it was now raining. 'In all my life,' said an old lady of the village, 'I never saw rain like this so long after monsoon.' It crashed onto her corrugated-iron roof like wild applause, and went sheeting off into the garden. The insects, I noticed, were continuing their disappearing act from the walls as if it were any old December. You could measure their departure into winter limbo by the way the geckoes followed suit. Half of them were gone, too, leaving the remainder with more territory to cover – but also with their tails, because there were fewer turf wars now to lose them in.

Christmas was two days away. The bar had its decorations up; a choir made its yearly visit to sing 'We Three Kings of Orient Are' and collect tips in a Santa Claus jug. Out on the roadside by the shops, five of the six cars bore Maharashtra licence plates, and I passed a driver returning with cigarettes, Marlboros at $2 a packet, for his passengers invisible behind smoked glass. Mumbai people. They come down in April and May, and the hotels discount tariffs for the monsoon season (an extravaganza of water, the torrent from above pounding the breakers below, drowning fields, overflowing wells), but now Christmas-New Year is also becoming fashionable. Indian tourists are not easily put off by Gulf Wars or other passing panics. Around fifty thousand foreign tourists visit Goa every year – but there were that many Indian tourists thirty years ago. The change is in where they go.

In Panjim the budget bus tours arrive, the commerce-college boys hollering with excitement, changing into their holiday finery even as the bus pulls in. Fifteen hours from Bangalore and they are still awake, shuttling up and down the aisle. They have paused now and again to strike heroic dance poses to the technopop and rap and film songs – 'East, West, India is Best' – and to check out the video as the ads sponsored by underpant firms in Dubai scroll endlessly across the bottom of the film.

In a body they will rush out of the bus and into Panjim, towards the companionable dormitory room, the cut-price bottle shop, the ice-cream parlour, the bazaar. They will tour the beach, but for them, living beachside is too expensive. So what delights hoteliers great and small out along the coast is the new interest in sand and sea being shown by more prosperous Indian tourists. They will take family meals. And unlike many Western tourists, they are decorous dressers and early risers who will not insist on watching European football on satellite TV at two in the morning.

The people from Pune have had their ten days and are off in the morning. You hope they slept last night. For miles around, parties are beginning to break out, and I find my landlord has locked my bicycle in his shed. New Year's Eve is *Janeiro*, traditionally a night for things to be removed by stealth from porches and compounds, and strewn round the landscape. *Balcao* furniture has been known to end up on the beach. But the Pune teenagers are not intrigued by this old custom. It merely confirms their belief that Goa is not modern at all, but old and sleepy and yes, quaint, if you like quaint. They don't. 'Goa,' they say, 'is a holiday. It's not serious.'

In the early eighties Goan buses stopped playing Konkani music, at least along the trend-sensitive northern coastal belt, and switched to film music, sung in Hindi. Candolim fishwives going to Mapusa market didn't care for it. They didn't know Hindi, but their children did, because of school and television. The talents of a small place are obviously confined. It cannot expand and is therefore likely to retract. It is tempted to retreat into quaintness, while at the same time yearning for the cosmopolitan life, trying to keep its own culture from atrophy by embracing everything the big places send.

The big places are tempting; emigration beckons. The emigrants take their education and talents and leave, and the little birthplace becomes a repository of loss and nostalgia. 'Goa! That dream destination from times immemorial . . . The lovely lady of the Indian subcontinent has failed in making her sons and daughters cling on to her bosom and drink the milk of happiness.' The same *Goa*

Today cover story notes that in recent times, emigration has preferred Canada without giving up on much-nearer Africa. 'A large percentage of those who chose to settle abroad are the Africanders . . . grabbing the opportunity with both hands, they plunged headlong to their destiny.'

Of the twelve émigrés interviewed in that article, ten were Christians. They continue to emigrate in numbers: in 1910, 51 per cent of Goa's population was Christian; in 1980, it was 33 per cent. Another third of that year's total population of 850,000 consisted of recent arrivals from greater India. The incomers are Hindu, culturally closer to Goan Hindus, so it tends to be the Christians who get that shrinking feeling, identity-anxiety. Not that everyone does. 'I'm not a snob,' Lucio Miranda told me, 'but sometimes I do feel that a little learning is a dangerous thing . . . I think this identity worry is coming from a class that only ever absorbed the superficial trappings of Western culture. Nevertheless, they were brainwashed by the Church into believing that they were superior. As if a few table manners and the speaking of English constituted an identity . . . It's an outer skin.'

The Portuguese language that carried the culture of the West to Goa was only ever taught to a minority, and instruction ended with the Portuguese departure. The values that Lucio was brought up with 'are now being totally sidetracked by a society of the new rich. My social circle today is of successful, predominantly Hindu, Goan businessmen who model themselves on successful Mumbai businessmen. They are Westernised too, though the influence is not Portuguese but Anglo-American. There is one Goan Hindu family with a Portuguese connection, but they're the exception.'

Christianity stayed on, its clergy now all Indian, its instruction all in Konkani, Church and State finally sundered. Portugal survives as a mood. The 'everyday currency' of the Portuguese-speaking world is *fado*, 'Portuguese blues, and *saudade*, the spirit of futile yearning that infects it . . .' A new estate may be called *Saudades*; a heritage name. Meanwhile in Panjim, the Portuguese-speaking Christian elite that Lucio Miranda grew up with 'in their minds or hearts refuse to make the transition to the present. To a great extent they live within themselves. They try to go on as if nothing has happened. They do not accept reality. To them, Goa is lost. They can certainly afford to go on like this, but they are the last generation that will wish to. In fact, it isn't so difficult to adapt to Indian Goa. There was always a solid Hindu culture here.'

To me, Goa remains that one bus with two names, *Mahalaxmi* and *Mother Mary*. A society of compatible incompatibilities. I suppose it is sentimental to say that. But between them they have seen off the worst demons, so far. Goan society is somehow indivisible, perhaps because it is still supported by the steel frame of an ancient social system. To this day, Christian Mhars are drummers in the church and Hindu Mhars are drummers in the temple.

Goa's equilibrium was achieved because it is one of those 'small patches' where 'local realities might exorcise atavistic phantoms' – which is to say that there may be a few old ghosts around, but few of the living believe in them. Political exploiters have not succeeded in turning community competitiveness into tribal neurosis. Contention is tempered by indifference, a quality essential to toleration. Toleration, after all, means leaving people alone, being indifferent to what they do: it is the legacy of that ancient Indian social system, caste. In its traditional sense, caste was a matter of leaving others alone, of indifference, of not intermarrying or interdining. Hindus, whose lack of charity the Christian missionaries denounced, practised the toleration for the beliefs of others that the Christians of intolerant Europe could not.

23 SAUDADES

The spring-into-summer heat began to rise in the last week of February, on the new moon of Shivratri, the Nights of Shiva. Shivratri was simultaneous with the Carnival that saw in the fast of Lent. I noted this second religious coincidence of the season, the first having been in October, when Yom Kippur fell on the peak day of Dussehra. I asked my neighbour if he fasted for Lent. No, he didn't, but he did fast every Friday. Fridays, he ate only fish. And what did he eat for the rest of the week? Usually, fish.

For Carnival there were costume parades along festive streets, every band worked every night, and the church complained about commercialisation. In Calangute the marquee sponsored by a champagne company was nearly the length of the football ground it was pitched on.

It was a time to revive old acquaintance. After years in Bangalore, FX was back in Goa, sequestered at his sister Hilaria's place on the coast near Margao. I had hoped to catch up with him while attending the wedding of Hilaria's granddaughter in mid-May, but I had to leave for London just before it. May is the wedding season. Sometimes you hear two or three parties all going at once; the hotter the weather, the wilder the party. There is feasting, the big beat, humid evenings lit and scorched by fireworks. This summer was always going to be a hot one. Already the prognostication for the mango crop was gloomy; too few flowers were appearing, because it wasn't cold enough.

Hilaria's granddaughter was in her mid-twenties; the 'boy', as FX called him, was ten years older. 'The right age, and a love match, too.' The nuptial day would be decided in the Christian way, without benefit of astrology. Any day other than a Thursday or Friday would be fine; these days were considered unlucky.

In Goa, following the religious marriage ceremony, the church (or temple or mosque) has to inform the registry office, and the official papers are signed there. This is a reflection of Goa's distinctive Civil Code, which deals with matters of marriage, divorce and inheritance. A Portuguese import, the Civil Code treats the adherents of all religions impartially. On the death of a man whose marriage has been registered in Goa, half his property goes to his wife and the other half is divided equally amongst his children. The original intention was to safeguard the rights of widows, though the long migration which has dispersed heirs across the globe has complicated matters. Land and property cannot be sold without the consent of all the heirs. Goans overseas are regularly asked to release their share of title to disputed properties – too many of which lie empty for years, rotting under litigation.

At the end of February, I took a bus to Panjim, another (a hellish affair of contralto horn shrieks and conductor attitude) to Margao and finally an autorickshaw for the few kilometres to Hilaria's. In the past, when you had to change buses for ferries at every river, this was a tedious trip. The new bridges have ended all that, with the result that I arrived far too early. Down the road a litany was being said before a modern cross shielded by a corrugated-iron rainshade. Dawdling under a tree, I heard the PA speakers delivering what you would have to call Christian pop, while worshippers from the neighbouring houses gathered and found their places. Glimpses of the crucified figure set up before the worshippers revealed, as often seemed to be the case, that He was calm. He displayed no torment, perhaps because Indian craftsmen for centuries had been importing into this religion of suffering and martyrdom a style of divinity derived from Hinduism. Goa adapted Iberia to India, India to Iberia. A lemonade stand on wheels arrived to tempt the ladies in their neat frocks; they sang hymns that were lilting and sad and slid through Indian quarter-tones.

Long ago, the arrival of Europe in Goa had been a shock; but in time an equilibrium had been found. Now the shock of the new had come again, abrupt and dislocating, but this time Goa was directed by Mumbai, not by the West. Her exemplar was a day's train ride away.

The changes, the dislocations and contemporary tumult were unlikely to upset poor people, for whom any change brought hope. To most other people, me included, change seemed to bring nostalgia. But that was useless. Nostalgia obscured any understanding of the past that one was being nostalgic about. It was nostalgia that encouraged the notion that Christian Goa had emerged from the past culturally maimed, an awkward hybrid; that an ancient purity had been lost. But societies acquired more than they ever invented. Diffusion and cultural interpenetration and migration, the dislocations of the past – in the end, they produced composite, adaptable societies, and freed up individual lives.

The singing ended and a stentorian bingo caller took over the microphone just relinquished by the priest. I was ready to call on FX.

Hilaria and her lawyer husband had prospered in Bangalore. FX's retirement home was an upstairs room in a substantial house in a big walled compound with papaya trees, a score of coconut palms, fat chestnut hens, sheds, a well – an old-style, self-sufficient place. Here too was the last home of the ancient Ford Popular, over by the shed under a palm-leaf shelter. I rounded a banyan, a beauty with its head in the sky and its feet in the garbage, and opened the boundary gate.

At ground level the compound was a garden, while up at coconut height it was alive with jungle birds: golden orioles, woodpeckers, tiny wrens momentarily visible against that soundscape of birdsong whose makers you can never see. Framed in FX's big unglazed window, a palm trunk climbed upwards, banded in shades of brown. A paradise-flycatcher sashayed by, streamer-tailed and crested, the star of the jungle.

So far his view had been that frame, FX said from his daybed, and that palm. Come April or May he'd look up, and there'd be a plucker climbing it. The coconuts had to be cut, before the stems dried out. Until then, his afternoon entertainment would be the chat drifting up in instalments between dozes from the *balcao* down below.

'Gone are the happy-go-lucky days. It's gone all serious now.' That was the theme: the fond past, the cusp of the present, the fraught future. 'Whatever Goa will be, it will not be what it was.' It was going to be Mumbai-on-Sea, or a free port with casinos and moral chaos; or with prices the way they were going, an enclave of the rich. That would be best. The rich kept things looking nice.

'Look at that. Cheeky sod.' A huge crow was hopping about by the balcony door, beadily waiting for FX to nod off and forget the biscuits.

In the sixteenth century the dour but attentive traveller Linschoten noted the particular audacity of Goan crows. They were said to be immortal. Legend had them representing the sages, or being inauspicious but useful as messengers to the other world. They didn't sing, but made remarks, and thereby found interpreters. I was glad to tell FX that even today there was still a little interpreting left to do: his days could be enlivened with *The Language of Ravens and Crows*, the definitive guide to crow-talk. The original was in Sanskrit, but I promised to photocopy him my version, an English translation from the eighth-century Tibetan.

I told him it was best to divine by ear. You didn't want to see your oracle on foot, that lurching, peering meander of the drunk hunting for his car keys. FX said he'd do a divination and phone it through to me on the very day I left; he liked the idea of a farewell prophecy.

We'd spent an hour or so on odd digressions, FX having begun the process by wondering why all the sidewalks in Panjim were

so high. This had tailed off, but the mention of Panjim brought up
the subject of Hilaria, and the time he had taken her to the vast old
inherited house. Which took him to the car, and the time he had
driven along to the sound of gunfire from Aguada. How mundane
were the things people found themselves doing on great occasions! At the moment of freedom he had been driving home with
a consignment of tartan car upholstery from old Naik's.

FX was reviewing his life in flashbacks, and at the wheel. At
some point he got to what I recognised as our first meeting, in
1983. 'She never did come along that road, dammit.'

'Mrs Thatcher?'

'She'd like it along there now, if she came back. All that busy-
ness. Everyone working away.'

'You don't approve.'

'I don't approve of them doing away with the bullfight and the
matka, the numbers racket. Every once in a while you'd win. It
was an excuse to go to the taverna. Of course, there are much
worse things to disapprove of. But what to do? What happens
everywhere else even happens here, now. It's on Hilaria's TV.
It's the same pressure now for everyone. We just got away with it
for longer. When I came back from Africa in '47, Goa was like an
island. If it had floated away no one would have noticed.'

'Wasn't it like that right up to the eighties?'

But FX was already on the road ahead. 'I may still be around
for the anniversary. Albuquerque's.'

'In 2010. Not too much to hope for?'

'Okay, too much to hope for. The millennium, then.'

'How does it look?'

'Look?' FX said, turning and dismissing with a single gesture
his bedside table and its mute exhibit, a stuffed mongoose wearing an ancient pair of sunglasses. 'He does the looking now. I
don't look around much any more. I'm not going out there.'

'I'm sorry. I didn't even know you were ill.'

'I'm a borderline case. Hilaria's had the priest round.'

'I didn't think you were a churchgoer.'

'I went. Doing the decent thing, the Captain used to call it. I said as much to the priest. I said: "Father, pray on. Do the decent thing for the family. Mustn't spoil the family name. But as far as I'm concerned, you're wasting your time." And he said he wasn't wasting his time, he thought of his prayers on my behalf as fire insurance.' As FX began to laugh, a long, hiccuping laugh, Hilaria appeared at the top of the stairs. It was time to go.

On the Vagator hill, where the wells are deepest and dry out first, people arriving for an evening's techno at the Nine Bar had seen a water tanker. Already, in the first week of March. And because the closing tourist season brought in the long months of the thin wallet, the police were expected.

At my local restaurant the frogs were out, at least half a dozen of them in all shades and sizes. Driven from damp repose by the drying ground, they would hop tastily about for another two months, waiting for the rains like the mysterious freshwater fish the restaurateur saw going to ground in the deep mud at the bottom of his well.

The restaurant's bar was closed but the restaurateur himself was working, renovating the kitchen. And the help? It was their compulsory day off for voting. There were to be six alcohol-free days for the elections, though no one could see why this little state needed six days to vote, or why they had to be dry. Out on the road an apprentice mafioso, his swagger and headscarf copied from his mentors, was loading a van with precautionary cases of beer.

Only recently the restaurateur had been obliged to give a waiter fifteen days off for the festival of Lord Ganesh, when he himself couldn't take fifteen minutes off for Lord Ganesh. And soon it would be Holi, the boisterous festival of colours. Like Goan elections, the Goan Holi went on for days on end, and his waiters would want time off for that, too. I noted that the full moon day, when the Holi fire was kindled, would be on Friday the thirteenth, marking the third religious coincidence – or in this case, conjunction of religion and superstition – of the season.

Now the restaurateur had to give six dry days to democracy. But it would be business as usual in the pub with no beer. 'Wet or dry, dry or wet, it is of no concern to me. Every day, I will serve,' he said, sounding like George Washington.

Lamentation comes from somewhere in the village, and the coucal in the tree outside my window gulps in alarm and takes off on russet wings. Women hurry from their houses; there's no time to waste in this weather. Early next morning the funeral band arrives, horns playing sad and low. The lamentation reaches its crescendo, clouds of incense and red dust drift over the mango tree outside; but soon the priest shuts his breviary and hurries to his Scooty. The mourners compose themselves. Young men in shirtsleeves take up the coffin and the cortège starts out along the sandy path, where a huge and grinning sow is suckling three abandoned puppies.

The wind has died. In March and then in April a fierce onshore gale turned the ocean to cruel-sea green, a misplaced Atlantic with whitecaps in the bay. It came roaring off the sea from the north-west, sweeping the sand into smooth contours, ironing out the footprints, burying the lost sandals. The beach became Arabian, pristine; but now people have reappeared, and the sand is pocked again from the shacks to the sea.

Even inanimate things smell the monsoon, now a bare month away. Clumps of plastic bottles wait in the flood channels along the beach. The drying ground behind the dunes evicts yet more nervous frogs, and unusual subterranean insects. In the distance, wedding bands are tuning up. In the compound over the way the chickens are well used to Konkani pop and film songs. Rap and technopop they can take; but the new wedding trend for American rock anthems drives them wild. Epic power chord, frantic cluckings, silence. Power cut.

The general crisis of infrastructure is most obvious in electricity outages. Tourism doubles the usual demand all winter, and in summer the cuts are incessant, with early evening the worst, when everyone comes home and switches on as the dark comes down.

Demand invariably peaks at shower time. Off go the lights, leaving you naked, towel-hunting, only to flicker on again as your neighbour appears at the window. Hello! Goodnight! In the shower ten minutes later off they go again, and so do the mosquito-repeller machines, leaving you covered in soap, a victim in the whining dark. Then there is light again, and you are suddenly reanimated like a toy with a new battery – but it fades, falters, recovers, and comes back low. The fridge convulses, and the lights quaver in shades of mustard.

The lights will slowly strengthen and brighten through the evening as people switch off and retire; and with the return of that bright light come deep thoughts. How transient are the things one takes for granted, like electricity – and how spiritual is the so-called material world, to remind one of it. The two mosquito-repellers are little domes of plastic which when switched on, heat up and emit an insecticide. There are two power sockets in the living room: one machine works off both of them, the other off only one of them. Why? In the kitchen, both machines work off both sockets.

At times like this you suspect that some principle beyond the merely electrical is operating. Inanimate things are showing signs of life. They are exhibiting the properties of the animate, just as plastic bottles and frogs alike await the rain. Everything has life, just as the ancients believed. This is evident in just one week's reading matter. In one book on Goa, a road speaks to the writer; in a history of Calangute, the sea upbraids humanity for polluting it. In an article on tourism, a beach shack speaks.

The next morning, as I pick up the paper in Guru Communications, the power goes off: so much for deep thoughts. Power cuts are a fearful nuisance. In the gloom I read that there will be a shutdown of the entire state today. They are calling the power minister the

Prince of Darkness. Everyone without a generator – the vast majority – will have no fans or well-pumps or refrigerators in 36-degree heat and stifling humidity. The reason is 'pre-monsoon maintenance'. At least it's on the front page.

The phone rings in its sweltering booth. It's FX calling, right on time. 'The crow book, you know? I did a divination for you. It isn't great, but there's no getting away from it. Bird has spoken. I heard it twice yesterday, loud as you like. When a crow caws at sunset from the south-east, the book says, "you will suffer a loss." '

'Well, I do have to leave.'

'See you next season.'

There is a picture on the paper's entertainments page, the same impassive photo that I have been seeing for years, of a veteran actor in the Konkani theatre. So many photos look as if they were taken long ago. In the newspaper files I've seen back issues from even recent times that were bound between big hard covers and already felt as weighty as memorials. On yellowed paper, antique people frolicked on the beach. One day soon in the obituary section, FX himself will appear, gazing intently out of a black-bordered frame. He too will be dressed for the past; probably it will be the photo from the thirties he showed me, his lounge-lizard phase, he called it, with sharp white shirt, narrow face, oil-slick hair, hair-thin moustache.

I put the thought away, folding it back into the paper with the rest of the lost past. This is leaving day, and the taxi is waiting.

Notes and Sources

Prologue

p. 3 *a "dry adhesion"*	J. C. Daniel, *The Book of Indian Reptiles* (Mumbai,1983), p. 33.
p. 5 *Graham Greene*	'Goa the Unique', *Reflections* (London, 1991).

Old Conquests

1   INTO GOA

p. 17 *Goody Servai*	C. de Souza, *In Search of Sands* (Panjim, 1997), p. 23.
p. 21 *In its range of deleterious effects*	C. Alvares (ed.), *Fish Curry and Rice* (Ecoforum, Mapusa, 1995) p. 155.
p. 22 *hanging over Goa*	Afonso de Albuquerque in D. F. Lach, *India in the Eyes of Europe* (Chicago, 1965), p. 389.
p. 22 *like mounting*	Duarte Barbosa in Lach, *India in the Eyes of Europe*, p. 371.
p. 22 *'diverted'*	In 1998 there were newspaper reports of 9000 hectares of forestry land (maintained by the Forestry Department of the State Government and supposed to be inviolable) being 'leased out' for mining.
p. 23 *the great destroyer of customs*	N. Lewis, *An Empire of the East* (London 1993), p. 3.

2 THE MARGINS

p. 24 *Oceans unite*   F. Fernández-Armesto, *Millennium*
(New York, 1995), p. 682.

p. 25 a*lmost unique form of*   D. D. Kosambi, *Myth and Reality*
(Bombay, 1962), p. 165.

p. 25 *gruesome and beautiful*   Ibid., p. 10.

p. 27 *In fact, they are not*   K. S. Singh (ed.), *People of India*
only backward   *– Goa* (Anthropological Survey
of India, Mumbai, 1993), p. 75.

p. 27 *tribal people's unsatis-*   Lewis, *An Empire of the East*,
factory existences   p. 23.

p. 28 *Many nameless village*   Kosambi, *Myth and Reality*, p. 110.
gods

p. 29 *The unwilled is the*   Sir James Campbell in R. E.
spirit-caused   Enthoven, *The Folklore of Bombay*,
1925 (New Delhi, 1990), p. 10.

p. 30 *My grandfather is*   Kosambi, *Myth and Reality*, p.170.
certainly

p. 31 *the chicken sucked the*   F. S. Gracias, *Health and*
venom   *Hygiene in Colonial Goa* (New
Delhi, 1994), p. 160.

p. 31 *whose nomad tracks*   Kosambi, *Myth and Reality*, p. 108.

p. 32 *cross in Moadys was*   O. J. F. Gomes, *Village Goa*
built   (New Delhi, 1996), p. 29.

p. 32 *to appease those spirits*   Ibid.

p. 32 *the collective ghost*   Ibid.

p. 33 *As a matter of fact*   Kosambi, *Myth and Reality*, p. 159.

p. 34 *The people whom*   Ibid., p. 100.

p. 34 *They believe evil spirits*   Singh (ed.), *People of India*, p. 35.

p. 35 *Christian aboriginals*   Gomes, *Village Goa*, p. 20.

p. 35 *monkey-like figures*   E. Waugh, *Diaries* (London,
1979), p. 708.

3 SWORD AND HAZARD

p. 39 *as many as four arms*   Vasco da Gama in Lach, *India in the Eyes of Europe*, p. 361.

p. 43 *as one leaving this world*   L. de Camoens, *The Lusiads*, 1572, trans. and intro. W. C. Atkinson (London, 1952), p. 17.

p. 44 *If cultures and civilisations*   Fernández-Armesto, *Millennium*, p. 20.

p. 45 *at times*   C. Barros, in Lach, *Decadas*, *India in the Eyes of Europe*, p. 389.

p. 45 *precisely a protection racket*   M. N. Pearson, *The New Cambridge History of India*. Vol 1.1, *The Portuguese in India* (Hyderabad, 1987), p. 78.

p. 45 *And if there had been more*   L. de Camoens in D. J. Boorstin, *The Discoverers* (London, 1986), p. 255.

p. 46 *no contempt for subject peoples*   N. C. Chaudhuri, *The Continent of Circe* (New Delhi, 1966), p. 321.

4 THE RIGOUR OF MERCY

p. 51 *able to compete in magnificence*   Missionary letter in Lach, *India in the Eyes of Europe*, p. 449.

p. 51 *spiritual conquistadors*   Fernández-Armesto, *Millennium*, p. 298.

p. 52 *Some were burnt down*   Missionary letter in T. R. de Souza, *Goa to Me* (New Delhi, 1994), p. 94.

p. 52 *We are here on a battlefield*   Jesuit letter in Lach, *India in the Eyes of Europe*, p. 445.

p. 52 *Many Christians from these parts*   Missionary letter, ibid., p. 381.

p. 53 *men without law*	Jesuit letter, ibid., p. 445.
p. 53 *At our coming*	Ralph Fitch in R. Hakluyt, *Voyages and Discoveries*, ed. J. Beeching (London, 1972), p. 256.
p. 56 *So far, being a member*	Ibid., p. 172.
p. 56 *set up a habit of mind*	T. Zeldin, *An Intimate History of Humanity* (London, 1995), p. 173.
p. 56 *Garcia da Orta*	Worked in Goa between the 1530s and 1570s on his famous *Colloquies on the Simples and Drugs of India*.
p. 57 *The same faith*	Boorstin, *Discoverers*, p. 116.
p. 58 *bagatelles*	Giovanni Maffei in Lach, *India in the Eyes of Europe*, p. 450.

5   GOA DOURADA

p. 59 *It is a fine city*	Ralph Fitch in Hakluyt, *Voyages and Discoveries*, p. 256.
p. 61 *the population of a single*	J. N. Fonseca in J. M. Richards, *Goa* (New Delhi, 1982), p. 65.
p. 61 *Goa was then at its zenith*	Capt. F. Marryat, *The Phantom Ship* (London, 1839), p. 223.
p. 64 *utterly at variance*	R. F. Burton, *Goa, and the Blue Mountains* (Oxford, 1991), p. 102.
p. 64 *At Goa all men are equal*	Ibid., p. 106.
p. 64 *The Portingales*	Jan van Linschoten in Lach, *India in the Eyes of Europe*, p. 483.
p. 65 *Many husbands are fed datura*	Ibid.
p. 65 *very slowly forwards*	Ibid.
p. 66 *The Indians eat everything*	John Newbery in Hakluyt, *Voyages and Discoveries*, p. 257.
p. 66 *I am astonished*	St Francis Xavier in Pearson, *The New Cambridge History of India*. Vol. 1.1, *The Portuguese in India*, p. 140.

6   THIS BABYLON

p. 68 *the dominant caste families*   De Souza, *Goa to Me*, p. 90.

p. 71 *The conversion of unbelievers*   E. Hobsbawm, *On History* (London, 1997), p. 221.

p. 72 *whose best-selling books*   P. Vallely, the *Independent, on meditation*London, 5 Dec. 1998.

p. 72 *massy, handsome pile*   Marryat, *Phantom Ship*, p. 23.

p. 72 *At Goa the accusations*   Ibid., p. 29.

p. 73 *most zealous bigots*   Alexander Hamilton in Burton, *Goa and Blue Mountains*, p. 54-55 .

p. 73 *Its prisoners*   N. Lewis, 'Goa', *A View of the World* (London, 1986), p. 111.

p. 77 *Reflected in hopeful eyes*   Fernández-Armesto, *Millennium*, p. 247.

p. 78 *This Babylon*   De Camoens, *Lusiads*, p. 17.

7   RESISTANCE

p. 80 *He may be ill-bred*   A. Huxley, *Jesting Pilate* (London, 1926), p. 4.

p. 82 *There had developed three layers*   Lucio Miranda, interview by author.

p. 82 *The Goans, very much against*   C. de Noronha, *The Conspiracy of 1787 in Goa* (Panjim, 1994), p. 6.

p. 84 *out of the bazaar*   De Souza, *Goa to Me*, p. 138.

p. 86 *This sect, embraced*   A. Crabtree, *From Mesmer to Freud* (New Haven, 1994), p. 96.

p. 87 *developed with art*   Ibid., p. 107.

p. 88 *waded through the bitter*   Noronha, *Conspiracy of 1787*, p. 8.

p. 90 *pouncing like a great*   Greene, 'Goa the Unique', p. 231.

8   GOA BRITANNICA

p. 91	*is a rhubarb-coloured*	Burton, *Goa and Blue Mountains*, p. 17.
p. 92	*mongrel men*	Ibid., p. 97-103.
p. 92	*It has lost the Portuguese*	Ibid., p. 88.
p. 92	*was concentrated round Panjim*	Miranda, interview.
p. 92	*Everyone knows*	Burton, *Goa and Blue Mountains*, p. 158.
p. 93	*what today would be called*	Pearson, *The New Cambridge History of India*. Vol. 1.1, *The Portuguese in India*, p. 145.
p. 93	*An unmistakable Lakshmi*	Burton, *Goa and Blue Mountains*, p. 111.
p. 93	*There was tremendous vision*	Miranda, interview.
p. 94	*Even the dark faces*	Burton, *Goa and Blue Mountains*, p. 93.
p. 94	*very fair*	Ibid., 124.
p. 95	*formerly a village of*	Waugh, *Diaries*, p. 709.
p. 96	*a synthesis of the Italian*	Gomes, *Village Goa*, p. 334.
p. 96	*Goan composers had begun*	Miranda, interview.
p. 96	*such a proficient*	Burton, *Goa and Blue Mountains*, p. 128.

9   GEOGRAPHY AND DESTINY

p. 98	*diversity in customs*	Kosambi, *Myth and Reality*, p.157.
p. 98	*cultural tragicomedy*	De Souza, *Goa to Me*, p. 160.
p. 99	*By now, we have a Goan*	M. Cabral e Sa, *Great Goans* (Panjim, 1985), p. ix.
p. 99	*The far-ranging Goan*	Greene, 'Goa the Unique', p. 230.

p. 100 *In Goa the British found* — Miranda, interview.

p. 100 *The Goans who have settled* — V. P. Chavan, *The Konkan and the Konkani Language* (New Delhi, 1924), p. 58.

p. 101 *strikingly lax* — Kosambi, *Myth and Reality*, p. 153.

p. 101 *managed to live on* — Ibid., p. 155.

p. 103 *not in lorries* — Lewis, 'Goa', p. 112.

p. 104 *a mellowed authoritarianism* — Lewis, 'Goa', p. 113.

p. 104 *the choicest vocabulary* — De Souza, *Goa to Me*, p. 16.

p. 104 *One can walk about all day* — Lewis, 'Goa', p. 112.

p. 105 *noise absolutely infernal* — Waugh, *Diaries*, p. 706.

p. 105 *the horrors of Hitler's* — Ibid., p. 710.

p. 107 *We would be giving* — Salazar in T. Gallagher, *Portugal, A 20th Century Interpretation* (Manchester 1983), p. 155.

p. 108 *in Asia that God's* — De Souza, *Goa to Me*, p. 93.

p. 109 *totally ecstatic about* — Pearson, *The New Cambridge History of India*. Vol. 1.1, *The Portuguese in India*, p. 161.

p. 110 *Our soldiers and sailors* — Salazar in Gallagher, *Portugal*, p. 156.

p. 111 *Nor the next* — M. Hall, *Window on Goa* (London, 1992), p. 205.

10   VILLA PORTUGUESA

p. 113 *strong and liturgically* — De Souza, *Goa to Me*, p. 70.

p. 113 *dressed as usual* — L. de Noronha, 'Uncle Peregrine', in *Ferry Crossing*, ed. M. Shetty (New Delhi, 1998), p. 264.

p. 114 *device for opening up* — J. Pereira, *Baroque Goa* (New Delhi, 1995), p. 120.

p. 114 *sixteen great windows*   Greene, 'Goa the Unique', p. 233.

p. 115 *There were Shiraz*   H. Ribeiro, 'At the Shrine of Mary
   carpets   of the Angels', *Ferry Crossing*, p. 239.

p. 115 *as a matter of course*   Greene, 'Goa the Unique', p. 232.

11   THE EMPIRE OF HIP

p. 122 *You're losing*   P. Bowles, *Their Heads are*
   your colour   *Green*, 1963 (London, 1990), p. 13.

p. 124 *They are mainly*   C. Alvares (ed.), *Fish Curry and*
   lower-class   *Rice*, p. 182.

p. 127 *The road was not the*   Kim Morarji, interview by
   way   author, March 1999.

p. 130 *Perhaps the planners*   De Souza, *In Search of Sands*
   p. 10.

12   FROM UTOPIA TO ARCADIA

p. 134 *Then there were*   Eve Green, interview by author,
   the Italian   July 1997.

p. 137 *The guy had something*   Brendan and Kate, interview by
   author, July 1997.

NEW CONQUESTS

13   THE NEW FRONTIER

p. 145 *The stories of*   J. C Daniel, *The Book of Indian*
   monitor lizards   *Reptiles* (Mumbai, 1983), pp. 58–9.

p. 146 *a well-defined idea*   Burton, *Goa and Blue Mountains*,
   of what   p. 35.

p. 146 *interested in anything but loot* — The Maratha historian A. R. Kulkarni thought that the people of the Konkan coast never had much sympathy for the Maratha movement. Quoted in de Souza, *Goa to Me*, p. 158.

p. 147 *a poorer but surely a happier* — Greene, 'Goa the Unique', p. 234.

p. 148 *Ranes* — D. D. Kosambi called the 18th-century Ranes 'robbers claiming feudal titles'. Quoted in de Souza, *Goa to Me*, p. 59.

14   THE CHAISHOP YEARS

p. 150 *Would you ever sell the gods* — P. Naik, 'The Turtle', in *Ferry Crossing*, p. 25.

p. 151 *The tree is called the palm* — R. Fitch in Hakluyt, *Voyages and Discoveries*, p. 255.

p. 152 *The wine doth issue* — Ibid.

p. 153 *When the Aryan colonizers* — Chavan, *Konkan and the Konkani Language*, p. 6.

p. 154 *she should have been praying* — Greene, 'Goa the Unique', 235.

15   SUSPECT WITH A SONG

p. 159 *You got sick of the world* — Eve Green, interview.

p. 160 *Relatively cheap sunny places* — Fernández-Armesto, *Millennium*, p. 719.

p. 163 *a little datura seed* — Burton, *Goa and Blue Mountains*, p. 82.

16   SPEED

p. 168 *Speed is the form*   Milan Kundera, *Slowness*
       of ecstasy   (London, 1996), p. 4.

17   THE RISE OF TOURISTHAN

p. 175 *It will be on one of*   R. Neville and J. Clarke, *The Life*
       those lazy   *and Crimes of Charles Sobhraj*
                          (New Delhi, 1987), p. 351.
p. 178 *Cohen's Tourist*   M. Kumar, *Tourism Today* (New
       Purposes   Delhi, 1992).
p. 178 *Smith's Categories*   Ibid.
p. 179 *Vigilant Goans' Army* Tourist morality is a concern for
                          some of the organisations involved
                          in environmental causes. See *Fish,*
                          Curry and Rice, 'Tourism'.
p. 180 *to defy even the*   De Souza, *In Search of Sands,*
       strongest   p. 25.
p. 181 *The match witnessed* Ibid.
p. 182 *some negroid elements* Gomes, *Village Goa*, p. 88.
p. 183 *slavery was not a*   Kosambi, *Myth and Reality*, p. 15.
       recognised
p. 183 *even today employed* J. Pinto, *Slavery in Portuguese*
                          India (Mumbai, 1992) p. 131

19   GÉNÉRATION TECHNO

p. 195 *Techno brought out*   Dry Ice, interview by author,
       in people   March 1999.
p. 196 *Goa is a major venue* Ibid.

20   IN TOURISTHAN

p. 201 *more than 4300*   R. Botelho, *On a Goan Beach*
       Country Liquor   (Panjim 1984), p. 162.

p. 203 *In the first half of the*   Miranda, interview.
      twentieth

21   A GOOD PLACE TO END UP IN

p. 209 *People want to get on*   Morarji, interview.
p. 213 *The first characteristic* Zeldin, *Intimate History of*
      of travellers   *Humanity*, p. 304.

22   MOST DANGEROUS ANIMAL

p. 219 *Today Goa is pulsating* *Goa Today*, January 1998.
p. 221 *Goa! That dream*   *Goa Today*, March 1999.
      destination
p. 222 *everyday currency*   *Index on Censorship*, 'The Last
                        Empire', 1999, p. 40.
p. 223 *small patches*   Fernández-Armesto, *Millennium*,
                        p. 585.
p. 223 *caste.*   'Toleration means leaving people
                        alone. Caste means keeping away
                        from people who might pollute
                        one. The two ideas are related.'
                        Zeldin, *Intimate History of*
                        Humanity, p. 263.

23   SAUDADES

p. 232 *you will suffer*   *The Language of Ravens and
                        Crows*, trans. and ed. Tsering and
                        Mullens (Dharamsala, 1980), p. 4

LONELY PLANET JOURNEYS

JOURNEYS is a unique collection of travel writing – published by the company that understands travel better than anyone else.

It is a series for anyone who has ever experienced – or dreamed of – the magical moment when they encountered a strange culture or saw a place for the first time. They are tales to read while you're planning a trip, while you're on the road or while you're in an armchair, in front of a fire.

These outstanding titles explore our planet through the eyes of a diverse group of international writers. JOURNEYS books catch the spirit of a place, illuminate a culture, recount an adventure, or introduce a fascinating way of life. They always entertain, and always enrich the experience of travel.

'Lively, intelligent and varied . . . an important contribution to travel literature' – *Age (Melbourne)*

LONELY PLANET UNPACKED
Travel Disaster Stories
By Tony Wheeler and other Lonely Planet Writers

Every traveller has a horror story to tell: lost luggage, bad weather, illness or worse. In this lively collection of travel disaster tales, Lonely Planet writers share their worst moments of life on the road.

From Kenya to Sri Lanka, from Brazil to Finland, from the Australian outback to India, these travellers encounter hurricanes, road accidents, secret police and nasty parasites. Reading these funny and frightening stories from the dark side of the road will make you think twice about a career as a travel writer!

'Lonely Planet celebrates its road-stained wretches in . . . a collection of tales of delightful disaster' – *Don George, Travel Editor, salon.com*

A SEASON IN HEAVEN
True Tales from the Road to Kathmandu
David Tomory

In Iran and Afghanistan, in Rishikesh and Goa, in ashrams, mountain villages and dubious hotels, a generation of young people got hip, got busted, lost their luggage, and sometimes found themselves. From confusion to contentment, from dope to dysentery, *A Season in Heaven* presents the true stories of travellers who hit the hippie trail in the late 1960s, taking the trip overland from Europe to India, Pakistan and Nepal.

Only available in Canada and the USA

IN RAJASTHAN
Royina Grewal

As she writes of her travels through Rajasthan, Indian writer Royina Grewal takes us behind the exotic facade of this fabled destination: here is an insider's perceptive account of India's most colourful state, conveying the excitement and challenges of a region in transition.

'a vibrant portrait of the state of princes, snake charmers and astrologers' – *Tatler*

GREEN DREAMS
Travels in Central America
Stephen Benz

On the Amazon, in Costa Rica, Honduras and on the Mayan trail from Guatemala to Mexico, Stephen Benz describes his encounters with water, mud, insects and other wildlife – and not least with the ecotourists themselves. With witty insights into the phenomenon of modern tourism, *Green Dreams* discusses the paradox at the heart of cultural and 'green' tourism.

Provocative and absorbing reading.

SHOPPING FOR BUDDHAS
Jeff Greenwald

In his obsessive search for the perfect Buddha statue in the backstreets of Kathmandu, Jeff Greenwald discovers more than he bargained for . . . and his souvenir-hunting turns into an ironic metaphor for the clash between spiritual riches and material greed. Politics, religion and serious shopping collide in this witty account of an enlightening visit to Nepal.

'Greenwald's quest reveals more about modern Nepal . . . than writings that take themselves much more seriously'
– Chicago Tribune

THE LONELY PLANET STORY

Lonely Planet published its first book in 1973 in response to the numerous 'How did you do it?' questions Maureen and Tony Wheeler were asked after driving, busing, hitching, sailing and railing their way from England to Australia.

Written at a kitchen table and hand collated, trimmed and stapled, *Across Asia on the Cheap* became an instant local bestseller, inspiring thoughts of another book.

Eighteen months in South-East Asia resulted in their second guide, *South-East Asia on a shoestring*, which they put together in a backstreet Chinese hotel in Singapore in 1975. The 'yellow bible', as it quickly became known to backpackers around the world, soon became *the* guide to the region. It has sold well over half a million copies and is now in its 10th edition, still retaining its familiar yellow cover.

Today there are over 350 titles, including travel guides, walking guides, language kits and phrasebooks, travel atlases and travel literature. The company is the largest independent travel publisher in the world.

The emphasis continues to be on travel for independent travellers. Tony and Maureen still travel for several months of each year and play an active part in the writing, updating and quality control of Lonely Planet's guides.

They have been joined by over 80 authors and 400 staff at our offices in Melbourne (Australia), Oakland (USA), London (UK) and Paris (France). Travellers themselves also make a valuable contribution to the guides through the feedback we receive in thousands of letters each year and on our web site.

The people at Lonely Planet strongly believe that travellers can make a positive contribution to the countries they visit, both through their appreciation of the countries' culture, wildlife and natural features, and through the money they spend. In addition, the company makes a direct contribution to the countries and regions it covers. Since 1986 a percentage of the income from each book has been donated to ventures such as famine relief in Africa; aid projects in India; agricultural projects in Central America; Greenpeace's efforts to halt French nuclear testing in the Pacific; and Amnesty International.

'I hope we send people out with the right attitude about travel. You realise when you travel that there are so many different perspectives about the world, so we hope these books will make people more interested in what they see.'
                                                                    – Tony Wheeler